THE WORKING CLASS IN EUROPEAN HISTORY

Sweated Industries and Sweated Labor

James A. Schmiechen

Sweated Industries and Sweated Labor

THE LONDON CLOTHING TRADES
1860–1914

University of Illinois Press

URBANA AND CHICAGO

*Publication of this work was supported in part by
a grant from the Andrew W. Mellon Foundation.*

Published simultaneously in Great Britain by Croom Helm Limited.

This book is printed on acid-free paper.

Library of Congress Cataloging in Publication Data

Schmiechen, James A., 1940–
  Sweated industries and sweated labor.

  (The Working class in European history)
  Includes bibliographical references and index.
    1. Clothing trade — England — London — History.
2. Clothing workers — England — London — History.
3. Sweating system — England — London — History. 4. Trade-
unions — Clothing workers — England — London — History. 5. Labor
laws and legislation — Great Britain — History.
I. Title. II. Series.
HD9940.G82L67 1983   331.7′687′09421   82-17357
ISBN 0-252-01024-8

For my parents
Kurt and Charlotte Schmiechen

Contents

List of Tables

Acknowledgments

This book is a much revised version of my doctoral dissertation, which was presented to the faculty of the department of history at the University of Illinois, Champaign-Urbana, in 1974. I gratefully acknowledge my debt to that group of workers, particularly Professor John McKay who first introduced me to the forgotten workers of the sweatshop, and to Professor Walter Arnstein who, for four years, guided me down the paths of British history. I thank them for their teaching, wise counsel, editorial help, and friendship. Another member of that faculty, Professor Bennett Hill, was equally generous in sharing his learning and in giving friendship and support in times of both plenty and want. The faculty kindly provided me with a Babcock Fellowship to support research in London in 1973–74.

I am indebted, as are all writers of history, to many librarians. Mr. Norman Brown, of the University Library at Urbana, was instrumental in acquiring a number of important newspapers used in my research; at the early stage of this work, librarian Nancy Anderson provided me with the luxury of a little workspace in Altgeld Hall. The library staffs of the British Museum, the British Museum newspaper library, the Trades Union Congress library, the British Library of Economics and Political Science at the London School of Economics, and the Institute for Historical Research at the University of London made my research in London not only possible but enjoyable. Mr. David Webb, librarian of the Bishopsgate Institute, provided me with important materials in the final stages of this project.

The American Council of Learned Societies provided a grant to support the revision of this book. My friend, Ken Carls, spent hours listening to my arguments, reading many of my drafts, and encouraging me to keep with the ship. I am also deeply grateful for the advice and criticism of the series editor, Professor Standish Meacham. My colleagues at Central Michigan University have shown me much kindness and patience. Professor David Macleod patiently undertook the reading of the entire manuscript at one of its later stages. I am also indebted to Ms. Susan Patterson, assistant editor at the University of Illinois Press, and its director, Richard Wentworth, for their invaluable labor.

Last, this book is dedicated to my parents whose lives have stood as powerful lessons to many in the search for the improvement of life and establishment of social justice.

Introduction

RIDING AN OMNIBUS through the bustling commercial districts of London at the turn of the century, one could hardly avoid noticing gaunt and harried women and children scurrying through the streets — there boarding a tram, here leaving a workshop, there entering a warehouse — alone and carrying heavy bundles. If one were to follow these creatures, one would discover that they were passing along from workroom to workroom the shirts, suits, blouses, ties, and shoes that soon would dress much of the world. This scene was the public face of the "sweating system" — long considered to be a terrible but inevitable part of the modern industrial order.

There are numerous horror stories in working-class history — every schoolchild knows of the "dark and satanic" textile mills and the debilitating mines of the nineteenth century — but few are as notorious as those of sweating. Nowhere was sweating more endemic than in clothing production. At its height in 1900, this system affected two classes of workers — the artisan craftsmen, whom it threw into the streets, and the semiskilled workers, many of them women and Jewish immigrants, whom it devoured. The heartache of artisanal decline is well documented: Charles Kingsley's novel *Alton Locke* is a graphic picture of the fallen artisan, as is Robert Tressell's *The Ragged Trousered Philanthropists*. Similar glimpses emerge from the social investigation of Henry Mayhew at mid-century and Charles Booth in the 1880s and 1890s.[1]

Nor has the sweated worker escaped documentation. The sweated woman is one of the most prominent female figures of nineteenth-century literature. A timeless figure, she turns up everywhere: in the paintings of Richard Redgrave and George Frederic Watts, as Giacomo Puccini's Mimi, in George Bernard Shaw's plays, in the writings of Kingsley and Guy de Maupassant. Elizabeth Gaskell's heroine Ruth was a seamstress, as was Charles Dickens's Jenny Wren in *Our Mutual Friend*. Tom Hood's poem "Song of the Shirt" was probably as well known as anything by Alfred, Lord Tennyson, the poet laureate of the Victorian age.[2] Sweating, it seems, was as Victorian as the railroad and the music hall.

But sweating has been consigned a marginal position in labor and economic history. This is somewhat understandable, considering the general course of industrial development away from the home and backroom workshop, but it points to our incomplete understanding of industrial life and work in the mature industrial society. On the one hand, it is commonly accepted that the long-term character of nineteenth-century industrialization was centripetal, that is, the dominant tendency was to centralize production and labor within the factory, which has been seen as representing the natural progression to greater and more sophisticated economic organization. On the other hand, this trend toward factory production does not always stand the test of local history. As Peter Hall, Gareth Stedman Jones, and Duncan Bythell have shown,[3] in some regional and local economies (and London was perhaps chief among these) the centralizing movement of industry was neither uniform nor self-sustaining but existed side by side with opposing centrifugal movements, namely, the decentralization of production and fragmentation of the working class. Therefore, an underlying theme in this book is how in one local industry, the London clothing trades,[4] this centrifugal tendency manifested itself in the spread and growth of nonfactory outwork production of goods, or, as it was known because of the sordid conditions under which it was done, the sweating system. As a result, a sweated workshop and homework labor force grew alongside the factory labor force and a symbiosis developed between factory and nonfactory production. It became increasingly common in London, at the close of the nineteenth century, for employers to shift production back and forth between the factory or artisan shop and the home or small outwork shop.

The term sweating originated in the tailoring and shoemaking trades. London tailors used it in the 1840s to describe changes that had crept into their trade since the early 1830s, and by the 1850s the investigative journalism of the *Morning Chronicle* and *Punch* insured that the word would become a part of the nineteenth-century vocabulary. Sweating meant long and tedious hours of labor, abominably low wages, and degrading and unhealthy surroundings. It was usually found in trades like tailoring, furniture-making, and chainmaking, which technology was making less skilled and more seasonal. Above all, sweating meant the movement of work into unregulated premises, often the worker's home, but just as often any backroom, basement, or garret shop — any place beyond the policing eye of the respectable artisan, manufacturer, or government inspector. It was here that one could disregard all restrictions on hours, pace and conditions of work, and quality of goods; it was here that the system acquired its reputation for squalid misery.

Almost all sweated workers in the clothing trades were outworkers: they took work out from the employer's shop or factory to be worked up into goods in unregulated premises. Outwork in the clothing trades was a euphemism for sweating; it is something of an enigma, for it is difficult to fit it into any of our existing notions of the stages of economic growth or to reconcile its growth with other features of a mature economy, such as Britain's after 1860. At first glance, outwork production seems similar to the old putting-out system of the premodern cottage industry in which goods were produced in part or in their entirety in the home. Like the outworkers of old, the modern industrial outworkers acquired raw materials or partially made goods from a middleman and then applied their labor to these goods on a piecework basis. These newer outworkers, be they skilled or semiskilled, received relatively low wages, worked long hours in certain seasons and were unemployed at others, and usually had no contact with unions. But because outwork was so similar, in appearance at least, to the old domestic system, it has been difficult for historians to agree as to exactly what nineteenth-century outwork was: a remnant of the old preindustrial system or an appendage of the new factory system.[5] This book attempts to show that in the London clothing trades for the half century after 1860 outwork was not an outside department of the factory, but a substitute for it.

The evil most frequently set forth as both cause and consequence of sweated outwork was subcontracting, through which manufacturers let out work to middlemen who hired their own workers. This commonly accepted definition of sweating was first set forth by Kingsley in the 1850s and was used in much the same manner by Booth nearly forty years later, although he preferred to replace the word subcontracting with the phrase "employment at second hand."[6] In contrast, one of Booth's assistants, Beatrice Potter Webb, who had direct experience in the East End sweated trades, claimed that the sweater was not necessarily a subcontractor or middleman, nor were all subcontractors sweaters.[7] In 1888 the House of Lords committee on sweating came to somewhat the same conclusion: subcontracting through middlemen was the consequence, not the cause, of sweating. But four years later the Royal Commission on Labour insisted that there was a connection between subcontracting and sweating. It noted that sweating "exists very largely *wherever* the system of sub-contracting prevails, *though it is also found where sub-contract is absent.*"[8]

The debate over subcontracting illustrates the difficulty in untangling sweating's origin. Most Victorians and Edwardians knew what sweating meant, but few agreed on why it grew and flourished. The first half of this book, chapters 1 through 3, centers on the causes of the sweating system. Some historians and reformers have attributed the evil to an oversupply of labor, particularly the entry of women and immigrant Jews into the labor market; others pointed to the sewing machine and a host of other technological innovations that made many skilled jobs obsolete while they provided sweated work for others. Not a few blamed sweating on a growing popular taste for material goods, and there was always a voice to be heard putting the blame on some greedy capitalist.

The second half of this book, chapters 4 through 6, focuses on the role of the trades unions and the state in the long struggle to end sweating. Because sweated work was largely women's work, an examination of women as wage earners and unionists is crucial to a study of this battle. The sweating system, with its propensity to isolate the worker and to force workers to exploit other workers, promoted racism and sexism and pitted women — and Jewish immigrants — against white English males in a vicious labor competition. The end result was that women and the immigrants found it difficult to rise above intraclass struggles. As these subjects are explored, I try to make clear the relationship between the workplace and working-class culture and politics in the last quarter of the nineteenth century.[9]

The history of sweating also illustrates how the poor survived in a prewelfare society. Poverty and sweating were a vicious cycle. The sweatshop was the only means of existence for thousands of people left indigent by the recurring unemployment of a husband, the death of a marriage partner, old age, or sickness. It became increasingly apparent to reformers that sweating would survive as long as there was available a ready army of workers who under other circumstances should not have to work. At the same time, it became equally apparent that poverty was not chiefly a Malthusian certainty or a result of moral weakness, but the outgrowth of an exploitive industrial system. By the first decade of the twentieth century the failure of the unions to organize the workers and of the state to legislate the abolition of sweating forced the nation to adopt an elementary form of a national minimum wage.

NOTES

1. Kingsley (London, 1850); Tressell (1914; reprint ed., New York, 1962); Mayhew, *London Labour and the London Poor,* 4 vols. (London, 1851–61); and Booth, *Life and Labour of the People in London,* 9 vols. (London, 1882–97).

2. See Helene E. Roberts's essay, "Marriage, Redundancy or Sin: The Painters' View of Women in the First Twenty-Five Years of Victoria's Reign," in Martha Vicinus, ed., *Suffer and Be Still: Women in the Victorian Age* (Bloomington, Ind., 1973); see also Wanda F. Neff, *Victorian Working Women: An Historical Literary Study of Women in British Industries and Professions, 1832–50* (New York, 1950). Hood's poem is found in *Punch,* Dec. 1843.

3. Hall, *The Industries of London since 1861* (London, 1962); Jones, *Outcast London: A Study in the Relationship between Classes in Victorian Society* (Oxford, 1971), ch. 1; Bythell, *The Sweated Trades: Outwork in Nineteenth-Century Britain* (London, 1978). Lewis Mumford (*The City as History* [New York, 1961], 455) has noted that the decentralization of industry had an impact on urban development as early as the seventeenth century.

4. Throughout this study I am using the following categories for the clothing trades, taken from census reports: boot- and shoemaking, dressmaking, tailoring, mantlemaking, shirtmaking, cap- and bonnetmaking. The census reporters often changed their definitions of clothing trades from decade to decade. Laundresses, furriers, haberdashers, wigmakers, and hairdressers have been excluded from this study. Dealers have been left in, and female machinists and female drapers have been added. "Shoemakers' wives," which were included in the 1861 census, were excluded because they were not counted in subsequent returns. Historians generally regard the 1861 census figures as too high. For the most part, I have used the guidelines set out by Alan Armstrong in E. A. Wrigley, ed., *Nineteenth-Century Society: Essays*

in the Use of Quantitative Methods for the Study of Social Data (Cambridge, 1972), ch. 6.

5. For example, J. H. Clapham treats outwork as an extension of the old domestic putting-out system, which had not yet died off. See his *An Economic History of Modern Britain* (London, 1930), 1: 172–73, 179; 2: 85, 93, 131. David Landes, on the other hand, claims that technology often created outwork industry where it had not existed before and extended it where it already existed. See *The Unbound Prometheus* (Cambridge, 1970), 119. See also Hall, *Industries of London*, 53–57; Jones, *Outcast London*, ch. 5; Bythell, *Sweated Trades*, 143–51; and Pamela Horn, "Child Workers in the Pillow Lace and Straw Plait Trades of Victorian Buckinghamshire and Bedfordshire," *Historical Journal*, 17 (Dec. 1974), 774–76.

6. Booth, *Life and Labour*, ser. 1, 4: 330.

7. Beatrice Potter (Webb), "The Lords and the Sweating System," *Nineteenth Century*, 160 (Jan. 1890), 890. The same argument was presented five years later in "Sweating: Its Causes and Remedy," *Fabian Tracts*, no. 50 (London, 1895). See also Parliamentary Papers (hereafter P.P.), "Select Committee on Sweating," Fifth Report, 1888, vol. xvii, p. vi. Although the term sweater usually referred to the exploiter, not the exploited, in the boot and shoe trade it was used in the opposite sense — one who did sweated work. Thus, although perhaps misleading, Mr. Punch's use of the term in his 1851 cartoon is correct.

8. Emphasis added. P.P., "Royal Commission on Labour," Fifth Report, 1894, vol. xxxv, p. 535. The sweating committee's opinion is found in P.P., "Select Committee on Sweating," Fifth Report, 1888, vol. xvii, p. xliii. My research cannot substantiate the claim by E. P. Hennock ("Poverty and Social Theory in England: The Experience of the Eighteen Eighties," *Social History*, 1 [Jan. 1976], 83–85) that by 1890 conventional opinion had abandoned the idea that sweating was primarily a result of subcontracting.

9. For an excellent discussion of how the decline of the London artisan trades and its work-centered culture led to a conservative and nonpolitical working class, see Gareth Stedman Jones, "Working-Class Culture and Working-Class Politics in London, 1870–1900: Notes on the Remaking of a Working Class," *Journal of Social History*, 7 (Summer 1974).

CHAPTER 1

The London Artisan and the Origins of the Sweating System, 1815–60

WHEN THE WARS WITH FRANCE came to an end in 1815, London was known as the Athens of the English artisan. The journeymen tailors and shoemakers of London enjoyed active and vigorous control over their trades. The tailors had been organized for nearly a hundred years, and despite legislation against the unions (the Combination Acts of 1721, 1799, and 1800) and regulation of wages by both Parliamentary and local action (often to the advantage of the unions), the tailors had built strong unions, used strikes to set their wages, and held sway over production. The employer-masters were compelled to pay higher wages than the maximum allowed by Parliamentary statute; often increases in the statutory wage were a result of a local magistrate bowing to the pressures of the workers.[1] As early as 1764 the masters petitioned the government to break up the unions, but to no avail; London tailors, in fact, were so successful in protecting themselves that the wartime inflation, which had left many workers facing a drop in real wages, found their wages up by 63 percent in 1815. Here wages remained until the 1830s.[2] These tailors, claimed tailor Francis Place, were "more firmly united than any other class of journeymen." They successfully resisted their masters' attempts to have the Combination Acts enforced, and then, under the guiding hand of Place, in 1824 they led the fight in getting the acts repealed — a remarkable display of labor power in this postwar depression period, which brought ruthless oppression of unions, economic distress for the working class, and nearly universal wage reductions. By 1830, when a great labor revival was underway in Britain, the tailors of London claimed to be 100 percent unionized — and unscathed by wage reductions.[3]

Tailors were among London's most politically radical working-class citizens, and few workingmen of the period were as well known as Place. Until the 1840s London artisans were "almost to the man red hot politicians" — a situation that would change, however, as artisan-ship declined.[4] The flood of unskilled cheap labor, often pauper children, that inundated the early textile mills and scandalized Parliament in 1802[5] was not a problem in the tailoring trade. As long as their union was strong, the tailors could determine their wages and the labor supply. These tailors enjoyed higher wages than most working people of the metropolis, and it is not until later that tramping — leaving home in search of work — became a common feature of tailoring work.[6]

The decline of the artisan

London tailors were not living in a utopia, however. Already by 1815 the trade had been divided into two branches — an honorable section called "flints," who worked only by hourly or daily wages and always in the master's shop, and a smaller dishonorable section made up of the "dungs," the predecessors of the sweated workers, who worked for lower wages, under a piecework system, and usually at home, where the tendency was to hire one's family and neighbors. But the dungs were a minority. The prevailing mode of clothing production continued to be that of the honorable artisan working in his master's shop and executing a single item for a single customer; and, although the dungs worked for lower wages, they often cooperated with the flints in strikes. The aim of the artisan was to equalize wages, that is, to have all workers receive the rates paid by the best firms. Such a result was nearly impossible, however, if workers escaped the union's notice by taking work for less pay outside the master's shop. Home-working, then, was the poison of London unionism, and warfare periodically broke out between the flints and dungs, but the flints were able to control the spread of dung work, and occasionally they got the dungs to join in resisting wage reductions. In this manner the tailoring trade remained in a somewhat precarious but generally good position until around 1830. "Sweaters," Henry Mayhew was told, "were scarcely known."[7]

No one seems to know exactly when the tailoring trade began its rapid descent, but it was sometime after 1824, when Place led the tailors in the repeal of the Combination Acts, and before 1834, when the union collapsed. The wars with France had placed heavy strains on wages and prices, and manufacturers saw outwork as a way to reduce wage costs. Although E. P. Thompson claims that artisanship was destroyed by the influx of cheap labor following the repeal of the old Elizabethan apprenticeship statutes (which had made it illegal for a master to employ nonapprenticed workers) in 1814,[8] it appears that as long as the tailors were able to resist piecework and homework this repeal was not harmful. Most tailors looked back not to 1814, but to the breakup of their union, the London Operative Tailors, in 1834 as the turning point in their history. An unsuccessful tailors' strike in 1834, when 20,000 of them protested pieceworking and homeworking, completely broke the union, leaving the tailors unorganized and weak for the next thirty years. Thus, the breakup of the London Operative Tailors Union and the fear of repression generated by the Tolpuddle Martyrs' deportation about the same time ushered in a long period of union weakness and employer hegemony.[9] This weakness was an invitation to employers to switch to piecework, homework, and cheap female labor, the evils the strikers were fighting. It was, then, after 1834 that the repeal of the apprenticeship laws and the end of the informal arbitration by local magistrates was felt. By 1849 only one in seven tailors belonged to the union, and Charles Kingsley could write that in London there "are two distinct tailoring trades — the 'honourable' trade, now almost confined to the West End, and rapidly dying out there, and the 'dishonourable' trade of the slop shops — the plate glass palaces where gents . . . buy their cheap and nasty clothes."[10] By the 1860s, London was known as the "ants' nest" of the tailoring trade, and the tailors of London would estimate that from a half to a quarter of the tailors in London had become outdoor workers and had thereby succumbed to the "monster evil" — the sweater.[11] Tailoring had become a sweated trade.

What was happening to the tailors was also happening to the shoemakers. Boot- and shoemaking moved from a strong artisan trade to a sweated industry in the 1830s and 1840s. In 1815 boot- and shoemaking, then the largest artisan trade in both London and Britain, was in London a healthy trade led by respectable pipe-smoking gentlemen "in their frilled shirts." Although their eighteenth-century reputation as drunken, thriftless, and reckless radicals had partly carried over into the nineteenth century, shoemakers were known for their intelligence, strong character, and political consciousness, and Mayhew describes them as "stern, uncompromising and reflecting." Not a few of them — like Thomas Hardy and John Ashley — could be found in the London Corresponding Society, the eighteenth-century harbinger of working-class political consciousness. The Grand National Consolidated Trade Union movement of 1832–34 and the Chartist movement that was to follow included many shoemakers, who also made up the core of several early socialist groups, such as the Spenceans and Owenites. Greatly influenced by French radicalism, early nineteenth-century shoemakers were an important part of "the nucleus from which the labour movement derived ideas, organization and leadership" and were among the last to stop using the word "citizen" and other Jacobin terms.[12]

Despite attacks by their employers and the law courts — as in 1799 when their union was temporarily disbanded[13] — like the London tailors, the boot- and shoemakers were powerful enough in the period of union illegality to disregard the Combination Acts. Through their union they were able to control wages and hours, while their London employers unsuccessfully petitioned the government to prosecute them.[14] Here in this "twilight world of semi-legality," as E. P. Thompson calls it,[15] armed with the idea of a just and fair wage and with union power and the statute of apprenticeship, they were able to protect themselves from invasion by the unskilled masses. Then, sometime after the union split of 1813 and by 1850, London shoemakers became a classic example of sweated workers; their protected status tumbled, and by 1849 they were describing themselves as starving, wretchedly overworked, and underpaid. Mayhew found that an artisan shoemaker working for the best shop in London could exist only with the assistance of his wife's labor; others who worked in the growing lower-class shops cursed "such a country as England" that allowed them to become paupers.[16] All the signs of sweating were present. Wages deteriorated by as much as half, and in all but the upper-class work the trade was invaded by cheap labor (mainly women, boys, and some German immigrants), the quality of goods deteriorated, and production centered in deplorable sweatshops.

"I wasn't born soon enough to see good times" was the rebuke of those who entered the trade after 1815.[17] Artisanship in shoemaking declined for many of the same reasons it declined in tailoring. The entry into the trade of women and unapprenticed boys after the repeal

of the statute of apprenticeship was devastating. These apprenticeship laws, while not needed in times of union strength, disappeared
just as the unions lost their power. Allen Davenport, socialist
shoemaker and member of the London union, lamented that when
the statute of apprenticeship was repealed the trade "was thrown open
to all."[18] Simultaneously, a series of strikes were lost, destroying the
unity of the shoemakers by 1830. The first of these strikes, the Great
Strike of 1812–13, was the last general strike by shoemakers for nearly
half a century. The goal of the union was to equalize wages, that is,
to "strike up" the already growing army of low-wage workers (called
refactories and scabs) to the level of those who worked for union wages.
Though the strike brought victory to the West End workers, who ended
up with a higher wage, it set the whole trade aflame — with the City
division losing and the union split into quarreling camps.[19] Although
the "society men" of the West End were able to defend themselves
for a few more years, further strike defeats and employer lockouts
in 1826 and 1830 meant wage reductions for them as well.[20] The rest
of the shoemakers were now at the mercy of the employers whose
organization and lockout tactics had paid off and who were now ready
to meet competition and increase their profits by putting out the work
to cheap labor.[21] Henceforth, London artisan shoemakers had to compete against the cheap labor of their wives and children.

But this was not all. The victory of the employer over the union
was partly a result of the rise of cheaper provincial and foreign manufacturers — although it is possible that the very militancy of organized
labor in London encouraged the growth of such provincial shoe production centers as Northampton and Stafford in the first place.[22] Prior
to the strike of 1812–13 not a single Northampton shoe was sold in
London, and all of London's boot and shoe exports were made locally.
The temporary success of the West End shoemakers in 1813 saw
employers turn to production outside of London, chiefly in Northampton; by 1849 there were several hundred shops in London known
by the names of Magazine, Depot, and Emporium, which daily received thousands of pairs of boots made in Northampton. It became
a common saying among London shoemakers that "every child in
Northampton has a leather apron."[23]

Also beyond control of the weakened union was the repeal of tariffs
on foreign-made, particularly French, boots and shoes in 1826, 1833,
and 1842. In the name of free trade, Englishmen now had access to

the cheaper and more fashionable French footwear. How much these tariff reductions resulted in lower wages and increased unemployment of London artisans is difficult to determine. The shoemakers claimed that a tariff reduction on boots and shoes in 1826 deprived "hundreds and thousands of their means of subsistence, and reduced them to such a state of destitution in 1828 that 120 shoemakers were in the workhouse of the parish of Westminster alone, whereas previous to the reduction there had been only three."[24] They were convinced that wage reductions and labor intensification were very much a result of free trade. There is, no doubt, some truth to this belief, for it appears that English manufacturers sought to meet foreign competition through expanding sweating in London and sending out orders to be done in the provinces. To make matters worse, the workers complained, there was no compensation in the repeal of the corn laws because cheaper food simply meant a reduction of wages.[25] To them free trade was a fraud.

It appears, then, that for tailors and shoemakers the deterioration of their artisan status was accelerated by the decline of their unions in the decade after the repeal of the Combination Laws in 1824–25. The Tolpuddle antiunion scare in 1833–34 and the breakup of the Grand National in 1834 dealt the final blow to an already weakened labor movement. When the unions lost their ability to control the labor market, the earlier repeal of the apprenticeship laws was felt, and another form of state protection, the tariff on foreign-made goods, was withdrawn. All of this took place amid a growing demand for cheap clothing.

Consumerism and the sweated trades

The fall of the unions and the rise of foreign competition and provincial production do not fully explain why one of London's most honorable trades became its least. The history of sweating, like that of Britain's industrial revolution, is inextricably linked to the history of mass consumption. The misfortunes of the artisan tailors and shoemakers were partly a result of a revolution in British taste and consumption and the inability of the industrial process to meet that demand without the sacrifice of some of its workers. There emerged, beginning in the early nineteenth century, an insatiable demand for ready-made, mass-produced clothing.[26] This production, although holding its own during the French wars, increased rapidly after 1815. This new "cheap and nasty" industry, as Kingsley called it, was at first the result of foreign demand, chiefly in India and the West Indies, but also in Europe, as markets reopened in 1815. At home the proportion of working-class income spent on clothing doubled in the sixty years after 1845, from an estimated 6 percent in 1845, to between 8 and 10 percent in 1889, to 12 percent in 1904, following, roughly, the doubling of working-class income for the same period. The number of retail shops in Great Britain also increased, from 544 to 5,681 between 1880 and 1915 — an average increase of about 65 percent every five years (Table 1). And retail clothing sales in Great Britain increased by 16.7 percent between 1900 and 1910, the first period for which we have data.[27] The export of leather goods, mainly footwear, increased threefold between 1855 and 1901, while that of clothing increased twelvefold between 1826 and 1914 (Table 2).

It was largely the change in home consumption that brought havoc to the old trade and opened the gates to mass consumer production. The growth of the middle class gave this process its initial boost. It was this middle-income group of substantial farmers, artisans, businessmen, shopkeepers, and professionals — those who were the most likely to postpone marriage until late and to limit their families — which came into affluence in the first decades of the nineteenth century and grew faster than the population as a whole. The professional occupations alone grew 2.5 times as rapidly as did the population between

Table 1. Growth of Ready-to-Wear Clothing Outlets, 1880–1915

A. Numbers Type	1880	1885	1890	1895	1900	1905	1910	1915
Men's and boys' wear	44	119	211	349	570	854	1,085	1,259
Women's and girls' wear	—	20	77	153	245	342	472	543
Footwear	500	757	1,231	1,967	2,589	2,962	3,544	3,879
Total	544	896	1,519	2,469	3,404	4,158	5,101	5,681

B. Percentage Increase Type	1880–85	1885–90	1890–95	1895–1900	1900–1905	1905–10	1910–15
Men's and boys' wear	170.4	77.3	65.4	63.3	49.8	27.0	16.0
Women's and girls' wear	—	285.0	98.7	60.1	39.6	38.0	15.0
Footwear	51.4	62.6	59.8	31.6	14.4	19.6	9.4
Total	64.7	69.5	62.5	37.8	22.1	22.6	11.4

Source. Calculated from James B. Jefferys, *Retail Trading in Britain, 1850–1950* (Cambridge, 1954), Table 85.

Table 2. Clothing Exports from Great Britain, 1826–1914

Years	Yearly Average	
	Apparel	Leather Goods
1826–30	1.0	0.35
1831–35	0.98	0.32
1836–40	1.36	0.38
1841–45	1.46	0.38
1846–50	2.0	0.38
1851–55	4.78	1.01
1856–60	6.16	2.06
1861–65	7.2	2.00
1866–70	7.6	1.74
1871–75	10.6	2.4
1876–80	7.9	2.08
1881–85	8.6	2.46
1886–90	7.9	2.62
1891–95	7.3	2.52
1896–1900	7.8	2.44
1901–5	8.3	3.18
1906–10	8.7	4.08
1911–14	12.2	5.84

Note. Data are in £000,000.

Source. Calculated from B. R. Mitchell and P. Deane, *Abstract of British Historical Statistics* (London, 1962), 302–6.

1841 and 1881.[28] This elasticity of demand, so important to Britain's economic growth, became more pronounced as more consumer groups arrived on the scene. Beginning in the 1840s there emerged an elite upper stratum of the working population — the so-called labor aristocracy — made up of skilled workers who enjoyed good regular earnings. This was a small but growing class (Eric Hobsbawm says it was about 10 percent of the working class between 1840 and 1890) whose skills were needed in the iron and steel industries, in shipbuilding, machine-making, and the like, as well as in some of the traditional artisanal trades.

After about 1870 and until about 1890, this upper stratum grew faster than the working class as a whole, and its wages grew even faster.[29] About the same time, this momentum toward a consumer economy speeded up with the expansion of the lower-middle-class, white-collar workers — those engaged in civil service, teaching, and management, and as clerks in banking and finance. Their pay was not very good, but they had social status above those who worked with their hands. This group grew from about 0.8 percent to 4 percent of the total labor force between 1851 and 1901. A large number of them, but not a majority, working in insurance, banking, and the civil service, earned double that earned by a manual worker.[30]

The new habits of these families, which included buying ready-made clothes once a year, meant a significant increase in the demand for clothing, which meant a revolution in taste. Clothing became the mark of those who had moved into the realm of Victorian respectability. Fostering the spending habits of these consumer groups was a general long-term fall in food prices. Thus, when the corn laws were repealed in 1846 or when William Gladstone cut the tea duty by two-thirds, the extra income could be spent on clothing. In short, the British consumer was aided by the general tendency over much of the century for import prices to fall more rapidly than those of manufactured goods. In addition, the fall of clothing prices encouraged demand. Some clothing, like underwear, had never been available to the masses before the nineteenth century, and other items, like suits for men, had been available only as a once in a lifetime item or as a hand-down from someone in the upper class. A coat formerly costing 18s. at a high-class West End bespoke shop could now be purchased for less than 10s. at a ready-made shop. "Turpin's 10/6 Trousers Astonish the World!" was the cry of the working-class neighborhood store.[31]

Production followed these demands, but we can only guess the increase as being somewhere between 40 and 500 percent between 1861 and 1911. Considerable increases in worker productivity lead us to believe that the increase in production was closer to the higher estimate of 500 percent. Table 3 estimates the growth in output (at 42.7 percent) simply on the basis of worker output as it stood in 1911. This method overestimates production for the earlier periods because it does not take into consideration the production speedup that occurred with the introduction of machinery and labor-saving practices. Thus, output per worker was much less in 1861 than in 1911. If, for example, we guess (as the evidence seems to allow us) that output per worker was two-thirds less in 1861, then the increase over the fifty-year period would be over 300 percent rather than 42.7 percent. In any case, we can safely say that there was no downswing in demand, either internally or from abroad, or in production during the so-called Great

Table 3. Estimated Output of the London Clothing Industry

Year	In £millions	Percentage Change for Decennial Period
1861	11.7	—
1871	11.5	− 2
1881	12.9	+ 12.1
1891	19.7	+ 52.7
1901	15.5	− 21.3
1911	16.7	+ 7.7

Overall increase, 1861–1911: 42.7 percent

Note. The data are calculated by multiplying the output per worker (from the 1907 census of production) by the number of workers (from the 1911 census). The output per worker for "clothing" and "boot and shoe" in 1907 was £62 and £71, respectively.

Source. Great Britain, Parliament, *Parliamentary Papers* (Commons), "Census of Production of the United Kingdom in 1907," 1912–13, 109:387. It is possible that the output per worker for London was lower than the national average. The 1907 census does not include outworkers. The small scale and decentralized nature of these industries did not lend itself to the collection of statistics. For example, the standard index of industrial output (the Hoffmann Index) does not include any clothing except footwear; thus, I have taken the output per worker for these trades in 1907 and multiplied it by the number of workers from the occupational census for the decennial periods. But this estimate only reflects the occupational trends and does not account for changes in output per worker. Technology and remuneration customs of the industry point to a steady increase in output per worker, thus making the estimates for the earlier decennial proportionately lower, and the overall increases in output much greater, than estimated. Also, the estimate above is based on 1907 prices, which were lower per unit of production in 1901 than, for example, in 1871, further weighing the index in favor of the earlier periods and thereby underestimating the true growth of the clothing production in London. See ch. 2 herein.

Depression. On the contrary, the London clothing trades showed a remarkable ability to meet the demand for ready-made goods, and, although often mistakenly described as an industry in decline, it was actually an industry of significant growth and a leader in the consumer-goods revolution.

It was also consequential for the artisan that, for several reasons, the new ready-made clothing industry did not, in London at least, become a factory industry. Labor and industry were subject to problems indigenous to the city's growth. The building of railroads and the construction of new warehouses and commercial streets in inner London combined with other physical changes to reduce available housing and to contribute to rising rents and scarcity of land, which, in turn, made the factory system of production largely prohibitive. Ready-made clothes could be easily stitched by workers in their homes or in a dirty backroom shop. Central London became the center for this trade — crowded with the offices and small workrooms of clothing firms, which each day put out work to laborers who entered the City by omnibus from the East End, or walked over London Bridge from London Bridge station, or, after 1863, were brought to the edge of the City by the metropolitan line of the inner-London railroad. Every day thousands of these workers moved back and forth, carrying their bundles of work. As this industry grew, every room, basement, garret, and backyard of London became subject to invasion by those looking for a place to work. Bridgeways and covered hallways connected existing houses to new workshops. The City was teeming with small workshops, sometimes with "two or three men in different branches" occupying one room. "There are few back streets," observed one Londoner, in which from almost every house one cannot hear "the whir and rattle of sweater machines."[32]

Meanwhile, the tailors could do little to reverse or control these changes, except, as some did, to set themselves up as subcontractors of labor and go into the business of making ready-made goods themselves. In the short run, at least, some tailors used the sweating system to move up the social scale and become small-time capitalists. Nevertheless, for most tailors, like most shoemakers, the movement was down rather than up. Little is known of the London tailors in the three decades following the collapse of their union in the 1830s. They formed a new union in 1843 and helped in the creation of a National Association of Tailors in 1846. Both were short-lived and had little impact. By 1859 there were twelve tailors' societies in London, but none was strong enough to revive the union that had been broken a quarter of a century earlier, although the trade did continue to produce leaders for the London labor movement. The turning point was 1865, when the London tailors joined to form the London Operative Tailors Association, and in the following year the London tailors entered the new Amalgamated Society of Tailors (the AST), which was founded in Manchester by Peter Shorrocks. This new era in unionism for tailors corresponds roughly with a new era in sweating (see chapter 4, herein).

Life and work in the clothing trades

Life and work in the clothing trades in this period between the fall and recovery of unionism is best described by Mayhew, whose investigation at mid-century was Britain's first empirical survey of poverty.[33]

Mayhew wrote a series of now famous articles on life and work in London for the London newspaper, the *Morning Chronicle,* in 1849 and 1850. This statistical but compassionate work was a chilling exposé of the sweating system, which, as he predicted, proceeded to get worse. In the 1830s and 1840s, Mayhew showed, tailoring was taken over by sweating. Of some 21,000 tailors in London in 1849, 3,000 were in the honorable trade, while the rest labored wretchedly in the "slop" trade carried on in homes and hidden workshops.[34] He found that between 1844 and 1849 the number of traditional shops in the West End declined from seventy-two to sixty, while the number of "slop and show" shops doubled from 172 to 344. Most telling, the number of sweated workers increased threefold. Working on Sunday, once regarded as the "most iniquitous of all impositions on the honourable part of the trade," became commonplace and an eighteen-hour day not uncommon. The "cheap show and slop shops," as one tailor told Mayhew, "have ruined thousands . . . have cut down the prices so that men cannot live at their work."[35]

The most important change in production in this period was the switch from day to piecework following the defeat of the workers in the strike of 1834. Masses of women and children were brought into the trade, as piecework could be done outside the master's shop.[36]

Although traditional, honorable work continued for a few "intelligent artisans" who lived in comfortable houses "redolent with . . . perfume," most London tailors by mid-century were living in squalor. By the time the AST was founded, 80 percent of London's tailors were outworkers — sweating themselves, their families, and their neighbors, and living a life of "incessant toil, wretched pay, miserable food, and filthy homes." Most of them lived, worked, and raised their families in one room.[37] Medical officers found that over 70 percent of all tailors were under thirty-five years of age, largely because they either died at an early age or they lost their jobs because of failing health and eyesight. For example, the death rate for London tailors between the ages of forty-five and fifty-five was nearly double that of agricultural workers.[38] Average weekly earnings for a West End tailor working in an honorable shop in 1849 were 18s. 9½d., whereas wages for those who worked at home, for longer hours and under deplorable conditions, were half that. Wages fell from 36s. per week in 1813 to 11s. per week in 1849.[39] Through his hero-tailor, Alton Locke, Kingsley told of the decay of the London tailoring trade. Locke's employer was representative of the old honorable trade. He was:

> One of the old sort of fashionable West-end tailors in the fast decreasing honourable trades; keeping a modest shop. . . . He paid good prices for work, though not as good, of course as he had given twenty years before, and prided himself upon having all his work done at home. His workrooms . . . were not elysiums; but still, as good alas! as those of three tailors out of four. . . . At all events, his journeymen could live on what he paid them.

But when the old master died, he was succeeded by his son, who was a man of the new age of "cheap clothes and nasty." He was, he told Locke, "resolved to make haste to be rich. . . . Why should he stick to the old, slow-going honourable trade? Out of some four hundred and fifty West End tailors there were not one hundred left who were old fashioned and stupid enough to go on keeping down their own profits by having all their work done . . . at first hand."[40] The new fashion, of course, was subcontracting and piecework. Thus, Kingsley argued and Mayhew showed that a new sort of capitalist was busy taking advantage of the new opportunities for gain.

The comfort of the respectable working Victorians was in exchange for the growth of a class of sweated workers. The engineer, the builder, and the clerk who earned about £1 a week for eight to ten hours of work were able to buy stylish garments and footwear at two-thirds the former price "at the expense of poor wretches who work eighteen hours a day for a bare existence."[41] But what happened between 1813 and 1860 was merely the beginning. The system of sweated production was to grow even more with the coming of machinery in the clothing trades. Sweating was to remain a London institution until well into the twentieth century.

NOTES

1. See C. R. Dobson, *Masters and Journeymen: A Pre-History of Industrial Relations, 1717–1800* (London, 1980), chs. 5, 6. Dobson states that "the London society of journeymen tailors was the most militant and effective trade union in eighteenth-century England" (60).

2. The increase was from 22s. per week in 1795 to 36s. per week in 1813. M. Dorothy George, *London Life in the Eighteenth Century* (New York, 1925), 163, 368.

3. Place's quote is cited in F. Galton, *The Tailoring Trade* (London, 1896), 148–51. For the general history given in this paragraph, see ibid., lxxiii; A. E. Musson, *British Trade Unions, 1800–75* (London, 1972), 24; G. D. H. Cole, *A Short History of the Working Class Movement* (London, 1927), 74; Sidney and Beatrice Webb, *History of Trade Unionism* (London, 1911), 82; and Eric J. Hobsbawm, *Labouring Men: Studies in the History of Labour* (London, 1964), 77.

4. Henry Mayhew, letter XIX to the *Morning Chronicle,* in P. Razzell and R. Wainwright, *The Victorian Working Class: Selections from the Morning Chronicle* (Portland, Oreg., 1974). George Rudé notes the prevalence of artisan craftsmen, such as tailors, cabinetmakers, and locksmiths, rather than the casual laborers, criminals, or slum poor, as the faces in the revolutionary crowd of the eighteenth and early nineteenth centuries (*The Crowd in History, 1730–1840* [New York, 1964], ch. 13). The participation of tailors in the Chartist movement is fairly well known. Charles Kingsley, in the edition of *Alton Locke* published in 1881 (p. 179), noted that in 1851 the improved morality of the tailors was due to the influence of Chartism; conversely, Gareth Stedman Jones has noted that the decline of artisanship resulted in a "remaking" of the working class by 1900 ("Working-Class Culture and Working-Class Politics in London, 1870–1900: Notes on the Remaking of a Working Class," *Journal of Social History,* 7 [Summer 1974], 460–508).

5. The Factory Act of 1802 limited the daily work of poor-law apprentice children in cotton factories to twelve hours.

6. John Wade made the observation on wages, cited in E. P. Thompson, *The Making of the English Working Class* (New York, 1963), 257. See Hobsbawm, *Labouring Men,* 36.

7. Galton, *Tailoring Trade,* lxx, lxxiii, 151; G. D. H. Cole, *Attempts at General Union* (London, 1953), 7; Mayhew, letter XVIII to the *Morning Chronicle,* in Eileen Yeo and E. P. Thompson, *The Unknown Mayhew* (New York, 1971), 219.

8. Thompson, *Making of the English Working Class,* 257. When Mayhew tried to uncover the cause of the tailors' distress, none of the tailors he interviewed mentioned the repeal of the Elizabethan apprenticeship statute. Dobson, *Masters and Journeymen,* 60–61, suggests that the tailors were not greatly affected by the apprenticeship laws.

9. The Tolpuddle Martyrs was the name given to six English farm laborers who were sentenced in March 1834 to seven years' banishment to a penal colony in Australia for organizing trade unions in the Dorsetshire village of Tolpuddle. Mayhew, letter XVI to the *Morning Chronicle,* in Yeo and

Thompson, *Unknown Mayhew,* 181–227. See also Margaret Stewart and Leslie Hunter, *The Needle Is Threaded: The History of an Industry* (London, 1964), 35.

10. Charles Kingsley, *Cheap Clothes and Nasty* (1849), 2. The estimate on union membership is Mayhew's (letter XVI to the *Morning Chronicle,* in Yeo and Thompson, *Unknown Mayhew,* 182).

11. "The Sweating System and How to Cure It," *The Tailor,* Jan. 12, 1867, 211.

12. Mayhew, letters XXXII, XXXIII to the *Morning Chronicle,* in Yeo and Thompson, *Unknown Mayhew,* 232, 241; George, *London Life,* 195–200; Thompson, *Making of the English Working Class,* 193, 614, 705; Pauline Gregg, *Modern Britain: A Social and Economic History since 1760* (New York, 1967), 172.

13. Webbs, *Trade Unionism,* 71.

14. Henry Pelling, *A History of British Trade Unionism* (London, 1963), 27.

15. *Making of the English Working Class,* 508.

16. Mayhew, letter XXXV to the *Morning Chronicle,* in Yeo and Thompson, *Unknown Mayhew,* 264.

17. Ibid., 241.

18. Quoted in Thompson, *Making of the English Working Class,* 254.

19. Mayhew, letter XXXIII to the *Morning Chronicle,* in Yeo and Thompson, *Unknown Mayhew,* 245.

20. Ibid., and Thompson, *Making of the English Working Class,* 255.

21. Mayhew, letter XXXIII to the *Morning Chronicle,* in Yeo and Thompson, *Unknown Mayhew,* 244–45.

22. R. A. Church, "Labour Supply and Innovation, 1800–1860: The Boot and Shoe Industry," *Business History,* 12 (Jan. 1970), 26–28.

23. Mayhew, letter XXXIV to the *Morning Chronicle,* in Yeo and Thompson, *Unknown Mayhew,* 255; see also letter XXXII, ibid., 239.

24. Letters XXXII, XXV, ibid., 236, 258.

25. Letters XXXIII, XXXIV, ibid., 242, 249. (Mayhew was won over by the bootmakers' protectionist argument and, as a result, broke with the pro-free trade *Morning Chronicle.* See ibid., 37ff.)

26. The mass-consumer markets in certain domestic products and foodstuffs had begun to appear about a century earlier. See Carole Shammas, "The Domestic Environment in Early Modern England and America," *Journal of Social History,* 14 (Fall 1980).

27. James Jefferys, *Retail Trading in Britain, 1850–1950* (Cambridge, 1954), 453, Appendix A, Table 85. This correlation between retailing and output may be criticized as reflecting buying habits, that is, a switch from bespoke to ready-made goods, rather than actual changes in output. It is more likely, however, that the increase in retailing reflects the switch from hand-down, handmade, and resale clothing than a switch from bespoke purchases — thus increased sales reflect an actual increase in production.

28. D. E. C. Eversley, "The Home Market and Economic Growth in England, 1750–80," in E. L. Jones and G. E. Mingay, *Land, Labour and Population in the Industrial Revolution* (London, 1967), 254; W. J. Reader, *Professional Men: The Rise of the Professional Classes in Nineteenth-Century England* (New York, 1966), 211. See also Harold Perkin, *The Origins of Modern English Society, 1780–1880* (London, 1969), 141–43.

29. Hobsbawm claims that "taken all in all, the general tendency for skilled wages to rise faster than unskilled over the long period is in little doubt" (*Labouring Men,* 295). On the other hand, Sidney Pollard argues that a "remarkable stability in the ratio of skilled and unskilled wages" existed ("Trade Unions and the Labour Market, 1870–1914," *Yorkshire Bulletin of Social and Economic Research,* 17 May 1965, 100–101). The experience of the sweated trades seems to be on the side of Hobsbawm, although S. G. Checkland (*The Rise of Industrial Society in England, 1815–1885* [New York, 1964], 26) claims that wages for women clothing workers rose as a result of the introduction of the sewing machine. See chs. 3 and 6 herein.

30. Hobsbawm, *Labouring Men,* 293. It is doubtful that trade unionism had much effect on the wages of the unskilled, particularly of women, between 1870 and 1914. Pollard claims that of the three periods of trade union expansion (1870–74, 1888–90, 1909–13) wages rose only in the first ("Trade Unions and the Labour Market," 104).

31. The lower classes traditionally acquired the cast-off clothing of their betters, either purchased in used clothing stores or handed down from master to servant, or they made do with clothing made at home. See Robert Roberts, *The Classic Slum* (London, 1973), 38.

32. P.P., "Report to the Board of Trade on the Sweating System in the East End of London," 1887, vol. lxxxix, p. 11.

33. For a discussion of Mayhew's methods see Eileen Yeo, "Mayhew as a Social Investigator," in Yeo and Thompson, *Unknown Mayhew,* 51–95.

34. Mayhew, letter XVI to the *Morning Chronicle,* in ibid., 181.

35. Letters VI, VII, XVII, ibid., 116–26, 129, 216–19.

36. Letter XVII, ibid., 196.

37. P.P., "Sixth Report of the Medical Officer of the Privy Council: Report by Dr. Edward Smith on the Sanitary Circumstances of Tailors in London," 1864, vol. xxviii, pp. 416, 425–26.

38. It is probable that at between the ages of twenty-five and thirty-five, the mortality of tailors and printers was even greater because many young men, if attacked by disease in London, returned to their country homes to die, and it would be there that the deaths would be registered. Ibid., 30.

Death Rates of London Tailors and Printers and Agriculture Workers
for England and Wales in 1863 (per 100,000 men employed)

Category	Age, 25–35	Age, 35–45	Age, 45–55
Agriculture Workers	743	805	1,145
Tailors	958	1,262	2,093
Printers	894	1,747	2,367

39. The figures for 1849 are from Yeo and Thompson, *Unknown Mayhew,* 218; for 1813, from George, *London Life,* 356, 386.

40. Kingsley, *Alton Locke,* 293–94. This edition was published in 1910, although the novel was first published in 1850.

41. This was the observation of John Williamson, a tailor, as quoted in Stewart and Hunter, *Needle Is Threaded,* 62.

CHAPTER 2

Sweating and the Machine

THE MOST IMPORTANT CONSEQUENCE of the invention of the sewing machine was the speedup in work and production, which, in effect, caused a proliferation of the sweating system. This chapter first examines how the sewing machine and related innovations brought about a revolution in the production process and the organization of the labor market. Then the speedup in the pace of work and the amount of displacement of the traditional English male artisan by a new sweated labor force are discussed. The rest of the chapter sketches the growth patterns in the London clothing trades from the 1860s, when the sewing machine became widespread. An attempt is made to establish the size and makeup of the sweated labor force in the London clothing trades and to measure the shifts in production from the traditional centers of production to sweated premises, particularly in the East End.

The sewing machine

Unexciting when placed alongside the gaslight or the electric street-car, the sewing machine was nevertheless one of the most momentous inventions of the second half of the nineteenth century: it revolutionized the consuming habits of the nation and changed the lives of a multitude of workingmen and women. The falling price of clothing (in 1900 a shirt cost one-fourth as much as it did fifty years earlier[1]), the increase in clothing exports, and the influx of workers into the clothing trades were a result, in part at least, of the widespread use of the sewing machine.

Introduced into Great Britain from the United States at the Great Exhibition of 1851, the machine was not widely produced until after the first patents expired in 1861. Machines were being used in London by the 1860s in Whitechapel in the East End, in the homes of workers living about Seven Dials, and at the Army clothing factory at Pimlico. Still, Andrew Ure reported that there were only about 500 sewing machines in all of England in 1869. The first machine was operated by a hand-driven crank wheel, but with the development of Singer's treadle mechanism most sewing machines were operated by foot power. Steam-powered machines were being experimented with by 1864, but it was not until the development of the oscillating shuttle in 1879 that the replacement of the treadle became practical. By 1870 the sewing machine was being mass-produced on an enormous scale. Annual worldwide production of the sewing machine grew from 2,266 machines in 1853 to 139,312 in 1867 and to over half a million in 1871. A large number of the six million sewing machines made in Europe by the Singer Company from 1853 to the end of 1896 were produced in the Singer factory in Kilbowie, Scotland.[2]

There were two basic types of machines used for sewing cloth: a chain stitch machine and a shuttle machine. The former employed a circular needle to produce a back stitch on the surface and a loop or chain stitch on the underside; the shuttle stitch used less thread and was formed by an upright needle passing up and down through the material and a shuttle passing through on the underside to form a loop.[3] Although technically these were the only two basic types of sewing machines, there was no dearth of styles of machines available for clothing work. One American concern in 1900, for example, manufactured 400 different types of machines. Each firm made claims of excellence, but the important factor in selecting a machine was the kind of clothing to be made. For example, tailors, staymakers, and bootmakers as a rule used heavier machines than did shirt- and collar-makers or dressmakers.[4]

The sewing machine saved the worker much of what was called the "slaving," that is, the seaming and stitching found in the old hand-sewn production. The shirt of a mid-Victorian gentleman had over 20,000 stitches. Sewing this shirt by hand, the sewer could average thirty-five stitches a minute; with a machine the worker could complete between 1,000 and 2,000 stitches per minute,[5] or thirty times as many as a hand stitcher. In hatmaking it was estimated that one machine could do the work of five to six women. A staymaker claimed that the sewing machine allowed for a 90 percent reduction in hand work.[6]

In the very early stage of sewing machine production (1862) one manufacturer claimed that the machine, when compared to hand labor, could speed up production by six to eleven times, depending on what sort of article was being made.[7] All in all, it appears reasonable to guess that the sewing machine speeded up production perhaps 500 percent — although much depends on the type and quality of product discussed.

The sewing machine was the "first domestic appliance."[8] Early predictions that the sewing machine would encourage the centralization of production in the factory[9] turned out to be unfounded: most machine-made clothes were not made in a factory. Other machines were developed for high-speed stitching, band-stitching, machine-felling, collar-padding, buttonholing, cutting, lacemaking, and embroidery, but with few exceptions these, too, were machines for the home and small workshop, "no larger than a neat small work-box, very portable and convenient." The Reece buttonhole machines, for example, patented in the United States in 1881, was no larger or heavier than the average sewing machine. Using this machine at home, the woman machinist cut the buttonhole and then transferred it to the stitching device. In this manner she could make over 10,000 buttonholes in a single workday, resulting in savings of "several hundred percent" in labor cost to the manufacturer.[10] Even beltmaking was done with special machines used by women homemakers. As late as 1915 there was probably no industry as untouched by factory production or in which the methods of production had been standardized so little as the manufacture of clothing.[11]

Most of the sewing machines used in the sweated trades were purchased on the hire system by homeworkers or proprietors of small workshops, who made weekly installments over many months until the machine was paid for. The machine manufacturer often provided machining lessons, usually for a fee and the unpaid labor of the student. The installment purchase system was first introduced by the Singer Company in 1856. The whole of East London, by 1888, was mapped out in sales districts with regular armies of collectors, who visited the customers each week to collect the installment payment; the Singer Company had thirty collectors in the East End alone. The weekly payment in 1888 for a Singer machine was 2s. 6d.; for a Bradbury it was 1s. 6d. Although it allowed many women who would otherwise never have purchased a machine to do so, the system was harsh and brutal. Workers frequently lost their machines when they were out of work and unable to keep up payments. This was the case of a woman homeworker who lost four machines on the hire system, having paid £1 to £5 on each of them; another homeworker, a blouse-maker, lost her machine and her £4 investment when she missed two of the weekly payments. To avoid such disasters, the Jewish Board of Guardians for a time sold or rented machines to workers.[12] The hire system of Singer and others insured that the sewing machine became the most widely used invention of the second industrial revolution. "Probably no organized piece of machinery has ever been so systematically exploited, so thoroughly advertised, so persistently canvassed, and so extensively sold as the sewing machine."[13]

The speedup in sewing forced the cutter to look for new ways to cut materials faster. Hence, clothes were cut out by a power-driven band saw from thick stacks of cloth after their patterns had been chalked or soaped out. Although the band saw was not a home machine, it facilitated and generated outworking. First developed for cutting veneer wood in the furniture trade, the band saw eventually cut leather for boots and shoes and cloth for shirts, trousers, vests, and other garments. The manufacturer — and this could be anyone with a bit of experience and a bit of cash — could, with one or two cutting machines jammed in his shop, cut out hundreds of coats or trousers a week.

Other innovations in production

This quickening of the pace of production was accompanied by two other labor-saving and task-simplifying devices: subdivision and subcontracting of labor. The subdivision of labor was a system whereby the functions of production were minutely divided into single tasks, each performed by a worker who did nothing but an assigned operation. The system was, to a large extent, introduced by Jewish entrepreneurs. The advantages it provided were numerous, not the least of which was increased output at a lower cost. It was cheaper to subdivide the work among a team of women and boys, who needed only to become proficient at one task, than it was to assign the work to a highly skilled artisan, who was capable of constructing the entire garment himself. It was not necessarily true that subdivision of labor meant shoddy goods. The journeyman bootmaker may have been a

"jack of all trades," but often he was "the master of none" as well.[14]
Indeed, the end result of the new methods was "cheap" but not necessarily "nasty" goods.

Yet the subdivision of labor was highly disturbing to the artisan.
Like the butty system in coal mining, it encouraged workers to exploit
one another. Although the subdivision of labor in tailoring had existed
in some form long before the advent of the sewing machine, it was,
like subcontracting, a natural outgrowth of machine production. The
artisan, of course, opposed the system not only because the worker
was learning a very small portion of the trade but also because it
allowed the work to be done by relatively unskilled laborers who would
depress wages, working conditions, and job status. The artisan-tailor
found all the functions in coatmaking so divided that instead of one
person working on a coat, there would be many: one to do sleeves,
one to do cuffs, one to sew pockets, and so on. In addition, the other
functions in coatmaking, like fixing, basting, and pressing, were all
subdivided, as they were in all other tailoring work, so that by 1888
tailoring had been subdivided into at least twenty-five divisions. The
"art of the English tailor," Beatrice Potter noted, "has been exchanged
for the perfect mechanism of Jewish organizations."[15]

Even more controversial and subject to debate among workers and
reformers was the system of subcontracting of labor, often pointed
out as the source of the sweating system. It was a process whereby
subcontractors, called middlemen or sweaters, would arrange with
a large wholesaler, shopkeeper, or manufacturer to produce a certain
quantity of specified goods. Many of these subcontractors neither
maintained work premises of their own nor had any expertise in the
trade itself, both facts that were obnoxious to traditional craftsmen.
After receiving the contract and paying a security deposit to cover
the cost of the cut-out pieces of material, the subcontractor then found
a number of workshop owners or homeworkers to do the work, perhaps
keeping some of the work to be done by himself or his employees in
his own workroom. Some of the workers under subcontract, in turn,
would contract a portion of their work to others, either smaller sweaters
or outworkers who worked in their homes or small garret shops. Not
infrequently, the work would be subcontracted yet another time by
the outworkers. (See ch. 3 herein for a more complete discussion of
these practices from the worker's view.)

Subcontracting had its origins in the bespoke trade but became a form of production extensively used in the ready-to-wear trade. This new industry was eventually subdivided into chains of retailers and wholesalers on the distribution end and a complex of manufacturers on the production end. Manufacturers in the ready-made trade put out goods that went through numerous contracts, while some of the old bespoke firms in the West End merely opened branches, that is, storage rooms and distribution centers, in the East End or elsewhere for putting out work. Others, like the London tailoring firm of Herbert and Company, subcontracted their work to East End middlemen, who then contracted the work out to a number of secondary middlemen who would let the work out to small shops that worked their laborers fourteen to fifteen hours a day — work that no union member would consider doing. On each level the workers would compete by agreeing to lower wages. In this manner Herbert and Company was able to get coats, which had cost 2s. 9d. in 1886, made for 1s. 8d. in 1888.[16] This system became more and more complex as there was a greater vertical movement of manufacturers into retailing and retailers and wholesalers into manufacturing. In short, the clothing trades were able to expand and contract easily as market demand, fashion, and other factors, including operation costs and, as we shall see, government regulations, changed. Hence, for the laborer the work was erratic and highly seasonal — what the Victorians called "casual labor" — and because of subdivision and subcontracting, it was highly decentralized: an industry of the streets. "Our so-called factories," claimed the London boot- and shoemakers, "are nothing but private houses, pulled and nailed about to suit some petty employer's purposes, and are mostly situated in the worst of neighborhoods, and have not enough room for workmen to stand much less to do their work properly."[17]

The footwear trades

As in the other clothing trades, technology and innovation in the boot and shoe trades led to the mechanization of outwork. To see this change, we need only briefly look at the four major steps in footwear production, clicking, closing, making, and finishing. Clicking was cutting out the various parts of the boot or shoe; it sometimes involved as many as thirty to forty pieces. It was a highly skilled job that under the bespoke system was done in its entirety in a separate room of the workshop by an artisan. Since clicking was most always done on the premises of the employer, it was the division of the footwear trade least subject to sweating and homework. But clicking slowly changed, beginning in the 1860s and 1870s with the so-called American kit of cutting knives, which simplified and subdivided the cutting process. Through this process a large number of ready-made boots and shoes could be cut out by one or two skilled cutters with the aid of several unskilled or semiskilled helpers. The privileged position of the cutter lasted longer — at least until the mid-1890s, when cutting machines, such as the cutting press, leather splitter, leather roller, lift cutter, and sole rounder, were introduced.[18]

Closing was sewing together the upper parts of the boot or shoe. In the traditional bespoke trade this was done by hand by a skilled worker. However, because it could be easily done by a machine, it was one of the first sectors of the footwear industry to become sweated. Machine-closing was first done in the early 1860s but was limited to "short work," or low-cut footwear. By the 1890s it had so infiltrated the "long work," or high-boot sector of the trade, that most bespoke and ready-made boots and shoes were machine-closed. As in tailoring, the machinery used in closing was small, cheap, and relatively easy to operate; hence, machine-closing was rapidly taken over by out-workers. Although electric power was eventually applied to machine-closing, the foot-operated treadle machine was still widely used in the home in the first decade of the twentieth century.[19]

Once a male occupation, closing became, even in the bespoke sector, dominated first by women and after the turn of the century almost entirely by immigrant Jews. By the late 1880s closing as an artisan craft "was fast dying out";[20] machine-closing had all but completely replaced hand-sewing.

Making was attaching the sole and heel to the uppers and was under the purview of the laster. It consisted of two steps: the first was to last or tack the insole to the shoe last and then shape the uppers over the shoe last and attach it to the insole; the second step was to attach the insole and the upper, now one piece, to the sole and heel. This process was one of the last bastions of hand work, and not until 1888–91 did lasting begin to succumb to machine work. In 1891 an American machine manufacturer advertised that his lasting machine could be operated by women.[21] Lasting became, for the most part, an outwork task.

The next step in making up the shoe, attaching, was previously done either by hand-riveting or by hand-sewing. This process was revolutionized in 1861 by the McKay shoe-sewing machine, an American invention that allowed for the production of comfortable and strongly sewn shoes at much less than the price of the coarse and clumsy pegged shoe. With the McKay machine a single operator was able to sew between 500 and 600 pairs of shoes in a ten-hour day. After the adoption of the Goodyear sewing machine in 1871, even high-class footwear began to be attached by machine, although it was not until the 1890s that the process was perfected enough to be used on a widespread basis in the production of high-class goods. Last, the attaching of the heel was done by hand until the mid-1890s, when heeling machines were developed. None of these were yet, however, factory machines; they were used mainly in small workshops.[22]

The final step in boot- and shoemaking was finishing, a series of subprocesses that required a moderate degree of skill. Knifing, socking, cleaning, lining, sewing on buttons, and packing were all steps in the process. Finishing had always been a homework process and remained so with the advent of portable machinery, such as a machine for setting eyelets, one for cutting decorative patterns on the leather, and other labor-saving tools patterned after the American system of production. These innovations allowed the finishing process to be subdivided into some twenty different parts, most of which could be done by women at home or by boys under the so-called team system.[23] Hence, as the ready-to-wear trade grew, thousands of new outworking jobs in finishing were created.

Like the garment industry, the ready-made footwear trade was based on the assumption that a single worker could most economically do one task in the production process. For example, by 1888 closing was no longer a one-person job but had been subdivided into pattern-cutting and clicking and then further divided into fitting, machining, then buttonholing, and, finally, sewing on the buttons. The workers in most of these occupations were women because the skill requirements were low and they were willing to work for lower wages.

All in all, subcontracting and subdivision were nearly as widespread in the footwear trades as they were in the garment trades. The easy manner of acquiring a machine led to a continuous augmentation of the system. Aspiring entrepreneurs, with little capital, cheap material, and a few rented machines could start manufacturing by employing a few unskilled workers, all on the basis of subcontract and all without a physical plant or even a moderately sized workshop. Although subcontracting could mean survival for the artisan who was being squeezed out of the trade, many subcontractors were of a different sort, having little or no experience with the trade. Credit was provided by the leather distributors, and the machine distributors welcomed purchases on the installment plan. The subcontracting chamber master, as he was called, did his own clicking with the assistance of his family. Closing was often done by women machinists in the master's home or by women who took the work to their homes or gave it out to subordinate labor. After being returned to the master, the boots or shoes were given out to low-paid workers to be finished. As in the garment trades, the production of a single shoe might well stretch across London, from the chamber master's shop in Hackney or Bermondsey to its final destination in an Oxford Street shop. Although frequently pointed to as the cause of sweating, the middleman chamber master often had an income that was little more or even less than that of his sweated workers.[24]

Job displacement

These technological innovations provided jobs for some thousands while they left others, largely skilled artisans, un- or underemployed. While the shortage of workers in America had led to labor-saving devices and job practices, for the London industry, with an abundance of labor, this approach had dreadful consequences. The number of women, working at much lower wages, in tailoring increased from one in seven in 1841 to one in three in 1871. The sewing machine, noted a government official in 1864, was striking a death blow to both factory and skilled laborers: "The labour-tide seems to have reached its highest in the factory system, and to be now receding towards the homes of the journeymen."[25] Concurring with this observation were London shoemakers, who complained that the sewing machine was driving their work "outdoors." Thinking to improve their condition, one shoemaker said that some of his fellow workers "have left the workshop and taken their work out; they have freed themselves from the restraint of the Association; they have bought a machine, and got young women to work it."[26] Speaking of the tailoring trade, a London factory inspector observed that some workers were leaving their masters "and taking two rooms in a back street, competing with their former masters, eluding the Factory Inspector and becoming a sweating master. The facilities offered for the hire of sewing machines and other necessary tools are so numerous that a workman starting without any capital becomes a master in the space of a week or two."[27] Similarly, a London tailor, in looking back to ascertain the origins of the outwork system of production, concluded that "I can scarcely tell how this outdoor working began, but it would seem to be coeval with the introduction and use of machinery; one thing is certain, that side by side with the cheapening of machines and the extension of the weekly payment system there is an ever-increasing number of outworkers."[28] A few years later this tailor, James Macdonald, lamented again that the machine was "a source of danger to the trade" because of the large number of unskilled workers it had brought into competition with "the educated workman."[29] In the same manner a factory inspector noted in 1903 that homework was becoming universally practiced because of the system of subdivision of labor, and Edward Cadbury, writing in 1907, claimed that "the cheapening of machines and supply of female labor tend to make [outwork] advantageous to the ordinary tailor" and "have driven the men to make their own working environment."[30]

Adding to this problem of easy entry into the trade was a dramatic increase in Jewish immigration. Between 1880 and 1914 tens of thousands of East European Jews were either expelled from their countries or fled to escape persecution. Finding themselves unwelcome in most of Europe, many of them sought refuge in London. During these decades more European Jews entered London than any other city of the world, and, although many of them went on to North and South America, large numbers stayed in London (mainly in the East End), so that, like New York and Chicago, London found itself with a large Jewish settlement. The immigrants came in three major waves. The first group came as a result of a pogrom in Russia from 1881 to 1886 and a period of anti-Semitism in Germany about the same time. The second wave occurred in 1890–92, when renewed anti-Semitic activity in Russia pushed thousands of Jews into London; this flow was accelerated ten years later (the third wave) as a result of internal turmoil and war (1905–6) in Russia. Russians and Poles (mainly Jews) living in London increased from 1,709 in 1881 to 26,742 in 1891, 53,539 in 1901, and 68,420 by 1911.[31]

How severe was the contraction of work for English male artisans and how easily they found work in the new ready-made sector are difficult to determine. Ben Tillett's estimate that 25 percent of the London dockworkers were former shoemakers and tailors partially confirms the often-heard claim that artisans were not easily assimilated into the new ready-made trades. Likewise in 1892 the Royal Commission on Labour was told that the use of machinery resulted in an exodus of bootmakers into dock labor.[32] Of all the clothing trades, job displacement was most severe in the London footwear trades, due to the departure of part of that industry from London to the provinces, particularly Northampton, and to the widescale introduction of machinery in the 1890s which opened the door to Jewish, female, and then boy workers. Until the early 1890s the industry in London was fairly healthy, and its male labor force was growing. But from then on the total number of workers employed in the trade declined. Production shifted from the old centers in south London to the bedrooms and kitchens of the north London and East End neighborhoods. The boot- and shoemakers often protested their employers' introduction of machinery and blamed the machine for the reduction in wages and the high levels of unemployment among union members. Machinery, claimed the union, had "upset everything."[33] The London branch of the National Union of Boot and Shoe Operatives reported nearly monthly that its members were losing jobs because of machine production. Typically, in 1897 the branch reported that "our men . . . are being discharged through the introduction of machinery." T. F. Richards, Member of Parliament and a boot-and-shoe unionist, claimed that a chief reason for the lack of jobs in the footwear industry was "the rapid introduction of machinery into our trades." And still, in 1906 the union reported that machinery "is unfortunately throwing a large number of men out of employment" while giving jobs to youths and boys and forcing true breadwinners to walk the streets.[34]

Machinery meant that cheap labor—mainly women and alien Jews—were more employable than the English male worker. "Women are able, in these days of machinery," noted the *Women's Trade Union Review,* "to learn in 14 days all that is required of them to manage their machines, therefore the market is always over-crowded with them, and they not only hurt themselves by the wages they accept, but they injure their husbands and brothers by undertaking to do for 5s what the men can get 13s a week for and whom they, therefore, push out of employment."[35] One assistant factory inspector claimed that unemployment among men was largely due to the increased employment of women in industrial occupations formerly reserved to men.[36]

Consequently, male workers tried to prevent the reductions of wages and elimination of jobs that followed the introduction of machinery. London tailors fought with their employers over how to adjust their wages to machine work. When skilled workers balked at the unilateral decisions of employers, they were frequently replaced with cheap labor, often outworkers. For example, the decision by a London bootmaker in 1892 to bring a lasting machine, a hobnailer, and a standard screwer into his shop resulted in a refusal of the union men to produce more than their contract called for. The men were replaced, a strike ensued, and boy labor was brought into the shop to work the machines.[37] The London boot- and shoemakers became so desperate for jobs that they dared not fight the machine nor turn down work at reduced wages.[38] Time and again the boot- and shoemakers were warned by their leaders of the encroachment of women and girls into the trade, and the union protested the use of "cheap labor." The executive of the National Union of Boot and Shoe Operatives passed a resolution stating that "this Council hereby protests against the introduction of females into the clicking, roughstuff, lasting, and finishing departments, and any branch or branches knowing of such . . . must immediately acquaint the Central Office with the circumstances."[39] Immediately the London branches began to inform the council of women being employed in the London trades.

By 1900 some trades, such as coatmaking, vestmaking, and trousermaking, were almost exclusively in the hands of Jewish entrepreneurs and workers. Boot- and shoemakers constantly complained that they were being thrown out of a job because Jewish workers did the work for less pay.[40] Consequently, by the turn of the century a noticeable amount of anti-immigration sentiment greeted the heavy influx of Jewish immigrants into London. The Jewish worker, viewed by many English workers as the source of sweating, blacklegging, undercutting, and scab labor, was regarded not only as a threat to English jobs but also as a threat to traditional production practices. As the Paddington branch of the Amalgamated Society of Tailors noted, the use of Jewish labor, at reduced wages, by some British employers meant that other employers of skilled English labor were forced to cut their costs by using machines and female labor to remain competitive.[41]

Despite these frequent and often vicious attacks by male English workers on their co-workers, it is hard to determine how frequently English workers were displaced by women and Jews. Some displacement took place simply because the traditional bespoke firms went out of business because of the lower costs of the Jewish entrepreneurs in the ready-to-wear trades. In other cases the bespoke firms remained alive by adopting some of the labor-saving devices and organization of production of the Jewish entrepreneurs, but the effect on the artisan was the same: no job or a job at substantially reduced wages. Hence, by 1906 it was reported that there was scarcely a British artisan in Soho;[42] in most of the clothing trades the number of English male workers declined both in absolute numbers and as a percentage of the total labor force. The male labor force in the footwear trades, for example, decreased by more than 4,000 between 1891 and 1901, a reduction of approximately 13 percent of the male labor force. In the other clothing trades during the same period, and with the exception of dressmaking, the number of English males decreased while the number of Jewish males increased. Over a forty-year period from 1861 to 1901, the proportion of immigrant Jewish workers in the clothing trades, particularly in tailoring and footwear, increased dramatically. In 1861 approximately 3 percent of the male London tailors were Jews. In 1901 foreign-born Jews made up 36 percent of the male labor force in tailoring. In absolute numbers there were 8 percent fewer male English tailors in London in 1901 than there had been in 1861 (21,861 in 1861 as opposed to 20,014 in 1901). In the boot and shoe trades the proportion of male Jews increased from less than 1 percent of the male labor force in 1861 to 12.3 percent in 1901. In absolute numbers English males decreased over this period by 28 percent, from 33,435 to 24,004.[43]

The proportion of females in the tailoring trade for all of London increased from 38.6 percent in 1871 to 51.3 percent in 1901; in the boot and shoe trades the proportion of women increased from 13.1 percent to 19.8 percent for the same period. These changes were greater or lesser in certain parts of London. In the borough of Hackney between 1901 and 1904, for example, the number of male workers in the clothing trades declined by eighty-eight, while the number of girls increased by 243 and the number of women by 283.[44]

If we use trade union statistics and operate on the premise that some correlation exists between union membership and the number of English males employed in the trade, an even more gloomy estimate of the level of technological unemployment in the footwear trades emerges. Records for the London branch of the National Union of Boot and Shoe Operatives show a 75 percent decrease in membership for the period 1894 to 1901,[45] leaving the impression that the 13 percent decrease in male employment shown in the census figures for the footwear trade for approximately the same period underestimates the amount of job displacement that English males in that trade suffered, even though it cannot be concluded that all 75 percent of those who left the union also left the trade.

The size of the sweated labor force

Although after about 1860 almost all observers of the sweatshop claim that the number of its victims was growing, the Victorians and Edwardians had difficulty in measuring the sweated population of the metropolis. The modern historian faces the same problem.[46] Among the few sources available are the occupational returns of the decennial census, which, although they must be used only with care and as an approximation, illustrate the growth of the clothing industry from 1861 to 1911 and give us a rough idea of the number of workers in the sweated clothing trades. The proportion of London workers engaged in the clothing trades nearly doubled, from 6.8 percent of the employed population of London in 1861 to 12.4 percent in 1911 (Table 4). This increase is significant because the percentage of employed workers in England and Wales engaged in the clothing trades actually decreased, from 10.1 percent in 1861 to 6.6 percent in 1911. In absolute numbers the clothing trades workers in London grew by 41.5 percent in the fifty years from 1861 to 1911, whereas the growth for the nation as a whole for the period was 17.0 percent. London's share of the clothing industry of England and Wales increased from 20.5 percent in 1861 to 24.9 percent in 1911, the greatest increase taking place between 1901 and 1911.

Although at least half of these workers can be generally categorized as sweated workers, the clothing industry was made up of a number of complex and separate industries, each with its own wage customs, growth patterns, and social standing; high-class dress work, for example, paid well and was at the top of the social ladder for women; shirt-finishing was lower on the scale; and trouser-finishing was at

Table 4. Employment in the Clothing Trades: London vs. England and Wales, 1861–1911

	London		England and Wales		
Year	No. of Workers in Clothing Trades	Percentage of Employed Population	No. of Workers in Clothing Trades	Percentage of Employed Population in Clothing Trades	Percentage of All Clothing Workers in London*
1861	190.2	6.8	913.7	10.1	20.5
1871	186.2	8.5	899.1	9.1	19.8
1881	208.3	12.2	933.4	8.7	21.5
1891	236.9	12.1	1,034.3	8.7	21.5
1901	249.4	11.8	1,125.6	8.3	20.9
1911	269.3	12.4	998.4	6.6	24.9

*"All" means those in England and Wales.

Note. Absolute numbers are in thousands.

Source. Great Britain (Parliament). Parliamentary Papers, "Census Returns—Occupations," *for 1861,* 1861, vols. li-lii; 1863, vols. liii, liii.1; *for 1871,* 1873, vol. lxxii, pt. 2; *for 1881,* 1883, vol. xcvi.1; *for 1891,* 1893–94, vols. civ-cvi; 1890–91, vol. xciv.1; *for 1901,* 1902, vols. cxx, cxx.1, cxxx; 1903, vols. lxxxiv, lxxv.1; 1904, vol. cvii; *for 1911,* 1912–13, vols. cxi-cxiii; 1913, vols. lxxvii-lxxx.

the bottom. During the fifty years after 1861 over 80 percent of the clothing industry was dominated by four trades: dressmaking (including millinery), tailoring, boot- and shoemaking, and shirtmaking and seamstress work (Table 5). Dressmaking, the largest of the four trades, enjoyed considerable growth until the early 1890s. In absolute numbers the dressmakers of London increased from 54,870 in 1861 to nearly 80,000 in 1911. Dressmaking absorbed approximately 30 percent of the labor force of the London clothing industry until the early 1870s, increased to nearly 35 percent by 1881, remained stationary until the 1890s, and then tapered off again to around 30 percent. London's share of the total dressmaking trade of England and Wales increased by 1.5 percent between 1861 and 1871 and remained stationary at about 20 percent for the remainder of the century. The popularity of the bicycle in the 1890s, for example, decreased the demand for the cumbersome dress of middle- and upper-class women and thus caused a shift to tailor-made clothing.[47]

The London tailoring trade grew from 34,678 tailors in 1861 to 64,993 tailors in 1911, an increase of 87.4 percent (compared to an

Table 5. Percentage of London Clothing Workers Engaged in Specific Trades, 1861–1911

Year	Dressmaking	Tailoring	Boot- and Shoemaking	Shirtmaking and Seamstress Work
1861	28.8	18.2	22.5	14.7
1871	31.9	20.6	19.1	14.4
1881	34.5	19.8	17.8	13.0
1891	35.2	22.1	16.4	7.8
1901	29.6	25.9	13.7	13.0
1911	30.2	21.9	10.4	9.9

Source. See the source note to Table 4.

81 percent growth for the same period for England and Wales as a whole). The number of tailors in relation to the rest of the London clothing industry grew only slightly, from 18 to nearly 22 percent, and the proportion of the nation's tailoring done in London remained the same. In short, as in dressmaking, the number of tailors grew in real terms, and tailors held onto their relative share of the clothing industry for the period 1861 to 1911.

Shirtmaking encompassed those working in the manufacture of shirts, collars, ties, underclothing, and other related items and the general category of seamstress. Collarmaking, for example, was one of the trades that grew because of the new fashion interests of workers, namely, the passion of the affluent workers for respectability as they took to wearing stiff collars in the workshop.[48] A precise analysis of this shirtmaking sector of the trade is difficult because a large number of those counted in this division, such as buttonholers, stitchers, glovers, or simply sewing machinists, actually belong under another heading, such as dressmaker or tailor. Hence, the more accurate the return in categorizing the labor force, the smaller will be this class of workers. This is apparently what happened in 1891 and 1911 — the census numerators were more careful in their counting. In any case, the category shirtmakers varied from around 8 percent to as high as 15 percent. In numerical terms the largest number of shirtmakers and seamstresses reported was 32,577 in 1901.

The number of workers in the London boot and shoe industry fell from 42,828 workers in 1861 to 27,940 in 1911, a decrease of 34 percent in fifty years. In the same period the number of boot and shoe workers on the national level decreased only 3.5 percent. The largest decreases took place between 1861 and 1871, when the industry in London lost 16.6 percent of its workers, and between 1901 and 1911, when another 18.2 percent of the boot and shoe workers left the trade. In between, however, from 1872 to 1881, the industry grew slightly faster in London than it did in England and Wales (Table 6). It was not until after 1891 that London's share in the national boot and shoe trade began to drop appreciably, from 16.7 percent in 1881 to 11.3 percent in 1911, just about half of what it had been a half century earlier. Until late in the century, London remained the center for "slop" — cheap footwear production.

Table 6. Percentage of All Boot- and Shoemakers in England and Wales Working in London, 1861–1911

Year	Percentage
1861	16.7
1871	15.9
1881	16.7
1891	15.7
1901	13.6
1911	11.3

Source: See the source note to Table 4.

Many of these new workers were women. The movement of women into the London clothing trades was most marked in the case of tailoring, where the percentage of women workers increased from approximately one-third in 1861 to one-half by 1901 (Table 7). The percentage of women boot and shoe workers increased by nearly 7 percent between 1871 and 1901. As a whole, the proportion of women workers in the clothing industry in London rose from approximately 63 to 67 percent — much less than the national increase that was from approximately 60 to 76 percent for the same period.

In truth, however, the outworking wife and widow were statistical mysteries. While the census picture of more and more women moving into the clothing industry on the national level probably reflects the introduction of the factory system of clothing production outside of London, it is equally likely that the census greatly underestimates the number of women working. Many women were simply not included in the census returns. They were not organized in factories but isolated in the home or small shop, and because so many of them worked

Table 7. Percentage of Women Engaged in the Various Clothing Trades in London, 1861–1911

Year	Clothing	Dressmaking	Tailoring	Boot- and Shoemaking	Shirtmaking and Seamstress Work
1861	63.4	100.0	35.7	21.5	84.2
1871	63.8	98.4	38.6	13.1	86.0
1881	67.8	98.0	44.8	17.9	85.1
1891	67.5	97.5	47.5	19.3	81.5
1901	67.4	99.0	51.3	19.8	82.2
1911	67.6	98.2	48.4	19.3	72.4

Source: See the source note to Table 4.

only casually—often for each other or for small employers—they escaped union records and evaded the census-takers. They did not report themselves as being employed simply because they worked part-time or were in seasonal work that was not operating at the time the census was taken.[49] Charles Booth noted that shirt-finishers, out of a general working-class fear of any kind of state official, often hid the fact that they were employed and would not talk about their work.[50] Others were simply not counted. For example, in 1861 some 13,000 women were counted in the occupational census as "shoemakers' wives"; in 1871 they were transferred to the category "domestic" workers, and in 1881 they were returned to the category of boot- and shoemakers. But then they disappear. The practice of counting them was probably discontinued because of the growth of the provincial factory system, but for certain production centers, like London, the number of nonfactory jobs for these wives increased, and thus we can be certain that the number of boot and shoe workers fell less drastically than the statistics indicate and that here and in the clothing trades in general the number of women entering the labor force was probably greater than the statistics indicate.

The statistics that exist, then, allow the historian to give nothing but a reasonable guess as to the numbers in and the growth patterns of the sweated labor force. The only statistical data on nonfactory (often sweated) jobs are the local government medical officer's outwork lists after 1901 and the occupational census category "working at home." Although the accuracy of these are questionable, a general statistical picture can be presented. The medical officer's outwork lists indicate that the number of outworkers in London increased from about 7 to about 12 percent of the labor force of the clothing trades between 1904 and 1909; the occupational census shows that the number of those "working at home" was 25 percent of the clothing trade workers in 1901 and nearly 20 percent in 1911. Recognizing that a large number of outworkers went unreported (see above and Appendix A), it is more probable that as many as half of the workers in the London clothing trades were outworkers—either in their own homes or in the homes of others.

These estimates, however, do not tell us anything about the shifts from district to district within London. We know that sweating expanded rapidly in some neighborhoods while it hardly affected others. A rapid growth in outworking and a contraction of living space in the central city resulted in the shift of work to traditional working-class neighborhoods. The most notable change in the concentration of workers was a shift in concentration of male workers from the west and central districts to the east (Appendix B). The highest concentration of male clothing workers in 1861 was in the west district (which composed the West End, the center for London's fashionable bespoke trade) and the central district (which was for the most part the City ready-made trade). By 1891 a considerable shift to the East End, the reputed home of the sweating system, had begun, and by 1901 the East End had more than doubled its concentration of male clothing workers. Likewise, the decreased concentration of boot and shoe workers in the south, central, and west districts and the corresponding increase in male and female boot and shoe workers in the east indicate a shift of that industry to the East End.

Women clothing workers increased slightly in concentration in the west up to 1891 and then decreased by 1901. The only noticeable shift in female clothing workers was from the central to the north, most of which was a shift in concentration to the northeast residential boroughs of St. Pancras, Islington, and Hackney. Concentration of female clothing workers, particularly in boot- and shoemaking, in the East End remained high. Female workers in shoemaking shifted from the south and central districts to the north, where the concentration of female workers nearly doubled, and east.

In sum, then, we may draw three general conclusions about employment in the London clothing trades from 1861 to 1911. First, there was a fairly dramatic growth of employment in the industry; the portion of the London labor force engaged in clothing production in-

creased—largely because of the influx of women and Jewish immigrants. Second, it is likely that the total labor force of the clothing
trades was even larger, especially in terms of women outworkers, than
the available statistics indicate. Third, the work shifted from the traditional centers of production—the West End and the central City—to
the north and east, where many of the workers lived.

The clothing trades: growth or decay?

Although the subject is still vigorously debated, historians generally agree that the British entrepreneur during the last quarter of the
nineteenth century was less innovative and efficient than his American and German counterparts. The general consensus with regard
to worker productivity and industrial output is that the older British
industries, including the clothing trades, lagged behind not only the
new industries, but also foreign competitors.[51] Because the clothing
trades were the last capitulators to the factory system, the historian
has tended either to pass over them in any discussion of economic
growth or to regard them as backwaters of development. Some historians treat the clothing trades as an old industry, with all the conno-
tations of decay and stagnation, and others point to the low output
per worker as an indication of its decline.[52] An analysis of technological changes in the clothing trades, however, results in a conclusion that challenges these generalizations. Machinery and its concomitant labor-saving devices in the clothing trades in the last decades of
the nineteenth century tended to be labor intensive and of rather low
productivity. Thus, production was carried out in very small, scat-
tered, and decentralized locations by relatively unskilled workers and
entrepreneurs who had limited investment capital. The pace of change
was highly uneven and involved rather simple techniques. But the
clothing industry, which appeared to many to be in decline, was
actually in transition; it was the coalescence of the old bespoke and
the new ready-made trades that made the growth of the clothing
industry indistinguishable and hardly recognizable.

To a large extent, in terms of worker, product, and production methods, the clothing industry was a new industry, rising out of the old
artisan industry, and presents a picture of dramatic growth and change
as well as one of a continuity between the old and the new trades.
Industrial change, as J. B. Saul notes, "is always a complicated pro-

cess with growth and stagnation side by side between and within industries."[53] Still, economic change bore a price: The nation became better dressed and probably cleaner, but, as the new clothing industry grew, so did sweated labor. The nation, as Beatrice Webb once noted, was a sweater.[54]

NOTES

1. Edward W. Byrn, *The Progress of Invention in the Nineteenth Century* (New York, 1900), 192.

2. Ibid., 188, 193; P.P., "The Sixth Report of the Chief Medical Officer of the Privy Council," 1864, vol. xxviii, pp. 416, 417. See also Andrew Ure, *Dictionary of Arts, Manufacture and Mines,* 2 vols. (New York, 1869), 2: 594; P.P., "Children's Employment Commission," Second Report, 1864, vol. xxvi, pp. 186–88; P.P., "Report of the House of Lords Select Committee on Sweating," Second Report, 1888, vol. xxi; Ruth Brandon, *Capitalist Romance: Singer and the Sewing Machine* (Philadelphia, 1977), 101.

3. The chain stitch was considered the superior stitch for strength and durability and was less liable to ravel. It was easier to run, was faster, and favored for use in general seaming, quilting, sewing facings, and in instances where the underside would not be subject to friction in wear. The shuttle stitch was favored for work on edges where both sides would not be subject to heavy wear. Many workers preferred to employ both the chain and lockfast stitch machines in the workshop, although where only one of the two could be afforded, the lockfast machine was preferred. *Tailor and Cutter,* 29 Jan. 1870, 162. See also Clementina Black, *Married Women's Work* (London, 1915), 77.

4. Thus, the Singer, the Weed, and the Thomas machines, which were large and powerful and required both feet to work the treadle, were preferred for sewing heavy materials. Then in the 1880s a lighter machine was developed by Singer and became popular for use by women workers. Professional sewers recommended the Grover and Baker machine with its circular needle, but only when it was accompanied by a shuttle machine. The Wheeler-Wilson and the Elias Howe machines were easier to work but were not capable of doing some of the more general requirements of the men's tailoring trade. These machines, like the Wilson and Gibbs machine, were lighter and able to do a loop stitch, and thus were perfect for the lighter clothing trades and female work. Byrn, *Progress of Invention,* 189; P.P., "Children's Employment Commission," Second Report, 1864, vol. xxii, pp. 137, 164, 187; *Tailor and Cutter,* 17 Apr. 1869, 121; 29 Jan. 1870, 163; P.P., "Sixth

Report of the Chief Medical Officer," 1864, vol. xxviii, with reference to Dr. Ord's report on the London needle trades, pp. 370, 375.

5. *Tailor and Cutter,* 17 Apr. 1869, 121. See also J. H. Clapham, *An Economic History of Modern Britain* (London, 1930), 2: 93.

6. P.P., "Children's Employment Commission," Second Report, 1864, vol. xxii, p. 138.

7. Brandon, *Capitalist Romance,* 42, 67.

8. David Landes, *The Unbound Prometheus* (Cambridge, 1970), 294.

9. See, for example, P.P., "Report of the Inspectors of Factories for 1877," 1877, vol. xxiii, pp. 6–8; P.P., "Children's Employment Commission," Second Report, 1864, vol. xxii, p. lxviii.

10. Byrn, *Progress of Invention,* 190–91.

11. Not until 1906 do the factory inspectors begin to note any application of electrical power in the apparel trades of London. See *Report of the Chief Inspector of Factories and Workshops for 1906* (London, 1906), 189.

12. The complaints of the machinists are found in P.P., "Royal Commission on the Poor Laws and Relief of Distress," 1909, vol. xliii, and Appendix — vol. ix, Report of Miss Williams and Mr. Jones; and Women's Industrial Council, *Home Industries of Women in London* (London, 1897), 61. Information on the purchase-hire system is found in Byrn, *Progress of Invention,* 193; Beatrice Potter, "The Tailoring Trade," in Charles Booth, *Life and Labour of the People in London* (London, 1889), ser. 1, 4: 45; P.P., "Select Committee on Sweating," First Report, 1888, vol. xx, p. 3, and Q 1676; P.P., "Children's Employment Commission," Second Report, 1864, vol. xxii, pp. 70, 133.

13. Byrn, *Progress of Invention,* 192.

14. David Schloss, "Bootmaking," in Booth, *Life and Labour,* ser. 1, 4: 70.

15. For the opposition of workers to the subcontract system, see P.P., "Select Committee on Sweating," First Report, 1888, vol. xx, p. 943. Descriptions of the system are found in ibid. Another witness claimed that there were eight to nine subdivisions in coatmaking; see ibid., Q 8063. In collarmaking there were seventeen different processes. See P.P., "Report of the Select Committee on Home Work," First Report, 1907, vol. vi., p. 13, and Potter, "Tailoring," 54–55.

16. P.P., "Select Committee on Sweating," First Report, 1888, vol. xx, Qs 8063–74; see also *The Anti-Sweater,* Feb. 1887, 1.

17. Quoted in National Union of Boot and Shoe Operatives (NUBSO) *Monthly Report,* Mar. 1895, 9.

18. For the union's fears of new machinery, see ibid., Oct. 1896, 13. A discussion of these changes is found in John Leno, *The Art of Boot and Shoe Making* (London, 1885), 167–74.

19. NUBSO *Monthly Report,* Nov. 1905, 338. On closing up to 1890, see

P.P., "Children's Employment Commission," Second Report, 1864, vol. xxii, p. 164; Leno, *Boot and Shoe Making,* 74–75; Schloss, "Bootmaking," 71.

20. Schloss, "Bootmaking," 71. Some machine-closing was done in provincial factories and then sent to London for the remainder of production, but the majority of the closing was done by London outworkers in their homes or small shops. One of the first London firms to use machine-sewing was Hickson's, which in 1861 had sixty employees, most of whom were machinists, working on the firm's premises. By 1864, however, the advantages of outwork had been recognized so that these indoor workers had been cut to eight and the bulk of the work was put out to subcontractors. These men bought machines from Hickson and contracted the jobs to outworkers, to be done either in small outwork shops provided by the subcontractor or in the workers' homes. Thereafter, because putting out work was cheaper, few London firms employed closers on their own premises. P.P., "Children's Employment Commission," Second Report, 1864, vol. xxii, p. 164.

21. In the bespoke trade a shoe last was a wooden model of the customer's foot. In the ready-made trade the worker used a standard model. *Workman's Times,* 5 Jan. 1891, 8. The transition from hand- to machine-lasting is discussed in Alan Fox, *A History of the National Union of Boot and Shoe Operatives, 1874–1957* (Oxford, 1958), 132.

22. Byrn, *Progress of Invention,* 180–90; Fox, *History of the National Union,* 24; NUBSO *Monthly Report,* Nov. 1905, 338.

23. P.P., "Select Committee on Sweating," First Report, 1888, vol. xx, Q415. By 1903 some finishing was being done in special shops. See NUBSO *Monthly Report,* Dec. 1903; Schloss, "Bootmaking," 75, 97, 107–9. One of the most widely practiced forms of subdivision of labor was the team system, an American innovation consisting of a series of operations (formerly carried out by a single skilled worker) split up so that the skilled part of the work was entrusted to a worker of considerable ability and the remainder of the job was done by workers of lesser skill. The skilled worker was the center of the team and set the pace of production. The work was done either on the premises of the firm or, more likely, in the shop of the subcontractor. It was a novel utilization of labor because it greatly lowered the technical qualifications of the worker and so brought an indefinitely large supply of unskilled labor into the industry. It was especially prevalent in London, where it severely reduced the demands for skilled workers and placed great pressure on unionists to accept reductions in wages. "This 'team system,' " said the NUBSO, "is an attempt to evade the fixed prices we have laid down for labour . . . it simply amounts to the sweating system" (NUBSO *Monthly Report,* Feb. 1894, 37). Since the subdivision of labor system relied heavily on boy labor, it is not surprising that some unionists regarded boy labor

as "the greatest evil" in the trade (P.P., "Royal Commission on Labour," Fifth Report, 1894, vol. xxxv, Qs 15041–15047, 15955). Neither it is surprising that the first restriction of boy labor through the National Arbitration Conference was applied to the boot and shoe industry.

24. It was the ultimate employer—the wholesaler or retailer—and not the middleman or woman who got the advantage of low wages. See R. H. Tawney, *Studies in the Minimum Wage, No. 2—Tailoring* (London, 1915), 233–38.

25. P.P., "Children's Employment Commission," Second Report, 1864, vol. xxii, p. 83.

26. *The Tailor,* 26 Jan. 1867, 248.

27. P.P., "Report of the Chief Inspector of Factories and Workshops, 1894," 1895, vol. xix, pp. 56–57.

28. James Macdonald, "The West End Tailors," in Booth, *Life and Labour,* ser. 1, 4: 147.

29. *Tailor and Cutter,* 7 Aug. 1896, 98.

30. P.P., "Report of the Royal Commission on Alien Immigration," 1903, vol. ix, Q11731; Edward Cadbury et al., *Woman's Work and Wages* (Chicago, 1907), 96.

31. Until the 1880s, when this wave of Jewish immigrants into London generated considerable anti-Jewish sentiment, the Jewish community of London was of moderate size and of predominantly Dutch and German descent. In the late eighteenth and early nineteenth centuries, some social and labor prejudice had emerged as a number of Jews came to London to escape starvation and political and racial persecution on the continent, but by the middle of the nineteenth century these Anglo-Jews, as they were called, were regarded as respectable citizens. It was in the decades after 1880 that the Jewish-English labor conflict became violent and formed an important chapter in the history of sweating. Lloyd P. Gartner, *The Jewish Immigrant in England, 1870–1914* (London, 1960). The figures are taken from Hubert Llewellyn Smith et al., *The New Survey of London Life and Labour* (London, 1934), 1: 82.

32. Tillett's estimate is found in P.P., "Select Committee on Sweating," Second Report, 1888, vol. xx, Q 12664. Clapham suggests that machinery in the clothing trades resulted in little technological unemployment. He bases his claim on the 1885 observation of a bootmaker, John B. Leno, that there was very little suffering by the shoemaker because of machinery and that "there were all kinds of half machine jobs to which the less adaptable of them could turn." Leno, *Boot and Shoe Making,* vii, 210; Clapham, *Economic History of Britain,* 2: 459. See, too, P.P., "The Report of the Royal Commission on Labour Evidence, Group C," 1893–94, vol. xxxvi, Q 12659.

33. NUBSO *Monthly Report,* Jan. 1899, 9; Jan. 1904; Mar. 1906, 105.

34. The 1897 claim is in ibid., May 1897; Richard's statement is in ibid., Aug. 1903, 14; and the 1906 report is in ibid., Mar. 1906, 106.

35. *Women's Trade Union Review,* Oct. 1898, 16.

36. Ibid., Jan. 1909, 5.

37. P.P., "The Report of the Royal Commission on Labour," First Report, 1892, vol. xxv, p. 63.

38. NUBSO *Monthly Report,* Jan. 1904, 1.

39. Ibid., June 1903, 1.

40. Ibid. For examples of these complaints see ibid., Dec. 1904, 337; Jan. 1905, 2; Aug. 1909, 379.

41. *The Tailor,* 26 Jan. 1867, 250. Forty years later an arbitrator for the Board of Trade stated that alien Jewish labor was causing a decline in wages in the boot and shoe trades. P.P., "Report of the Select Committee on Home Work," 1907, vol. vi, G.R. Asquith, Qs 3950–60.

42. Ibid., Qs 3599, 3600–3, 3782.

43. P.P., "Census Returns, 1861," 1863, vol. liii, pt. 2, p. 51; "1901," 1902, vol. cxx, p. 168. The returns for 1871, 1881, and 1891 do not classify London's foreign-born workers according to occupation. It is most probable that the greatest part of these changes in the labor force occurred in the 1890s, when the influx of Jewish immigrants was at its height.

44. P.P., "Census Returns—Occupations, London, 1871," 1873, vol. lxxii, pt. 2; "Census Returns," 1901, 1902, vol. cxx; P.P., "Report of the Royal Commission on the Poor Laws and Relief of Distress," 1909, vol. xliv, Appendix 24, p. 599.

45. Calculated from the issues of the NUBSO *Monthly Report,* 1894–1901.

46. Recent historians of the subject claim that sweating was declining by 1900. See Duncan Bythell, *The Sweated Trades: Outwork in Nineteenth-Century Britain* (London, 1978), and James Treble, *Urban Poverty in Britain* (New York, 1979).

47. Phillis Cunningham, *Costume in Pictures* (London, 1964), 149–51.

48. Robert Roberts, *The Classic Slum* (London, 1973), 38.

49. The problem of part-time work makes consideration of census estimates difficult. In agriculture, for example, it is estimated that more than half of the women who worked were not reported because they worked less than full time (G. E. Mingay, *Rural Life in Victorian England* [London, 1976], 77). The census of 1911 is even more unusual because of a boycott of the census by the "suffragettes." I have not been able to ascertain how much, if any, this boycott distorts the census figures for working women. A brief description of the boycott is in George Dangerfield, *The Strange Death of Liberal England, 1910–1914* (New York, 1961), 162.

50. Booth, *Life and Labour,* Poverty Series, 4: 259.

51. For additional discussion on this problem of productivity and economic growth — the so-called era of the Great Depression, see herein, ch. 5.

52. See, for example, Phyllis Deane and W. A. Cole, *British Economic Growth, 1688–1959* (Cambridge, 1967), 296–97; William Ashworth, "Changes in the Industrial Structure: 1870–1914," *Yorkshire Bulletin of Economic and Social Research,* 17 (May 1965), and S. G. Checkland, *The Rise of Industrial Society in England, 1815–1885* (New York, 1964), 217–18. See also Charles Wilson, "Economy and Society in the Late Victorian Britain," *Economic History Review,* 2d ser., 18 (1965), 186*n2,* 192. In this respect Wilson has made an astute observation: "There is something, it seems, in the doctrine of 'high mass-consumption' which makes it doctrinally necessary to excommunicate from the ritual such commodities as ready-made clothes and corsets, boots and shoes, newspapers, cheap jam and patent medicines. The bicycle passes muster but a motor car is better. Most of these products came from relatively small plants. No single plant represented an essay in *massive* investment or even technological innovation of a radical kind. Hence perhaps the economist is apt to be unimpressed by them." Wilson's claim is that scholars have too often seen dramatic, technological innovation and massive investment as the "indispensable condition of economic growth" and have neglected to realize that large-scale heavy industry and the consumer-goods industry "were by no means the same thing." Therefore, because historians have been preoccupied with the deterioration of the old basic industries, they have missed the impressive growth in consumer-goods industries and have perhaps overemphasized overall economic decay.

53. "The American Impact on British Industry, 1895–1914," *Business History,* 3 (1960), 38.

54. P.P., "Select Committee on Sweating," 1888, vol. xxi, Mrs. Webb, Qs 3308, 3336. See also Beatrice Potter (Webb), "The Lords and the Sweating System," *Nineteenth Century,* 160 (Jan. 1890), 885–905. Webb regarded sweating to be a result of the "slowness of the industrial revolution" (891).

CHAPTER 3

Outwork in the Sweated Trades

MECHANIZATION OF THE LONDON clothing trades meant a
gloomy future of deteriorating work conditions and the prospect of
eventual unemployment for skilled male artisans and increased employment opportunities but a worse (or at least unchanging) work environment for semiskilled workers. But the growth of outwork placed
women in probably the most precarious position. As they became the
great reservoir of cheap labor, new opportunities for outwork meant
a continuation of their traditional role as supplementary wage earner
for the family—but only at starvation wages and under socially objec-
tionable conditions.[1] This chapter examines the conditions under
which outworkers were employed and the special link between outwork and women.

Working conditions and wages

When asked if she liked her work, a young blousemaker replied
that "there was not much use liking or disliking it as she had to do
it."[2] Unlike the new industrial middle class, she—and the rest of the
laboring poor—could not afford a subjective view of labor. This resignation to work did not mean, however, that there were no voices of
discontent. When the Children's Employment Commission of 1864
inquired into the attitudes and work experiences of women, many
of whom were machinists in the clothing trades, they heard working
women complain that the sewing machine had meant a work speedup
and unhealthy working conditions. Most of these women were employed on a piecework basis, which they claimed led to long hours
at the machine, physical exhaustion, back and shoulder pains,
deteriorating eyesight, and the "tremble"—a malady caused by the

constant vibration of the machine.[3] A decade later women still complained of long hours in machine work and expressed a desire that
the hours of employment for machine-sewing would be less than the
hours for hand-sewing.[4] The effect of sewing machine work on the
health of the worker was described by an employee in 1872:

> One must watch everyone of the hundred and twenty or more stitches
> that are put in per minute; her eyes are intensely and constantly fixed
> upon a line, her hands and feet must move with the regularity of any
> piece of mechanism, a turning of the eye, a slip of the hand or foot spoils
> the work. The same set of nerves are constantly strained, and over
> strained, while the rest of the body is enfeebled, perhaps paralyzed by
> inaction. What ravages the sewing machine causes among those who have
> to play it constantly for a living is not yet ascertained.[5]

Workers complained to the House of Lords committee on sweating
in 1888 and to a Royal Commission on Labour in 1892 that working
conditions were deteriorating and that the workplaces were deplorable.[6] Union organizers heard workers complain that treadle machining was very tiring and the cause of "internal trouble" and "pains in
the legs and chest."[7]

Observers of women's work reported similar circumstances: that
the introduction of the sewing machine led to a worsening of working conditions, poorer health, and long and irregular hours of employment.[8] Homeworkers frequently received work in the evening and
were required to return it, finished, to the factory the next morning.[9]
Many employers agreed that it was sewing machine work that led
to these long hours and believed that the solution was the limitation
of hours of labor by the state. One employer claimed that seven hours
a day was "quite enough" for a machinist because of the eye strain
from the close work.[10] These complaints were repeated by factory
inspectors as they reported on the health problems and accidents due
to machine production in the clothing trades. Mercury poisoning, for
example, was common among workers using sole-stitching machines
in the footwear trades. As the wax thread was heated by a gas flame
on the machine, the mercury used for sealing the thread evaporated,
and the worker breathed the fumes. The accident rate increased as
mechanization grew; over 40 percent of accidents involving women
in 1908, for example, were due to sewing machine punctures.[11]

Work conditions were dictated by the precarious and complex nature
of sweated outwork. Sweated outwork and sweated homework were

not necessarily synonymous. All homeworkers were outworkers, but
not all outworkers worked at home — some worked in the homes of
others or in some jerry-built workrooms. As the ready-made trades
grew and the space limitations of London presented greater physical
problems, every room, basement, garret, and backyard became subject
to invasion by outworkers looking for a place to machine a dozen shirts,
make up trousers, do the finishing work on cheap shoes, or carry on
some similar enterprise.[12] The process and the location of outwork
varied from trade to trade, but its general features may be sketched.
First, sweated work usually took place in unregulated rooms, either
in the worker's home, a small workshop or "sweating den," or the home
of another worker. While the invasion of work into the home may
have been regarded by the middle class as reprehensible, it was a fact
of life seldom questioned by the working class. Work and family were
inseparable. In the north central London borough of Islington, for
example, it was found that of 146 workers who worked at home, only
eight had separate workrooms. Most worked in their kitchens or bedrooms; half worked in the same room in which they slept (Table 8).

Table 8. Location of Industrial Work in the Home in the Borough of
Islington, 1901

Number of Homes Inspected	Location of Work
8	Workroom*
85	Kitchens and sitting rooms+
17	Bedrooms
36	Kitchen-sitting room-bedroom combined

*Used exclusively as a workroom.
+ Ten contained beds.
Source. *Women's Industrial News,* Sept. 1901, 255.

Invariably, the work shifted back and forth between the outwork
rooms and the contractor. In boot- and shoemaking, for example,
the cutting out of the uppers was usually done in the factory and then
sent to outworkers, usually women or immigrant Jews, for piecing and
closing. After the homework was completed, the uppers were taken
back to the factory or warehouse, where the bottoms would be cut
out. The bottoms and uppers would then be given out again to subcontractors, who would put the work out for the bottom lasting and
heeling. The completed piece would then go back to its point of origin,
and once again it would be given to subcontractors for finishing. Each

one of these steps involved both negotiation of wages and directions as to the type and quality of work to be done. Fines and penalties for inadequate or incorrect work would be determined by the employer, if necessary, at each of these stages. The time of day that the goods would be put out varied, but usually the common or cheap goods would be put out in the morning and the better class of goods given out at night.

Outwork in the garment trades also originated in the warehouse or the cutting room of the retailer or subcontractor where the fabrics were cut out. The cut pieces would be put up in bundles for the outworkers to pick up and carry to their workrooms. Unless the employer adhered to the "particulars clause" of the Factory and Workshop Act, which established that wages and other conditions of employment be stated beforehand, the rate of pay was not fixed until the work was returned to the contractor's shop. In either case the worker usually provided the machinery, needles, sewing materials (e.g., thread), and was subject to a long list of fines in case of incomplete or incorrect work. Frequently these outworkers would subcontract on their own, giving out work to neighbors or, in many cases, to members of their family. Children were often used to fetch and carry work, sometimes to the detriment of their schooling. Since outworkers seldom communicated with each other, there were no customs or traditions as to the conditions of work, wages, and particulars of labor.

Typical of how the system worked is the case of Mary Withers, a single woman living in the district of Clerkenwell and a mantlemaker for a firm in nearby inner London (called the City). She had two sewing machines, probably on a hire-purchase basis, and she provided the thread and needles for her work as well as a security deposit for the cut-out materials she took from the factory. Withers employed, at extremely low wages, another woman, Mrs. Jessop, the wife of an unemployed carpenter, to do the finishing off, that is, making the buttonholes and sewing on the buttons. Jessop was also employed to fetch the work from the warehouses and deliver it when it was finished.[13] Here was a case of only two layers of subcontracting: the City firm to Withers and Withers to Jessop. But it was not at all unusual for there to be three, four, or more sweaters or middlemen between the retailer or wholesaler and the maker of the goods. A factory order in 1885 to make up two dozen aprons passed through five contractors before it finally reached the woman outworker.[14] Indeed, it might take days to trace the origin of an order of shirts being worked on by a woman in Camden town, who received her work from another woman who went by tram to Finsbury to pick up her work from a City warehouse that belonged to a respectable West End firm on Conduit Street.

Diagram 1 shows the manner in which nine shirt-finishers were employed in the late 1880s by three City shirtmaking firms, how the work was given out, and where the labor was performed. In the case of firm A, shirt 1 was given out by its subcontracting branch in the East End (the firm also had a workroom in the East End) to a woman subcontractor, who in turn contracted the work to a machinist (a sewer). The machinist then put out the shirt to a woman outworker for finishing. Shirt 2 went through the same stage but was finished in the workroom (probably the home) of the machinist. Shirt 3 was finished by an outworker who received it from a machinist working in the workroom of the first distributor (contractor) after it left the branch. Shirt 4 was given out directly from the branch office to an outwork finisher. Shirt-finishing by firm B worked in somewhat the same way; a branch in the East End gave out the work to a woman machinist who worked in her home, while it gave shirt 6 directly to a subcontractor, thus bypassing the branch. These two then contracted with finishers to complete the work. Firm C is somewhat different because it did not have a branch in the East End but gave out the work to a man who had a workroom in the East End. Shirts 7 and 9 went through the hands of a machinist; shirt 8 was put out by the subcontractor to a finisher. In many of these cases neither the firm nor the subcontractor knew where the shirts were finished, nor did the finisher know where her work originated.

Two of the nine finishers were wives of dock laborers. The workers in all nine cases were either young girls or older, mostly widowed, women. Their wages varied from 2d. an hour to 5d. a day. Most of the women were on piecework and could make, on the average, about 5d. per day, less 2d. for tram fare spent in picking up the work. One woman's income was limited by the fact that she could not carry more than two dozen shirts at a time.[15]

Collarmakers worked in a similar manner, although there was generally less subcontracting and more of the work was done at first hand, that is, in workrooms of the wholesaler or the retailer. The process of belt- and tiemaking was generally the same as shirtmaking. Some

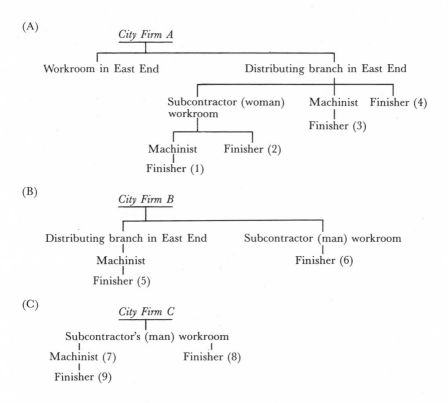

Diagram 1. The Paths of Production of Nine Shirts, London, 1888 (from Clara Collet, "Women's Work," in Charles Booth, *Life and Labour of the People in London* [London, 1889], ser. 1, 4: 260–63).

City firms gave out hundreds of dozens of ties to a single subcontractor who, in turn, gave them out again in smaller numbers to women who either had the ties made in their homes or gave them out to other women.[16]

Trousermakers worked in either the workshop of the master tailor or, in the case of more common work, in workrooms often managed by a woman subcontractor or in the outworker's home. Most workshops producing trousers, especially of a lower grade, were concentrated in Mile End Old Town, Whitechapel, and Stepney and were managed by German Jews. Typical of this type of shop was that of Mark Moses, a master tailor and member of the Mutual Tailors Association. Moses was an East End subcontractor who took work from City merchants to be done in his workshop or by his outworkers. In his shop he employed forty women and eighteen men. But it was, to a large extent, the City merchant who set the pace of competition within the trades and not a middleman like Moses. Moses and some of his fellow middlemen, for example, attempted to curtail low wages and long hours by joining with their workers to force factory owners and merchants to raise their prices so that the middlemen could improve conditions for their workers.[17]

Another major feature of outwork was that supervision of work was rather precarious and commonly led to disputes between the factory foreman or subcontractor and the worker, or between outworkers themselves. Those who opposed the outwork system did not have to look very far to find examples of an employer exploiting a worker or of a worker exploiting another worker. Such was the case of the boot-finisher who complained that his factory foreman purposely timed the giving out of work so that there would never be enough time to complete the goods and thus could reduce labor costs by fining the worker; or the case of the woman outworker who was brought to the Middlesex sessions court and sentenced to six weeks' imprisonment for stealing six jackets from another woman outworker who gave her employment.[18]

For many outworkers, like the nine shirt-finishers described above, outwork meant that they had to assume the expense and time involved in picking up and returning their work to the employer. Although in some cases this function was assumed by the subcontractor, in most instances it was the outworker who spent the time carrying the work to and from its place of origin or merely waiting for work to be given out. Outworkers were often required to ask at the factory every day and twice on Fridays. Mrs. B, a trouser-finisher in London, went to the shop twice a day. Mrs. G, another outworker, had her father carry her work from her home in Poplar to her employer in Stepney. More than half of the outworking tailoresses in West Ham in 1906 traveled outside of that borough (many to the City) to get their work, sometimes spending 6d. four times a week for a tram and sometimes returning home without work. Thus, a Southwark outworker took a bus to Soho, a three-hour round trip, to pick up and deliver her work. As already noted, children often carried the work to and from the factory or workshop, "often in great heavy bundles."[19] It was not uncommon in many parts of London, particularly in the east, central, and west boroughs, to pass outworkers and children of outworkers on the streets and trams, hurrying to employers with baskets of sewn uppers, stacks of finished trousers, or bundles of newly buttonholed shirts.

A large number of outworkers were employed by firms in boroughs other than the one in which they lived. For example, in 1904, 41 percent of the outworkers of London traveled outside of their borough to receive work; the figures for 1906 and 1908 are 68 and 61 percent, respectively. Two-fifths of the outworkers residing in Hackney in 1902 obtained work from outside of the borough, roughly one-third of them traveling to the City, one-third to the East End (Poplar, Bethnal Green, and Shoreditch), and the rest to Finsbury (one-sixth) and various other districts. By 1909, however, a shift in outwork had occurred: Hackney outworkers were obtaining most of their work from the East End and not the City. This may merely reflect the growth of City firms' distribution branches in the East End rather than a relocation of the firms themselves. There was an additional slight increase of Hackney workers who traveled to the north into Stoke-Newington and Walthamstow for outwork.[20] Similarly, there was a large number of workers traveling from the East End to obtain outwork, most likely from boot and shoe firms, in Hackney.

Of the hundreds of outworkers in St. Pancras who were employed outside of the borough in 1901, 22 percent, most of whom were probably employed in the dressmaking trade, traveled to nearby St. Marylebone. Others worked in nearby Hackney (8 percent) and Hampstead (10 percent), but others, probably shoemakers, worked for firms far to the south in Chelsea (8 percent) and Wansworth (8 percent). In 1894 St. Marylebone reported that almost all (96 percent) of its outworkers who received work outside of the borough were working for firms in Westminster.[21] By 1901 much dressmaking and tailoring had shifted to St. Marylebone, which then became a net importer of outworkers.

The outwork location quotient, which is set forth in Table 9, indicates the concentration of outworker premises (i.e., residences) and the premises of the giver out (i.e., employer) in all London boroughs for 1908. If the quotient is more than 1.0, the number of outworkers was greater than the number of outwork jobs offered by firms in the borough. A value of less than 1.0 indicates more outwork given out in the borough than outworkers residing in the borough. For every 100 outworkers living in Woolwich, for exam-

Table 9. Outwork Location Quotient for London, 1908

City of London	0.03	Hackney	1.29
Finsbury	0.27	Lewisham	1.30
Hampstead	0.27	Bethnal Green	1.41
Chelsea	0.39	Battersea	1.50
Kensington	0.49	Camberwell	1.56
Westminster	0.65	Bermondsey	1.60
Holborn	0.76	Greenwich	1.84
Marylebone	0.97	Shoreditch	2.05
Woolwich	1.00	Stoke-Newington	2.57
Paddington	1.06	Hammersmith	2.72
Poplar	1.08	Stepney	3.03
Wandsworth	1.09	Fulham	3.79
Islington	1.17	St. Pancras	4.32
Deptford	1.21		
Southwark	1.25		

Source. London County Council, *The Report of the Chief Medical Officer of Health, London County Council* (London, 1909), 72–73. The quotient is calculated by dividing the number of outworkers who live in the borough by the number of outworkers who work in the borough.

ple, there were 100 outworkers employed by firms in that borough. The outwork quotient for St. Pancras was the highest in London: 4.35 outworkers lived in the borough for every one outwork job in the borough. Most St. Pancras outworkers carried work into the borough from the outside. Conversely, the City of London had the highest ratio of outwork jobs to resident outworkers. Only three out of every 100 outworkers employed by a City firm lived in that borough; all of the rest carried their work into other boroughs. Finsbury, Hampstead, Chelsea, Kensington, Holborn, and (only by a small margin) St. Marylebone were net exporters of outwork. Conversely, more outworkers lived in the East London boroughs of Stepney, Bethnal Green, and Shoreditch than there was work given out by firms in these boroughs. Also the northern and southern boroughs tended to have a greater percentage of their outworkers obtaining work in other boroughs than within the borough of residence.

The quotient also suggests several other significant features of outwork. First, since some of the most notorious districts for sweating, namely Stepney, Shoreditch, and, to an extent, Bethnal Green, contained more outworkers than outwork jobs, the frequent contemporary claim that the source of sweating was the City and the West End rather than only the East End is substantiated. Second, the quotient suggests why so many of the late Victorian and Edwardian workers remained on the periphery of the central city and did not move to new jobs or new homes in the new suburbs. As long as outwork jobs were provided by firms in these areas, the worker had to live nearby and endure overcrowding and deteriorating housing. Occupational travel for the outworker was more than going to and from work. Since the product was bulky, workers who had to take it back and forth needed to live near the source of their outwork. As the ready-made trades grew, employers needed a larger outwork force nearby. All of this helps explain why geographic mobility was not characteristic of many of the urban poor. Because outwork often provided support (however minimal) for the families of men thrown out of work in the so-called declining trades, it delayed or even discouraged the movement of workers away from areas of chronic unemployment, such as the dock district of London.

Another feature of sweated outwork was its casualness. Most outworkers had only periodic employment. The employer, because he had limited outlay in fixed capital and paid his workers on a piece-work basis, had little incentive to keep his workers in times of depressed trade or in the off season. But outwork meant casual employment for the indoor worker as well. As long as the employer had a ready army of outworkers with machines to fill his orders rapidly, he was also reluctant to retain his indoor help in slack time. In this sense the machine, as it fostered outworking, caused the trades to become "more intensely" seasonal, and the season of a shorter duration.[22] In 1908 the Charity Organization Society reported that an increase in the supply of casual laborers followed the introduction of machinery, and, at about the same time, the Royal Commission on the Poor Laws argued that irregularity of work was partly a result of the industrialized outwork system.[23] Hence, the boot- and shoemakers complained that "permanency . . . means work for a few weeks at the most, never more; not one man in fifty stays in one place twelve months even on half time."[24] Thus, outwork tended to become not just a means for expanding and contracting the permanent labor force, but a replacement for it. As a result, according to Charles Booth, the chief factor in the financial status of the worker was the "greater or lesser continuity of employment." Said Booth, "In a majority of cases increased difficulty of obtaining full and continuous employment had done much to counteract the increase in the wage scale."[25]

Overall, the wages, diet, and housing of the late Victorian and Edwardian working classes had improved considerably since the first half of the century. The troubled and hungry post-Napoleonic decades had become, by 1851, the great age of "Victorian prosperity." Although it is clear that the working classes were beneficiaries of this prosperity, it has not yet been shown precisely who among the working class bene-fitted and who did not. Just as there was no uniform consumption pattern among the working class, there was no typical wage. Cer-tainly not all workers shared equally in industrial progress, and one of the most disquieting revelations of the 1880s was that for many members of society, particularly women, low wages and long hours of labor were facts of life. Poverty, as Booth and Seebohm Rowntree showed in their surveys of London and York, was still the woe of one-third of the population in 1900.

Nevertheless, a significant upswing in real wages for the British worker took place in the 1860s and early 1870s. This increase was largely enjoyed by the so-called labor aristocracy, the skilled and respectable upper strata of the working class, which made up about 10 percent of the labor population. The trend continued after 1873 and for the next twenty years but at a slower pace. This era, the enig-matic "Great Depression" of 1873 to 1895, saw money wages rise (with the exception of a short period of falling money wages in 1873–75) or at least remain stationary, while prices fell by one-third. The worker-consumers thus won a distinct advance in their standard of comfort. Then from 1896 to 1914 the situation reversed somewhat. Prices rose by at least one-fifth, while wages remained stationary for some and fell, or rose less rapidly, for others. Wages in the coal industry, much of the cotton textiles industry, and in public service rose with prices, but in other industries, such as building, engineering, and railroading, wages did not keep pace with prices; the result was a fall in real wages. Rapid price increases in 1900, 1907, and 1913, and increasing unem-ployment after 1902 pulled down real wages for some workers even further.[26]

In the early decades of the nineteenth century women's wages in-creased considerably, and then after about 1850 wages of unskilled women appear to have risen more slowly than those of skilled workers, so much slower, in fact, that the relative economic position of unskilled women most likely deteriorated. In some trades, like the worsted industry, the average wage increase for men between 1855 and 1868 was 66 percent, while that for women was 6 percent.[27] By 1906 women in the clothing trades still earned only half of what men made. Further aggravating this economic recession for women was a rising level of male unemployment after about 1900, which, along with declining real wages for husbands in some industries, meant that more women had to stay in the labor market or return to work after marriage in order for the family to maintain or improve its standard of comfort. "When we were very young," one woman recalled of her childhood, "my father's wage wasn't an adequate one for three or four children."[28] For many women it was only when wives and daughters worked that family comfort improved; this was the case with over 30 percent of the working-class families that Booth found in poverty.

Outworkers employed in the London sweated trades in the last half of the nineteenth century closely fit these trends. Henry Mayhew wrote that it was hard to believe that "there were human beings toiling so long and gaining so little, starving so silently and heroically, round about our very homes, as the thousands of women doing 'slop work' tailoring."[29] In his letters to the *Morning Chronicle* he described with Dickensian care the lives of London's sweated workers, making the link not only between sweated work and poverty but also between sweated work and prostitution, estimating that one-quarter to one-half of the women in the "slop" clothing work resorted to prostitution in order to survive. He met with sixty-five tailoresses and found their wages extremely low (twenty-one of them received less than one shilling a week), and he concluded that they aged faster than women in domestic service. Beginning work at age fifteen, they "are very much aged by the time they reach 30 or 40, being in constitution at least 10 years older than domestic servants," and their health had so deteriorated by then that they have difficulty finding employment.[30] A few years earlier another writer expressed shock not only at the wretched condition of young women of the metropolis who toiled from morning till night in the sweated trades but also that no one cared and that there was no public legislation ameliorating the condition of nonfactory women. He claimed that 37,000 women, mostly young and unmarried, with no other support, earned an average of 8s. per week and that many of them turned to prostitution in order to buy clothing.[31]

Table 10. Weekly Earnings of Women Employed in Factories and Workshops in England, 1906

Industries	Percentage Earning under 10s.	Percentage Earning under 15s.*
All textile (including cotton)	13.3	52.1
Cotton	3.0	23.9
All clothing	21.6	66.7
Paper, printing, etc.	26.5	78.7
Pottery	31.0	80.7
Food and tobacco	37.8	82.0

*Includes those earning under 10s.

Source. The 1906 census of wages and hours of labor, cited in B. L. Hutchings, *Women in Industry after the War* (London, n.d.).

Although substantial improvement came to many women in the following decades, Mayhew's sad tale could have been retold to describe the lives of many working women in London fifty years later. George Bernard Shaw's play, *Mrs. Warren's Profession,* initially banned in England, suggested that indeed it may have been wiser for a working-class woman to choose prostitution over industrial labor. As Table 10 shows, most English working women in 1906 earned less than the 15s. per week needed by a self-supporting woman to keep above poverty line. Only in the cotton trade did the majority earn over 15s. per week. Two-thirds of the women in the clothing trade earned less than 15s. per week; most men earned twice that much. For the half century between Mayhew's letters to the *Morning Chronicle* and the 1906 wage census, it is fairly certain that women in the clothing trades did not fare as well as the working class in general, and they probably worked harder for a decreasing share of the national wage. Real wages for women in the London clothing trades fell gradually in the 1870s and for the next twenty years.

Falling wages became the chief reason for the establishment of the Women's Trade Union League (WTUL) in 1874. Emma Paterson, its founder, claimed that the average woman worker, earning between 11s. and 17s. per week, was making poverty wages; except in the upholstery industry, wages for women in London did not follow the rise in the 1870s that workers in other industries participated in, and to Paterson this problem made it "urgent" that women organize.[32] The adoption of the sewing machine and the entry of girls into the shirtmaking trade in the 1870s resulted in the reduction of City shirtmakers'

wages from 28s. to 14s. per week. At about the same time wages at
the government clothing factory in London (Pimlico) were reduced
by 10 to 20 percent with an accompanying increase in hours.[33] In
1863 Dr. William Ord estimated that needlewomen were earning between 10s. and 22s. per week, but by 1883 only the best workers could
average 15s.[34] The select committee on sweating was told repeatedly
that wages in the sweated trades were declining.[35] A Board of Trade
survey in 1887 found that London tailoresses were making 13s. to
16s. per week and that homeworkers were making less.[36] By contrast,
English and Jewish women who had formed a trade union in the East
End in the late 1880s claimed that wages ranged between 8s. and 9s.
per week.[37] The wage census of 1886 (Table 11) reported that
tailoresses were making 20s. per week and that milliners, mantlemakers, and dressmakers (but excluding homeworkers and
apprentices) were making between 14s. 1d. and 15s. 6d. Booth found
that women's wages in tailoring ranged from 5s. to 13s. 6d. per week.
He surveyed 810 dressmakers, milliners, and shirtmakers in fifteen
London firms and found that skilled women earned 13s. to 20s. per
week, but, when apprentices were included, fully half of the women
and girls earned less than 12s. per week. He found that most milliners and dress- and shirtmakers earned from 12s. 9d. to 13s. 9d. But
like the wage census figures, these estimates did not exclude periods
of unemployment, which, for many of the casually employed, would

Table 11. Weekly Earnings of Women Clothing Workers in
London, 1886 and 1906

Clothing Trades	1886	1906
Dressmakers	14s. 1d.	14s. 1d.
Dress machinists (factory)	NI	15s. 5d.
Shirt- and blousemakers, etc.	NI	15s. 10d.
Milliners	14s. 3d.	15s. 8d.
Tailoresses, bespoke	20s. 3d.	16s. 2d.
Tailoresses, ready-made	NI	11s. 11d.
Mantlemakers	15s. 6d.	15s. 8d.

Note. The figure for mantlemakers is based on a time rate; piece rate was higher. These are
not yearly averages, but the earnings reported for the week that the census was conducted;
actual wages throughout the year were lower. NI = not included in 1886 survey.

Source. P.P., "Board of Trade Report on Earnings and Hours of Labour, II — Clothing," 1909,
vol. lxxx, pp. 51–53, 64–67, 20, 21, 28, and P.P., "Board of Trade Report on Wages, 1886,"
1893–94, vol. lxxxiii, pt. 2, pp. 126–27.

reduce the average by one-half. In drawing a rough picture of the most common lot of the London working class, Booth used 10s. as the typical wage of a working wife in the early stage of marriage. Finding that 40 percent of working-class families of London were at or below the povery line, he noted that it was necessary that "the women almost always earn some money."[38] Thus, taking into account that homeworking wages averaged 8s. to 9s.[39] and that there were wide differences in wages within the trades, it appears that the average weekly wage for a woman regularly employed full time in the clothing trades in the mid- and late 1880s was somewhere between 9s. and 15s. per week, with 11s. as a probable average. Because homeworking was the worst paid of employments, married women earned less than single women, and widows received less than either. Indeed, the wage of 9s. to 11s. for sewing machinists at the Pimlico factory and the 12s. earned by London machinists is close to the 10s. that Booth claimed was average for a young married woman or the 11s. we have set as an average.[40] Thus, Ord's estimate in 1863 of 15s. to 16s. as the earnings for London needlewomen is much too high for a period twenty or even thirty years later, although it is not known exactly what impact falling prices had on the well-being of working women — except that by the later part of the century workers were arguing that price declines were being cancelled by increased rent and higher unemployment.[41]

Through the 1890s and up to 1914, wages for workers in the London clothing trades remained stationary or declined; in some cases the decline even accelerated. Although wages for women in the textile trades rose by 18 percent between 1886 and 1906, those for women in the London clothing trades fell or increased only slightly (Table 11). This static wage picture, combined with a rising cost of living after 1900, gives support to the frequent observation that the economic position of women was "even worse" in the decades after the sweating investigation of 1888–91.[42] The average weekly earnings for women in the clothing industry after 1900 was 13s. 6d. — although this average does not include homework and does not consider seasonal unemployment (both of which increased after 1896[43]), it is hardly likely that wages were higher than the 11s. estimated as the average for the period 1873–96.

Instead, real wages had probably fallen — at least the workers thought this was so. They complained that, despite improved trade, there was little improvement in wages in the clothing trades and that rent and fuel had increased twice as fast as wages.[44] Although there were isolated cases of improvement in wages, such as the 1,500 women at the government factory at Pimlico, whose wages had climbed to 15s. 4d.,[45] it is doubtful that wages in the clothing trades came anywhere near the 13s. 6d. minimum, which was fixed by the first wage board in 1913. Over half the women employed in 1906 received less than 13s. 6d. In the late 1890s and the first decade of the new century almost every worker told the same tale of lowered rates.[46] One London shirtmaker claimed that, while wages had not changed since 1894, "there is appreciable more work required in making of the shirt" in 1906.[47] A survey of homework in London in 1887 and again in 1906 found wage grievances to be universal. One clothing worker lamented that "the whole trade is much worse paid than it used to be." A widow with two children at home and whose pay averaged 12s. per week claimed that wages had fallen by half in the past twenty years. Mantlemakers complained of falling wages, as did corsetmakers, tie- and glovemakers, shoemakers, waistcoatmakers, and shirtmakers.[48]

It was reported in 1863 that the needlewomen of London were exceedingly ill fed and were among the most malnourished workers in Britain. There is no evidence that their condition improved before 1914. Booth claimed that 12s. per week was not enough for a shirtfinisher to live on, and in 1906 it was estimated that the minimum sum required by a working woman living independently of relatives was 14s. 6d. to 15s. per week. This need had increased to 17s. to 18s. per week by 1915.[49] Although it was often claimed that single or self-supporting women spent their wages unwisely, the average self-supporting woman in 1910 spent approximately the same high percentage of her income on food and housing as did the average family in poverty.[50] It appears, then, considering that from 1873 to 1914 it was difficult for them to earn more than 11s. per week, that many working women in London continued to live at best at the subsistence level and that they had not shared in the increase in wealth enjoyed by most of the working class or the nation as a whole. Although in actuality this depends somewhat on how the other members of the family fared, many women appear to have suffered a decline in their standard of living, thus illustrating, perhaps, why the turn of the century was a "surprisingly unhappy transition period" for working-class women and why the working class felt increasingly confused, frustrated, and angry by 1914.[51]

Sweated labor, women, and the working-class family

All of the features of sweated work—long hours, low pay, and a personalized work environment—point to a view that the sweated woman worker was in more ways than not surprisingly similar to her preindustrial grandmother. In the preindustrial society most urban women worked in personalized surroundings, either in domestic industries, such as textiles, or as household servants. Work and marriage were fused because marriage was the only way for most women to secure their future against poverty. Not essentially a homemaker, she was a worker to whom wifely chores of cooking, cleaning, and raising children were dependent on and secondary to her work, her income, and her ability to manage the family economy. Although many preindustrial women held important positions in certain trades, and although they sometimes enjoyed the same job status as male workers, they usually toiled long hours for low wages (or no wages) and generally held a subordinate position in the agrarian-domestic economy. Nevertheless, the preindustrial woman stood at the center of the family economy. Before marriage she contributed to her parents' household and prepared for her own. In times of economic crisis it was the working wife and mother, "living on her wits," who enabled the family to survive. During marriage she was the manager of the household, not infrequently its chief breadwinner. Widowhood meant greater hardship, including raising children on one's own. All in all, the concept of womanhood was sharply conditioned by woman's economic role within the family.[52]

The traditional assumptions of Friedrich Engels and others were that all of these conditions changed in the nineteenth century with industrialization: a new industrial woman emerged as the home, formerly the economic and family unit, was broken by the industrial revolution. The working-class wife and child left the home, which had been the workshop, for the factory and became economically independent units, thus loosening the traditional family and the traditional attitudes of women toward marriage, motherhood, and womanhood.[53] "The family," E. P. Thompson has written, "was roughly torn apart each morning by the factory bell, and the mother who was also a wage-earner often felt herself to have the worst of both the domestic and the industrial worlds." But, Thompson and others have noted, the factory also meant increasing freedom, pin money, contact with other women, and new forms of entertainment, all of which contributed to a new individualism. The urban environment and new employment opportunities meant liberation. In short, it was the textile factories of the north of England that "gave rise to the earliest widespread participation by working women in political and social agitation."[54] On the other hand, it has also been assumed that as Britain entered industrial maturity after mid-century, with a resulting improvement for working husbands, an increasing number of working-class wives were able to escape from the labor market and emulate their middle-class sisters (rather than their working mothers) by staying at home.[55] Thankfully they exchanged their economic independence for release from work altogether and welcomed the opportunity to become Victorian ladies. Hence, it is argued, in both the early and later stages of industrialization the position of women changed compared to the preindustrial stage. Two models of industrial women emerge: the liberated factory worker, on the one hand, and the working-class homemaker liberated from the concern of wage-earning, on the other.

These assumptions are not true for the large number of women working in the sweated trades either in London or in the northern clothing centers of Leeds, Manchester, Sheffield, and Newcastle.[56] Most women played a role closer to that of preindustrial women than that of modern industrial women or middle-class wives: they had little economic independence, they fulfilled an important role in the family economy, they did not enjoy the release from work that marriage brought to women of the middle class, and they tended to be wage earners in a domestic setting. They were not, in a sense, modern women. The role that sweated labor played in the working-class family economy hardly supports the claim that industrial work for married women of the working class was rare. Certainly the Edwardians did not believe this; some of them even felt that the entry of wives into industrial work was pulling down the wages of unmarried women.[57] Indeed, the displacement of artisan husbands in the traditional crafts, the decreasing real wages of working men beginning about 1900, and a reduction in the size of the working-class family meant greater pressure on wives to enter the labor market. Equally so, becoming a widow meant a return to work — often to support young children.[58]

How common, then, was it for women with families at home to work? The census began to distinguish "married and widowed" from unmarried only in 1901 and did not classify "married" separately until 1911. Taken together, 18.5 percent of all married and widowed women of London worked in 1911, which was a slight increase over 1901 (Table 12). The percentage of married women who worked in 1911 was 13.2; for widows, it was 39.8. For working-class districts the percentage was higher: nearly 23 percent of the wives and 48 percent of the widows in ten London working-class districts worked. Not only did more working-class women enter the labor market after 1901, but also they did so at a rate of about three times that for women of all classes in London as a whole (3.5 percent vs. 1.3 percent). However, it is certain that a large number of working-class wives who were employed, especially those who did industrial work at home, went unreported in two sources of official government statistics — the census returns and the returns of homeworkers made by factory inspectors. Possibly as many as one-third of all married women workers were not reported in the outwork returns.[59] This discrepancy could mean that in working-class London instead of nearly one in five married

Table 12. Percentage of Married and Widowed Women Who Worked in Ten London Working-Class Districts, 1901 and 1911

Borough	Married and Widowed Who Worked		Widowed Who Worked, 1911	Married Who Worked, 1911
	1901	1911		
Bethnal Green	25.3	27.3	50.7	22.0
Finsbury	25.8	29.6	59.9	21.7
Hackney	15.9	17.9	57.1	13.4
Holborn	30.7	32.7	58.6	23.8
City	35.4	42.6	70.6	32.7
St. Marylebone	25.0	26.7	49.6	19.2
St. Pancras	17.9	19.8	44.7	13.6
Shoreditch	26.7	32.2	52.1	25.6
Westminster	25.3	27.7	54.2	19.1
Stepney	19.3	21.5	48.3	15.5
Average for these ten districts	24.7	27.8 (+ 3.5)	49.4	22.9
All of London	17.2	18.5 (+ 1.3)	39.8	13.2

Source. P.P., "Census Returns for 1901," 1903, vol. lxxxiv, p. 187; "1911," 1913, vol. lxxix, p. 293.

women at work, a more accurate approximation would be one in two, this being as many or more as in working-class neighborhoods in industrial towns such as Leicester, where 43 percent of all married women worked. It is possible, then, that in some urban centers like London, with considerable homework industries, the number of married women at work was greater, not lesser, than in the factory towns of Lancashire or the pottery towns of Staffordshire, where a quarter of the married women worked.

As a group in Victorian society, working-class widows were perhaps the poorest. It was twice as probable that a widow would need to find employment in pre-1914 London as would a wife. Although the census shows that at least half of all working-class widows needed to return to work, it is likely that, considering those left unreported, the City figure of 70.6 percent is close to the real average for working-class neighborhoods. This was especially true for the large portion of the working class that was never able to save adequately for old age and for whom the only alternative was the workhouse. Having to knock on the workhouse door was one of the greatest fears of British women, many of whom harbored childhood memories of the place. Many like Lucy Luck, a straw-plaiter who spent her married life in London, were determined never to return to the workhouse. "There my mother sat down on the steps with one of us on each side of her, and one in her arms, crying bitterly over us before she took us into the Union [workhouse]."[60]

Many of these working widows were young or of middle age with children at home, and they could look unhappily toward years in the sweatshop or the workhouse. This was the case with Mary Ann Farncombe, a young widow with two young children, who, out of desperation, applied for out-relief from the poor law officials in Poplar, where she lived. Mrs. Farncombe was a shirt buttonholemaker for a firm in the City, working on the firm's premises from 9 A.M. to 7 P.M., averaging 10s. per week. Poverty forced her to move in with a married sister, to whom she paid 3s. 6d. rent in addition to 1s. for washing and 1s. for child care. The older child was cared for by her mother-in-law, who lived across the street. The widow had formerly lived in two rooms, with a rent of 5s. 6d., which she had shared with an aunt who was eventually compelled to enter the workhouse where she was forced into "mixing with all sorts" — something Mrs. Farncombe viewed with abhorrence.[61]

Work before marriage was as common as work in widowhood. By 1911 women were delaying marriage until the age of twenty-five or twenty-six, so that they could work longer before marriage.[62] Single working-class girls certainly enjoyed some economic and social independence, but they also had to save for a dowry and contribute to their family's income. Over half of the income of the working girls surveyed by the Board of Trade in 1910 went to their families for board and lodging, and many girls paid "considerably more than their cost to their parents."[63] In London in 1911 over 72 percent of all girls between the ages of fifteen and twenty-five were employed, a figure that increased in working-class districts, such as Bethnal Green, to 80 percent.[64]

Nearly all wives of common laborers had to return to work at some point during marriage because their husbands did not earn enough to support the family. Clementina Black claimed that the situation in Leicester, where one out of four families in working-class districts depended on the mother for at least a third of its income, was typical of the entire country.[65] In the East London district of Bethnal Green over half of the women who worked did so to support their family, and, according to the Fabian Society, about one-half of all working women, including girls, had family dependents.[66] In Yorkshire 63 percent of women workers worked because of insufficiency of husbands' earnings, another 6 percent because they were widowed, and another 14 percent because of desertion or a drinking husband.[67] Women in the sweated trades had even greater economic responsibilities. In 1901 nearly 71 percent of the workers engaged in homework in the clothing trades were women. Although some outworkers took on employment only as supplement to their husbands' income, most outworkers depended on their work for their own and their family's subsistence. In Woolwich, Deptford, and Greenwich in 1891 most of the outworkers were English women, many of whom were wives or widows of soldiers or reserve men who worked in the royal arsenal. Many of these women were aided by their daughters. Among the families in London's Hackney district, as in many working-class neighborhoods, outwork was vital for the survival of the families. A survey of Hackney outworkers in 1906 (Table 13) found that of the new outworkers in that borough, 98 percent were women, of whom 74 percent were married or widowed. Significantly, 64 percent of these women needed to work in order to augment their husbands' incomes, indicating that insuffi-

Table 13. Economic Status of Hackney Outworkers, 1909

Category	Number	Percentage
Single women living with parents or family	56	19
Single women, self-supporting	20	7
Widows with young children to support	4 ⎱	7
Widows, self-supporting	17 ⎰	
Married women working to augment income	185 ⎱	64
Married women with invalid husbands to support	3 ⎰	
Workingmen assisted by wife or sister	7	2
Total	292	

Source. P.P., "Royal Commission on Poor Laws and the Relief of Distress," 1909, vol. xliv, p. 598, Appendix C.

cient family income threw women into an already glutted labor market. Among London homeworkers surveyed in 1897, over 40 percent were the sole breadwinners in the family.[68] Booth reported in 1901 that 20 percent of dressmakers, shirtmakers, and milliners were heads of households,[69] and in a sample of small London industries Black found that 28.4 percent of the married women workers supported a family and that another 64.5 percent of them worked because of insufficient family income.[70] It appears, then, that most late Victorian and Edwardian working-class women worked before marriage, many during marriage, and most after they were widowed, and so an industrial occupation was a fact of life, not an avenue to liberation.

But working-class women were warned about the evils of work: "Wife of the labouring man! Take warning in time. Try to make your home happy to your husband and children. Remember your first earthly duty, and, whatever the temptations to go out to work, STAY AT HOME!"[71] Had they wanted to do otherwise, many working-class wives could have heard these words with nothing but dismay. Certainly some women came to prefer the larger rooms and companionship of the factory to the home, but most working-class women worked before, during, and after marriage not for economic or social independence, but, as in preindustrial society, because their wages were essential to the survival of the family. The growth of sweated labor cannot be accounted for simply by a mechanization of the industry or by an expanded demand for ready-made goods. Sweating was both cause and effect of urban poverty. Certainly bedroom and garret shops grew up in the shadows of many London streets because relief for the distressed and indigent was inadequate and the wage of many primary breadwinners was altogether absent or insufficient. Sweating meant a job at a time of crisis. Sweated work required little skill, could be periodic, and, in many cases, allowed the worker to remain at home. Women are "working for rent," Margaret MacDonald told a parliamentary commission.[72] A sweated labor force was not just an historical aberration, but a part of the crisis in the late Victorian and Edwardian working-class family economy. With the pawn shop, it was the way out of poverty for many families.

NOTES

1. Although probably overstated, the common assumption is that industrialization brought about a decline in job opportunities for women. See Pam Graves and Joseph White, "An Army of Redressers: The Recent Historiography of British Working Class Women," *International Labor and Working Class History,* 17 (Spring 1980), 2-3.

2. Quoted in Women's Industrial Council, *Home Industries of Women in London* (London, 1908), 59. This was the second of two surveys; the first was done in 1897.

3. P.P., "Children's Employment Commission," Second Report, 1864, vol. xxii, pp. lxvii, lxix, lxxii, 102, 104, 133, 135.

4. P.P., "The Report of the Royal Commission on the Factory and Workshop Acts," First Report, 1876, vol. xxx, Appendix c — "Report of the Conference of Working Women, 28 April 1875."

5. J. G. Eccarious, *The Hours of Labour* (London, 1872), 27.

6. See, for example, P.P., "House of Lords Select Committee on Sweating," 1888, vol. xx, Qs 1894, 640, 745, 2549-51, 1634, 4481, 1066; Second Report, 1888, vol. xxi, Qs 10282, 11745, 13643, 11787; on deterioration of job status see ibid., First Report, 1888, Qs 3801, 4472; Second Report, 1888, Q 17970.

7. Women's Industrial Council, *Home Industries of Women* (London, 1897), 97, 103; (1908), 73.

8. P.P., "Children's Employment Commission," 1864, vol. xxii, pp. 118-20; *Tailor and Cutter,* 6 June 1868, 265.

9. On night work see Clara Collet, "Women's Work," in Charles Booth, *Life and Labour of the People in London* (London, 1889), ser. 1, 4: 263-65.

10. P.P., "Children's Employment Commission," 1864, vol. xxii, pp. 99-100, 111, 137.

11. P.P., "Report of the Chief Inspector of Factory and Workshops, 1895," 1896, vol. xix, pp. 35–36; "Report . . . 1907," 1908, p. 139; *Labour Gazette,* Sept. 1901, 1.

12. As late as 1901, for example, a factory inspector reported on the increased use of basement rooms for the purpose of boot and shoe work. "In one such room below the street level, reached by a ladder through an opening in the floor of a shop in Shoreditch, I recently found that five little girls, under 15 years of age, and seven men had daily been employed for 10 months. They worked by artificial light always for no day-light could penetrate into this cellar, neither was there any opening to the outer air, only the trap door into the shop as a means of 'ventilation.' " P.P., "Report of the Chief Inspector of Factories and Workshops, 1901," 1902, vol. xxi, p. 167. A local health inspector reported that there were twenty-two basement workrooms in Chelsea, which accommodated 180 workers. *Report of the Chief Medical Officer of Health, London County Council* (London, 1907), 74.

13. *Women's Union Journal,* Apr. 1882, 28.

14. *Charity Organization Review,* Feb. 1885, 63.

15. Based on a survey taken by Collet and included in her essay "Women's Work," 260–63.

16. Ibid., 263–65.

17. It was for this reason that Moses led the middlemen and East End workers in a strike against factory sweaters in the spring of 1890. P.P., "Select Committee on Sweating," First Report, 1888, vol. xx, Q87090; *People's Press,* 17 May 1890, 8; 14 June 1890, 5; 28 June 1890, 7.

18. The case of the boot-finisher may be found in P.P., "Select Committee on Sweating," Second Report, 1888, vol. xxi, Qs 11638–11640; the case of the woman outworker is reported in *Women's Union Journal,* Apr. 1882, 28. Poor outworkers frequently pawned materials entrusted to them, and, if they were unable to recover the pawned articles or compensate their employer, they often found themselves in prison. See Henry Mayhew and John Binney, *The Criminal Prisons of London and Scenes of Prison Life* (1862; reprint ed., London, 1972), 342. For the case of an outworker child charged with larceny, see *Women's Industrial News,* Dec. 1901, 273–74.

19. For these cases and others see Women's Industrial Council, *Home Industries of Women* (1897), 13; (1908), 30; P.P., "The Report of the Royal Commission on Labour," 1909, vol. xliii, Appendix 9; and Edward G. Howarth and Mona Wilson, *West Ham: A Study in Social and Industrial Problems* (London, 1907), 271, 265.

20. Hackney, *Annual Report of the Medical Officer for the Borough of Hackney, 1902* (London, 1903), 51–56.

21. St. Pancras, *Annual Report of the Medical Officer of the Borough of St. Pancras, 1903* (London, 1904), 62–82.

22. P.P., "Report of the Chief Inspector of Factories and Workshops for 1877," 1878, vol, xx, pp. 6–8.

23. Charity Organization Society, "Special Committee on Unskilled Labour," *Report and Minutes of Evidence, June 1908* (London, 1908), 83–84; also P.P., "Royal Commission on Poor Laws and the Relief of Distress," 1909, vol. xliv, Appendix 20, p. 598.

24. National Union of Boot and Shoe Operatives (NUBSO) *Monthly Report,* 6 Mar. 1886, 9.

25. Booth, *Life and Labour,* ser. 1, 4: 73–78.

26. John Burnett, *A History of the Cost of Living* (London, 1969).

27. Eric J. Hobsbawm, *Labouring Men: Studies in the History of Labour* (London, 1965), 293.

28. Cited in Paul Thompson, *The Edwardians* (Bloomington, Ind., 1975), 127.

29. Mayhew, letter VI to the *Morning Chronicle,* in Eileen Yeo and E. P. Thompson, *The Unknown Mayhew* (New York, 1971), 116.

30. Ibid., 116, 178–80.

31. —— Grant, *London Life* (London, 1891), 209–10.

32. *Women's Union Journal,* May 1878, 36; Feb. 1876, 1–2.

33. Ibid., Feb. 1876; Nov. 1876, 67–68; Apr. 1880, 43.

34. P.P., "Sixth Report of the Medical Officer of the Privy Council, 1863," 1864, vol. xxviii, "Report by Dr. William Ord," p. 376; Leon Levi, *Wages and Earnings of the Working Classes* (London, 1885), 131–32. Levi's estimates were high, as he did not include homeworkers in his samples. His low figure for bookbinding, for example, is the high wage paid by a large firm that claimed that wages for females had held stationary at between 10s. and 12s. per week since the 1840s, while wages for males had increased 20 to 30 percent (from 30s. to 36s. and 40s. per week).

35. *Women's Union Journal,* May 1890, 37.

36. P.P., "Select Committee on the Sweating System," First Report, 1888, vol. xx, Qs3874, 6077, 3874; Second Report, vol. xxi, pp. 569–80.

37. *Workman's Times,* 12 Sept. 1890, 8.

38. Booth, *Life and Labour,* 2d ser., 5: 320–21.

39. Estimates on homeworking wages may be found in Howarth and Wilson, *West Ham*; P.P., "Select Committee on Home Work," 1907, vol. vi., Q 681; P.P., "Royal Commission on the Poor Laws and Relief of Distress," 1909, vol. xliii, Appendix III; Women's Industrial Council, *Home Industries of Women,* surveys of 1897, 1908. The select committee on homework heard that the average weekly earnings of women homeworkers in tailoring were from 7s. 6d. to 10s. per week, and declining (1907, vol. vi, Q 3332).

40. *Women's Union Journal,* May 1879, 43. P.P., "Select Committee on Sweating," First Report, 1888, vol. xx, p. 19.

41. For example, see the criticism of Thomas Wood's analysis of wages and national income in *Justice,* 7 Mar. 1896, 3.

42. For example, see Robert Sherard, *The White Slaves of London* (London, 1897), 369.

43. The 1906 wage census overestimated the average wage of women in the clothing trades partly because the census was taken in a boom year and partly because the trades were highly seasonal (the wage given was merely the average received by all workers at work in the last week of Sept. 1906). The average shop milliner, for example, a month earlier would have received one-third less wages. Most important, the wage census did not include homework wages — which were notoriously the lowest in the industry. The inquiry was a voluntary one. Board of Trade President David Lloyd George suggested that employers not participate if they were so inclined, and it was suggested that only the best employers made returns, thus leaving lower paid workers unreported. Also in 1906 recorded earnings were reported, while in 1886 it was wage reports that were cited. A private study in Birmingham (Cadbury et al., *Women's Work and Wages*) found wages to be far below the estimates of the 1906 wage census. Dressmaking in Birmingham, for example, was found to range from 10s. to 14s. 6d. rather than the wage census report of 13s. 10d. and 15s. 5d. (319).

44. The Board of Trade reported that wages had gone up nearly 1s. from 1897 to 1901, but workers argued that rent and coal alone went up 2s. *Trades and Labour Gazette,* Sept. 1901, 1; July 1902, 3. L. Wyatt Papworth and Dorothy Zimmern, *Clothing and Textile Trades* (London, 1912).

45. *Women's Trade Union Review,* July 1904, 7.

46. Clementina Black, *Married Women's Work* (London, 1915), 79.

47. P.P., "Royal Commission on the Poor Laws and Relief of Distress," 1909, vol. xliii, 393.

48. These cases may be found in the *Home Industries of Women,* 1908 survey, 51, 63, 69. Outside experts expressed the same view. "This state of things seems to be getting worse," reported the WIC; "many of the workers say they would have scorned to do the careless work they are doing now ten or twenty years ago, and scorned too, to take the pay they are now receiving" (ibid., 7). G. R. Askwith of the Board of Trade testified in 1907 that wages in the sweated industries had gone down since the mid-1890s (P.P., "Select Committee on Home Work," First Report, 1907, vol. vi, 203). Constance Smith, an investigator for the Board of Trade, claimed that women's wages had fallen steadily for the past fifty years while men's wages had risen, a view shared by social investigator Edward Cadbury, who claimed that "as far as women are concerned, the workers have not shared in the progress of production of wealth and are still at the stage where capital is all powerful" (*Hasting News,* 20 Feb. 1909, item 21, Gertrude Tuckwell Collec-

tion, Trades Union Congress Library, London). Cadbury concluded his survey of Birmingham by noting that the existing level of wages was not sufficient for a girl or woman "to realize the standard of comfort of the working classes, low though that is, unless the woman is subsidized to some extent, or gets further income in some way or other" (*Women's Work and Wages,* 136). Despite some common feelings otherwise, few (2.5 percent) outworkers in West Ham received aid through the poor laws (Howarth and Wilson, *West Ham,* 268). One industrious homeworker in the boot and shoe trade, who worked twelve to fourteen hours per day for 7s. 4d. per week, claimed that wages had dropped by half in the years just prior to 1913 (Black, *Married Women's Work,* 65–67). In two London sweated trades, tailoring and box-making, wages were at the same level in 1912–13 as they had been in 1906. Between 1906 and 1913, 80 percent of the boxmakers received less than 15s., nearly one-third of them received under 10s., and it was not until after a minimum wage was established in that trade in 1913 that wages moved into the range 13s. to 15s. Likewise, wages for women in tailoring did not rise between 1906 and 1913, the year the first minimum rate was fixed by the trade board at 13s. 6d. per week. See M. E. Bulkey, *Studies in the Minimum Wage — No. 3: The Boxmaking Industry* (London, 1915), 3–4; R. H. Tawney, *Studies in the Minimum Wage — No. 2: The Tailoring Industry* (London, 1915), 75–76; *Labour Yearbook* (London, 1916), 260. A large Bermondsey (London) clothing firm employing 601 women in 1914 paid less than 11s. per week to two-thirds of its women workers, a figure not far from one estimate that the average woman factory worker in prewar 1914 was making about 11s. 6d. per week or the *Labour Yearbook* estimate that the average adult working woman earned 10s. 10d. per week. The Bermondsey case is cited in WTUL, *Annual Report of 1914,* 9, and the 1914 estimate is found in *Justice,* 26 Feb. 1914, 5.

49. The 1915 estimate is based on a Board of Trade survey, summarized in P.P., "Accounts of Expenditure of Wage-earning Women and Girls," 1911, vol. lxxxix; the Booth estimate is found in B. L. Hutchins, *Women in Modern Industry* (London, 1915), 227. The 1863 claim was that of Dr. Smith's, whose report is found in P.P., "Sixth Report of the Medical Officer of the Privy Council, 1863," 1864, vol. xxviii, No. 10, "Dressmakers and Needlewomen of London."

50. The percentage for the working woman was 62; the average family in Rowntree's poverty class spent 69 percent on food and housing. Burnett, *Cost of Living,* 271.

51. Peter Stearns, "Working Class Women in Britain, 1890–1914," in Martha Vicinus, *Suffer and Be Still: Women in the Victorian Age* (Bloomington, Ind., 1973), 103; Standish Meacham, *A Life Apart: The English Working Class, 1890–1914* (London, 1977).

52. Ivy Pinchbeck, *Women Workers in the Industrial Revolution, 1750–1850* (New York, 1930), ch. 1; E. L. Lipson, *The History of the Woolen and Worsted Industries* (1921), 65–66. Two related articles on working-class women in preindustrial France are by Olwen Hufton: "Women and the Family Economy in Eighteenth-Century France," *French Historical Studies,* 9 (Spring 1975), and "Women in Revolution, 1789–96," *Past and Present,* 53 (Nov. 1971).

53. P. Gaskell, *Artisans and Machinery: The Moral and Physical Condition of the Manufacturing Population* (London, 1936), and Friedrich Engels, *The Condition of the Working Class in England* (1845; reprint ed., Oxford, 1958), present the classic statement on the deterioration of the family. Engels wrote: "Since large-scale industry has transferred the woman from the house to the labour market and the factory, and makes her, often enough, the breadwinner of the family, the last remnants of male domination in the proletarian home have lost all foundation" ("Origins of the Family, Private Property and State," in *Marx and Engels: Selected Works* [Moscow, 1970]). In a similar vein, Sheila Rowbotham (*Hidden from History* [New York, 1974], 55) writes of the "separation of work and home and the new discipline of the factory." See also Harold Perkin, *The Origins of Modern English Society, 1780–1880* (London, 1969), 157: "The emancipation of women was in fact one of the most important and characteristic consequences of industrialization." The impact of industrialization on wives and families has been the subject of many studies, but two of the best are Margaret Hewitt, *Wives and Mothers in Victorian Industry* (London, 1958), and Joan Scott and Louise Tilly, *Women, Work and Family* (New York, 1978).

54. E. P. Thompson, *The Making of the English Working Class* (New York, 1963), 414–16. Edward Shorter, *The Making of the Modern Family* (New York, 1975), 259–62, has claimed that new job opportunities resulted in personal independence and sexual liberation for women.

55. It is frequently suggested that the working class, in emulating the standards set by the middle class, kept its wives out of the labor force. Patricia Branca (*Women in Europe since 1750* [London, 1978]) supports this claim, stating that only about 10 percent of all married women in the nineteenth century were formally employed; that "the working-class family, well into the twentieth century maintained itself on the wage of the husband and older children alone"; and that "the history of working women in nineteenth-century cities is the history of young single girls, spinsters, and widows" (32–33). Stearns states that work for married women in the early twentieth century was "a rarity" ("Working-Class Women in Britain," 114).

56. Factory work was not the typical experience of nineteenth-century working women — even in the industrial north, where sweated outwork still existed (Duncan Bythell, *The Sweated Trades: Outwork in Nineteenth-Century Britain* [London, 1978], 145). In reminding us that working women were

more typically employed in agriculture than in factories, Pinchbeck (*Women Workers*) challenges the view that the factory was breaking up the home. "The available evidence certainly suggests," she writes, "that detractors of the factory system overestimated and exaggerated its effects on home life" (198–99). She argues that fewer wives and mothers left the home for the factory than alarmists thought. For example, Lancashire cotton factories reported that 27 percent of their work force was women. Pinchbeck suggests that that figure is low in comparison to women in agricultural work and goes on to say that "hence, in the entire factory population the proportion of married women who worked, to those who remained at home, must have been far too small to justify the statement that the factory system destroyed the home life of the workers generally" (309). Another challenge to the traditional view that women were radicalized by industrialization comes from Robert P. Neuman, who has recently argued that the traditional sexual values of the preindustrial working class did not disappear as suddenly as heretofore claimed and did not differ radically from those of industrial workers ("Working Class Sexuality," in Mary Lynn McDougall, ed., *The Working Class in Modern Europe* [Lexington, Mass., 1975], 157–68). On the subject of family life, others have suggested that family life was not as disrupted by the changes of the nineteenth century as commonly accepted. See Virginia Y. McLaughlin, "Patterns of Work and Family Organization among Buffalo's Italians," and Elizabeth H. Pleck, "The Two-Parent Household: Black Family Structure in Late Nineteenth-Century Britain," both in Michael Gordon, ed., *The American Family in the Social Historical Perspective* (New York, 1973). Likewise, Elizabeth Roberts claims that the widespread belief that traditional English peasant cooking disappeared with the industrial revolution is not true for towns like Barrow and Lancaster, where women worked at home. Here it was possible for the traditional skills to be handed down from mother to daughter ("Working-Class Standards of Living in Barrow and Lancaster, 1890–1914," *Economic History Review*, 30 [May 1977], 311). Joan Scott and Louise Tilly argue that preindustrial values rather than a new individualistic ideology "justified the work of working women in the nineteenth century." Rural and domestic values, they claim, were imported into the new industrial environment as women regarded themselves not as individual workers, but as partners in the family enterprise. "Married women," they state, "in fact seem almost an internal backwater of preindustrial values" within the new industrial society ("Women's Work and the Family in Nineteenth-Century Europe," in Charles Rosenberg, ed., *Family in History* [Philadelphia, 1975], 151, 172).

57. See, for example, Margaret MacDonald's testimony before the Royal Commission on the Poor Laws in P.P., "Royal Commission on the Poor Law," 1910, vol. xlviii, p. 231.

58. Such was the case of the poor young widow, Mary Linden, in Robert Tressell's *The Ragged Trousered Philanthropists* (1914; reprint ed., New York, 1962): "Standing by the side of the dresser at one end of the room was a treadle sewing machine and on one end of the dresser was a pile of sewing; ladies' blouses in process of making. This was another instance of the goodness of Mr. Sweater, from whom Linden's daughter-in-law obtained the work. It was not much, because she was only able to do it in her spare time, but then, as she often remarked, every little bit helped."

59. See John Burnett, ed., *Annals of Labour* (Bloomington, Ind., 1974), 48–49, and E. Roberts, "Working-Class Standards of Living," 311; see also P.P., "Royal Commission on the Poor Laws and Relief of Distress," 1910, vol. xlviii, p. 231.

60. "Lucy Luck" in Burnett, ed., *Annals of Labour,* 67–76.

61. P.P., "Report of the Commission on the Poor Laws and the Relief of Distress," 1909, vol. xliii, Williams and Jones Report, Appendix, p. 28.

62. See P. Thompson, *The Edwardians,* 77, 302, 305. This is the average for Edwardian women and therefore possibly on the high side for working-class women — although by 1911 women of the unskilled working class were lowering their fertility (via late marriage) more rapidly than other classes. See John W. Innes, *Class Fertility Trends in England and Wales, 1876–1934* (Princeton, 1938), 43, 66–69, 97, 101.

63. P.P., "Accounts of Expenditure of Wage-earning Women and Girls," 1911, vol. lxxxix, p. 4.

64. P.P., "Report of the Census of Population, 1911," Occupations, Table 13, p. 203.

65. One woman made shoes in bed following childbirth, and another stitched twenty-five pairs of corsets in the morning of the day she lost a baby at childbirth. Black, *Married Women's Work,* 4, 160, 15, 224–26.

66. Cited in Hutchins, *Women in Modern Industry,* 234.

67. Black, *Married Women's Work,* 138.

68. Women's Industrial Council, *Home Industries of London,* 1897 edition.

69. Booth, *Life and Labour,* 1st ser., 4: 56, 64, and Black, *Married Women's Work,* 270.

70. Black, *Married Women's Work,* 9, 135–38. The Royal Commission on Labour found the same thing: women worked in order that the family could survive. These studies also dispelled the myth that working-class women worked because their husbands were drunk or lazy.

71. *British Workwoman,* 1 Jan. 1864, cited in Jenni Calder, *Woman and Marriage in Victorian Fiction* (New York, 1976), 73.

72. Testimony of Mrs. J. Ramsay MacDonald in P.P., "The Royal Commission on the Poor Laws and Relief of Distress," 1910, vol. xlviii, p. 230.

CHAPTER 4

Working-Class Power and Sweated Labor

WHAT WAS TO BE DONE? Could this virus of sweating be removed from the lifeblood of the nation? Among the workers themselves, both men and women, there were voices of hope. Some of those who lived and worked in the neighborhoods where sweating prevailed believed that the cycle of poverty and sweated labor could be broken by their own doing. In this they were encouraged by middle-class women. "No one," the Women's Trade Union League (WTUL) claimed, "can doubt that one of the main hopes of real improvement lies in the development of effective organization among female workers."[1] Unfortunately, the dreams of these Victorian and Edwardian women turned out to be unrealistic and remained unfulfilled as London, the center of the sweating system, remained a trade-union desert — "an amorphous zone of weak and fluctuating organization united only by its general poverty."[2] This chapter examines why trade unionism was unable to unify the clothing trades labor force and why sweated workers — particularly women and Jews — failed to develop a political or industrial consciousness.

Unions and sweating in the 1860s and 1870s

A primary issue facing the clothing trades unions throughout the last half of the nineteenth century was whether or not to bring outworkers into the union. As sketched out in chapter 1, the clothing trades unions in London collapsed in the 1830s. During the next forty years sweating rooted well and grew, so that when the tailors of London reestablished their union in 1866 they did so primarily as part of a war on sweating. Gradually, over the remaining third of the century, the unionists, making up but a few of the many, concluded that it was impossible to block the flow of labor into the sweatshops and decided, instead, that it was in their best interest to bring all sweated workers into the union, where wages and conditions could be monitored. The new union, the London Operative Tailors Protective Association, at once carried out a successful strike against the master tailors; soon after it boasted ten branches throughout London. A reaction to both the subcontract system and the influx of cheap labor into the trade, the union saw that its enemy was not only the master tailor but also the sweated worker who labored for practically nothing. As a consequence, the objective of the new organization, like its predecessor, was to unite the outwork labor force, which made up about one-quarter of the work force, with the indoor labor force. Its goal was to counteract, as described by a member of the Paddington branch of the union, the custom of the employer "to screw down" the wages of the indoor worker by telling him that the outworker would make the garments for less than he did.[3]

At first the union met with success. Outworkers cooperated with the union in the strike of 1866, which brought a wage raise for every union tailor in London. The southwest branch reported that they had made progress in converting the "miserable beings" in the sweating dens "into respectable and creditable" members of the society. No longer were the employers in control of the labor market. The masters who once used the outworker "as a tool" to depress wages were being deterred because of the unity among the outdoor and indoor workers.[4]

Ironically, however, the citywide wage scale or log, as it was called, that the union had won from the employers made it even more crucial that complete organization of the trade be accomplished. As long as all workers were not in the union, the log unwittingly put a premium on outwork because outworkers would work for less than union wages. In effect, labor power could be counterproductive—those who belonged to the union without ensuring that the entire trade be organized were damaging their interests. So the incentive for employers to put work out increased as workers insisted that the log be enforced. When a master tailor in Conduit Street was asked why he defied the log by putting his work out, he replied, "Do you think that I should be such a fool as to send my trade out if I could get it made as cheap in-doors?" Thus, to the union, the message was clear: The outworker could make or break the industrial action of the union. Without him the union would fail. In a letter to the outwork tailors of London, the executive of the London Operative Tailors wrote, "We would urge you [outworkers] to carefully consider that our interests being identical, and our case a common one, any lack of duty on the part of any section of the body must be more or less felt by the whole; and our united interests ultimately suffer."[5]

While the London men were sharpening their swords, a national union, the Amalgamated Society of Tailors (AST), was formed in Manchester. This new AST at first received only moderate support from the London union. Although the secretary of the London union, Charles Green, was vice-president of the new national, the London tailors had initial misgivings about amalgamation, especially with regard to the national's desire for a uniform national wage scale, which they feared would be lower than the London log. In the fall of 1866 a representative of the AST met with the London tailors to discuss the merger of the two, and by spring of 1867 the London tailors and the AST had agreed to a program of nearly full amalgamation through mutual memberships, mutual strike support, and the establishment of a uniform time log from which local wages could be set.[6]

In response to the new and potential power of the unions, employers outside of London joined with London employers (who made up the London Master Tailors Association) to form the Master Tailors Association (MTA) of Great Britain. The MTA, like the AST, wanted a universal log, and thus by late 1866 two logs, the master and the union logs, had been drawn up. A dispute between the masters and the union led to the strike and lockout of 1867, which lasted six months and ended at Old Bailey, where three members of the London Tailors Protective Association were found guilty of conspiracy to impoverish the master tailors of London.[7] In spite of this attack on the union, the London union had temporarily succeeded in achieving solidarity between outworker and indoor worker. In April a "Great Meeting of Outdoor Workers" was held in London, and the workers unanimously resolved that no work would be taken from shops on strike. Outworkers of the Nottinghill branch pledged to support the strike by not doing work for the struck firms. The outworkers met two more times that spring in support of the strike, one of the meetings being attended by 200 women outworkers. As a result of the strike, a "Ladies Branch" of the London Tailors was formed, but with initially only fifty outworkers from among the 200 to 300 women who supported the strike. Also joining the strike and responding to the organizing efforts of the London union were East End Jewish workers. "We must try and counteract," Mr. Neal of the London association told a Whitechapel meeting of East End workers, "that pernicious principle by which individuals look upon their men and their labour as they would upon a man selling some trifle in the streets—trying to buy at the lowest possible rate, and sell at the highest."[8] The Whitechapel tailors voted to support the strike and to set up their own branch of the union, although their membership was quite small.

But the strike failed. The London operatives withdrew their proposed time log and accepted, for the time being, the decision of the court that picketing was illegal. The masters proclaimed victory, and the union was split. The majority of the London men, disgusted with what they felt was less than full support from the AST, quit that organization; a minority, convinced that unity was "the great lesson taught by the past struggle," remained with it. In short, division and failure meant that the union was nearly extinct. The once enthusiastic movement to organize the industry went into a state of lethargy and neglect, and within a few years an "almost perfect state of disorganization existed among the London tailors." In 1872 the two London groups had less than 800 members between them.[9]

A new wave of union organization followed William Gladstone's Trade Union Act of 1871. Inspired by the unionization of the heretofore weak agricultural and railroad workers, once again the tailors declared war on the "large and continued increase" in outwork. The split between the two tailors unions was repaired in July 1872. This new London branch of the national AST set out to organize the entire trade, first by forming, again, an east London branch of Jewish workers. And again the London tailors announced that only "when the lowest portion of the trade were better paid, they might hope for improvement of the whole." As a result, a new and reorganized Jewish branch of the union allowed "trade" memberships, which made it possible for the poorer worker to bypass the expense of contributing for sick and funeral benefits. The goal was to build up an army of potential strikers. Had this "trade only" type of membership existed earlier, organization of the unskilled workers might have succeeded, and the Jewish workers would not have been forced into the "worst portion of the trade."[10]

However, "trade only" memberships went against the policy of the

national. The result was that the earlier conflict between the London
tailors and the national union resurfaced, centering on the continued
desire of the London union to organize the entire industry — which
meant, of course, a more aggressive unionism. But would this encourage or discourage the growth of cheap labor? Both parties, in
effect, were saying what Charles Booth and William Beveridge were
to say later: regulating the flow of workers into the trade is necessary
to end the casual labor-poverty syndrome; but they were not in agreement as to how it should be done — by the inclusion or the exclusion
of cheap labor. When the London union had been refounded, the
London men recognized that women working in the trade were a
problem, since so many male tailors themselves hired cheap female
labor, often their wives and daughters, as "a means of underselling
their fellow men." To many of them it was a matter of certainty that
if women remained unorganized, "the evil would increase to such an
extent as to destroy all the good that had been accomplished by unity
amongst the men."[11]

Sweating and unionism among women, 1874–88

The initiative to unionize women in the clothing trades came both
from the male unionists and through the work of two groups, the
WTUL and the Women's Industrial Council (WIC). Although the
cotton textile industry was the early stronghold in women's unionism,
the movement for the industrial rights of women was largely the outcome of the crisis in the sweated trades of London from the mid-1870s.
Here began a war against both male prejudice and female apathy and
a test of the proposition that unionization was the solution to the
problems of women's work. Emma Paterson, a woman of the upper
working class and founder of the WTUL in 1874, believed that the
solution to the problem of sweating was the "united effort of the workpeople themselves."[12] League member Emilia Dilke argued that it was
through unionization that advances for the working woman must
come, not through government regulation. Improved conditions of
labor, wages, and standard of comfort for men were testimony to the
advantages of unionization. Why not organize women as well? By
1878 the WTUL had established eight branches.[13]

The WTUL itself was not a union but a propaganda and educational agency, wanting to acquaint working women with the princi-

ples and knowledge of unionism and to provide leadership in organizing unions. For this reason the WTUL set up its own half-penny bank, library, swimming club, labor bureau, cooperative society, women's labor journal, and seaside resort house for women workers. It was not until 1906 when Mary Macarthur and the WTUL founded the National Federation of Women Workers that the concept of one great union of women workers was considered. Neither did the WTUL encourage militant unionism. From its inception the WTUL's interest was in welfare unionism — the workers taking care of their own in times of distress. At first it did not advocate the strike as a weapon to be used in advancing the interests of women workers. Its objectives were fourfold: to protect the trade interests of its members by preventing the depression of wages; to equalize the hours of work; to provide sickness and unemployment benefits; and to provide arbitration in disputes between worker and employer.

This movement among women in industry in the mid-1870s reflects some of the changing features of Victorian society, not the least of which was the women's suffrage movement. However, it also closely followed the general expansion of unionism in 1872–73, which emphasized the organization of the unskilled and semiskilled workers. But in the most immediate sense, Paterson's movement was a response to the widespread reduction of wages to which women workers were increasingly subject during these years. The "principal object" of the WTUL, it was reported in 1876, was "to promote a fair remuneration for labour, or rather to prevent a depression of wages which had been going on for some years." Women must unite, the WTUL's journal declared, in order to "prevent unskilled workers from working underprice." For example, a group of shirt machinists won the support of the WTUL in bringing suit against their employers who had reduced wages by 40 percent. The case, heard in the Guildhall Court in 1876, was decided in favor of the women, and led the women to found the London Sewing Machinists Society. In 1880 the organization of women employees, many of them outworkers, at the Royal Clothing factory at Pimlico (southwest central London) came after the reduction of wages and the discharge of a large number of workers. The women protested that over 200,000 garments, which ordinarily would have been made in the factory or by factory outworkers, were subcontracted to "the fever dens" of the East End.[14]

The Pimlico Tailoresses Union became a branch of the London

Tailoresses Trade Union, which had been organized by the WTUL, and the AST in 1877. Paterson, with the support of Peter Shorrocks and James Macdonald of the men's union, had persuaded the men to support the organization of women workers and to recognize the women's right to work. The head of the London AST addressed the women at their first meeting, held at the Tailor's Institute on Denman Street, and said that it was his opinion that it was "high time" that something was done to organize the tailoresses and went on to ask all those present "who might be well paid for their work to remember how many others there were who were not properly paid; they should take an interest in these less fortunate workers and try to help and protect them by union. If a woman did the same amount of work as a man and did it equally well she should receive as much as a man would for the same work."[15] This parent tailoresses union operated out of the league's headquarters, Industrial Hall, in Bloomsbury, while a branch was started in the East End. The women and the London branch of the AST got along fairly well. Macdonald, the London secretary, supported the WTUL in organizing other women in the clothing trades and was a member of its council. Other members of the London union regarded the organization of women "of great importance" and devoted time to the cause.[16]

But the partnership was an uneasy one. "A few individual members of the large Society of Tailors," noted the WTUL, "have given to the women's union movement earnest support, but the Society, as a body, has not yet given it much encouragement." When the AST conference of 1879 proposed to "protect" women by prohibiting them from working in the same workrooms as the men, the women's laconic response was that the solution would be for the men to get completely out of the trade, for "the men are clearly usurpers."[17] The men, they declared, were not concerned about the moral well-being of the female workers but wanted separate shop accommodations because they were afraid that women would learn too much of the trade if they worked with the men. Despite the protest, the men and women were separated.

Despite promotion by the London tailors, the national AST refused to open its membership to women. A woman correspondent for the *Workman's Times* asked whether the AST, in its lethargy, was going to "allow the men to be swamped" before bringing the women into the union and putting their wages on an equal basis.[18] The tailoresses did not want separate unions but wanted to organize with the men.

They believed that male fears of women "swamping" the labor market were unfounded and that women's participation in numerous tailoring strikes, especially the strike of 1891, was proof of their value as fellow unionists. To them the prejudices of the men had not changed since the 1830s, when the London tailors refused the plea of the tailoresses for a union. David Schloss charged that many male unionists were disinclined to help women raise their position because they were usually men in the prime of life, earning good wages "so that their wives were not obliged to work, and their daughters were too young to work and they did not care about their sisters."[19] Even the head of the MTA suggested that the national AST should organize women workers in order to prevent employers from taking advantage of them. The only way to stamp out sweating, wrote one critic of the AST, "is to make the women our equals, to associate with them, and let them know that the men working with them are comrades in arms." The AST delegates, by a vote of two to one, rejected the London tailors' proposal to admit women into the union.[20]

Union revival and the sweated trades, 1888–1914

The women's industrial rights movement received a boost from the union revival of 1888–89. Bringing nearly every occupational group into labor unions, this new unionism, as it has come to be called, advocated the organization of all unskilled workers and the use of aggressive strike tactics. The movement was inspired by a small but influential group of socialists who criticized existing unions and who preached labor militancy. In part, as well, this labor explosion was a women's revolt: it was the famous "match girls' strike" at the Bryant and May Company of London in 1888 that "turned a new leaf in Trade Union annals" and set the example for the great gas-worker and dock strikes of the following year.[21]

While it is true that the principles of open memberships, the full organization of labor, and an emphasis on strike tactics had existed in the London clothing trades unions long before 1888 (e.g., the London tailors' efforts to organize Jews and women in the 1870s), the new unionism of 1888–89 injected a new spirit and purpose into women's unionism. After fourteen years of a "dilettante" approach to organization, claimed the new unionist leader John Burns in 1890, the women were becoming more professional, and the men were becoming more willing to accept women's unionism.[22] Women began to reevaluate not only their movement but also their methods: "How was it they had done so little?" asked a charter member of the WTUL in 1889. New unionism, noted Lady Dilke, had given women's trade unionism "a lift" by showing that it was possible to combine the lowest forms of labor and break down a social prejudice against combination. Accordingly, the league changed its name to the Women's Trade Union League from the Women's Protective and Provident League and adopted a "new Policy," foremost of which was an aggressive organizing spirit and a reversal of its initial opposition toward government intervention in the labor market.[23] Henceforth, the WTUL was to be one of the strongest advocates of government regulation of labor and industry.

This new unionism had three direct results: first, with its new policy and under the leadership of Dilke[24] and her niece, Gertrude Tuckwell, the WTUL embarked upon a program of organization of women workers. Dilke's first action was to move the league's offices to "new respectable quarters" and to hire, at her own expense, the WTUL's first organizer, Mrs. A. B. Marland-Brodie. Within one year the league had grown from ten to over thirty unions.[25] Subsequent years brought increased organizational activity. In 1895, for example, five new unions were formed in London.[26] In addition, the WTUL began the practice of providing to any union, at a fee of one half-penny per year per female member, the services of a woman organizer.[27] The league's *Women's Union Journal* was replaced by the quarterly *Review,* largely because much of the WTUL news was being printed in labor weeklies such as Keir Hardie's *Labour Leader.* Finally, in 1890 Dilke's "scheme of affiliation" was adopted by the league, which took the WTUL to cities outside of London — thus giving the WTUL a "wider outlook and more experience."[28]

A second result of new unionism was the increased acceptance by men of female workers and female unionists. Never before, claimed the women in 1889, had men "shown themselves more ready and more helpful than they are showing themselves now." Skilled male labor was at last realizing that it was necessary that women organize and that male unionists step out from the circle of their own combination and participate in starting women's trade unions.[29] "Even in London" the WTUL reported, "where the organization of women is most difficult . . . the awakening interest shown by many trade union leaders

. . . stimulates us to fresh efforts and inspires us with the belief that, at no distant period we may rouse the women of this city from their apathy."[30] Similarly, Tuckwell expressed the optimism of the women when she announced that the "conservative elements of a narrower trade unionism" were giving way to the broader view that recognized that the industrial interests of men and women were "inseparably connected."[31] The London boot- and shoemakers led the London Trades Council in its pledge to "promote combination" among women wherever possible, and the league organized, in conjunction with the council, a twelve-month membership drive among women workers.[32]

In addition to the rejuvenation of the WTUL and the increased male acceptance of the idea of unionism for women, the new unionist enthusiasm resulted in a second women's labor organization in London, the WIC. Originally named the Women's Trade Union Association, the council was founded in 1889 by a number of liberals, socialists, and unionists, including Burns, Amie Hicks, a working-class woman, Clementina Black, former secretary of the WTUL, Sydney Buxton, a liberal Member of Parliament, H. H. Champion, the socialist leader, and Ben Cooper. Burns and Cooper were laborers and unionists. Although the formation of this new organization was "regretted" by the WTUL (the league did not feel that a new organization was necessary), there is little doubt that the more radical and socialist coloring of the new council pushed the WTUL into a more aggressive policy of its own.[33] The initial objective of the group was to organize East End working women, but in 1894 it professed its hope to help all working women and to watch over "all industrial matters which concern women."[34] One of its first acts was to found the East London Ropemakers Union under the leadership of Hicks.

From the beginning, the focus of the WIC was the London sweated trades. It embarked on a program to collect and publish information pertaining to women's work; to watch the activities and prepare legal matter for the House of Commons; to organize women and girls into the ranks of unions; to educate them in social, political, and economic matters; and to develop better skills among women workers. To do this the council functioned under four committees: investigative, legal, educational and technical training, and organizational. By 1906 there were thirty-seven Working Girls Clubs affiliated with the WIC; a legal services program had been set up for working women; and a strong lobbying position within the House of Commons had been established.

One of the most active members of the council, a tireless researcher, writer, and public speaker, was another former WTUL worker, Margaret Gladstone MacDonald. Largely because of her influence, the most vigorous spokesman for women's industrial rights within the House of Commons was her husband, Ramsay MacDonald, the future prime minister.

This unionist upsurge gave strength and encouragement to the men who had already worked hard for the organization of women. Among the men no one better represented the spirit of new unionism than did London tailor James Macdonald. Coming to London from Scotland in 1881, he played a leading role in the London labor movement for thirty years. During his stormy career Macdonald pushed the tailors union and the London Trades Council (he was secretary of both) into organizing the unskilled and semiskilled of the clothing trades.[35] When Macdonald and his London tailors presented the national union with a plan for rejuvenating the union — including the opening of the doors to women — they were turned down,[36] the conservative national union electing to wage a rearguard fight against changes in the trade, including female membership. Hence the trade magazine, the *Master Tailor and Cutters Gazette,* could note "how really little is the sympathy shown by the men for their toiling sisters."[37]

When Macdonald was expelled from the executive of the national AST in 1893, his London union, the London Society of Tailors, left in protest. Macdonald had wanted a censure of the national's executive committee for its neglect of unorganized workers and had moved that the national union adopt a policy stating that "the objects of this society are the protection and furtherance of the interests of its members and the complete emancipation of labour from the exploitation of capital." He wanted the union to separate strike funds from benefit funds and to lower its dues so to allow "strike membership" alone, thus enabling women to enter the union fold. He also proposed to split up the districts and decentralize the union. The rejection of his plan, along with his expulsion from the executive, generated "intense hostility on the part of London men," who asked why the AST had to exist at a "cast iron level" of membership.[38] The Londoners rejoined the union in 1901, only to leave that same year, again over the issue of open membership. The national union had allowed women into membership in 1900, but only if they would pay the same dues as the men. The Londoners wanted all tailoring unions to allow special (i.e., lowered) dues for women, which the national would not consider.

The work of these London men to organize women workers was important, for it provided much support for the WTUL and the WIC in their efforts to do the same. Beginning in 1892, Macdonald led the tailors in a renewed move to organize women and Jewish outworkers. For the tailors times had changed: "We must speak of conciliation—of working with the outworkers in the interest of the entire trade. In 1833 to 'work out' was the exception. In 1893 to 'work in' is the exception. . . . In London out-working is the tree; in-working is but the tender shoot, the young sapling."[39]

The answer was to organize, not exclude, the outworker before the sweating system moved in and took over the entire trade. Wages for outworkers had to be made uniform. With this objective, Macdonald, the tailors, and Black and Hicks of the WIC sought first (and unsuccessfully) to establish a minimum wage agreement between outworkers and contractors, and then (somewhat more successfully) to reorganize the London Tailoresses Trade Union, which had, for the past decade, consisted of only a few members. The men, with the aid of the WTUL and partly as a result of the participation of some 500 women in the tailors' strike of 1891, converted the old union into a branch of Macdonald's union, with a male president and treasurer, and two working-class women, Mary Elvery, a tailoress, and Hicks, became the paid organizers for it. Although the union remained the nucleus for the women's tailoring movement, in 1892 it was again described as weak, and by 1894 it needed reorganization again.[40] The most logical step, consequently, was to bring women directly into the men's union. In 1894 the London Society of Tailors reduced its entrance fee and opened its membership to immigrant Jews and women. Henceforth the London union was known as the London Tailors and Tailoresses Society with a West End Tailoresses branch for the women. As a result a large number of new members, most of whom were outworkers, was brought into the union: 230 in 1898, 170 in 1900, and 2,000 in 1901. Union pressure on the outworker was severe, and it was not unusual for the unionists to threaten and assault recalcitrant workers.

This effort to organize outworkers spread to other trades, as Macdonald used the London Trades Council to urge the organization of all workers heretofore unorganized.[41]

But the women's branch of the union continued to be unstable for a decade after its inception in 1894. In 1903 the union lamented that it had only "a handful" of members. In 1904 a new membership campaign, organized by Elvery, who was now the first woman member of the executive of the London Tailors and Tailoresses Society, brought hundreds of new members into the union. By 1905 it was reported that the West End tailoresses branch had over 1,000 members; it was so confident of its new strength that it proclaimed that the time had come when all firms employing women should only employ unionists.[42]

The East End Tailoresses Union had an even more capricious history than did the West End branch. David Schloss, bootmaker and onetime secretary to the Jewish Board of Guardians, served as treasurer to the organization for many years. In 1880–81 the union, with a Miss Browne as paid WTUL organizer, formed a branch in Whitechapel; ten years later, again under the leadership of the WTUL, the union attempted to organize English and Jewish girl tailoresses in Spitalfields. But the movement in the East End remained small; by 1890 its membership was forty and "decreasing." Hicks attempted to revitalize the union in 1892, but it was disbanded in 1893 and did not come back into existence until 1896. In that year the WTUL complained that "the members have apparently forgotten the lessons previous adversity should have taught them."[43] In 1904 the union became a branch of the London Tailors and Tailoresses Society and began a healthy rivalry with the West End women's branch.

In other sectors of the clothing trades, where there were no men's unions to give help, the women's union movement fared even less well. The WTUL was instrumental in the formation of a number of other unions, but none enjoyed even the limited success achieved by the tailoresses. A Shirt and Collar Makers Union was founded in 1875, initially with forty members, but, although it enjoyed some early growth and enthusiasm, it was dissolved "after continuing for some time in a state of limited usefulness."[44] A Dressmakers', Milliners and Mantle Makers Society was founded by the WTUL in 1875; after suffering through three years of limited success and corruption on the part of its male secretary, it was reorganized in 1878 with thirty-three members. By 1881 it had only sixty members—a depressingly small portion of the over 70,000 dressmakers and milliners in London in that year. The union revival of 1888-89 gave a boost to the dressmakers' efforts, but again with limited success. Reorganization of the dressmakers' union occurred in 1890, but the union could report only twenty members two years later.[45] A second dressmakers' union, the Society of Scientific Dressmakers, was organized by the WTUL in Marylebone, where over 4,500 women in that trade lived in 1888. It attracted no more than a fraction of the London dressmakers.[46] By 1892 it was claimed that "nothing is worse paid" than dressmaking and that organization of the trade was badly needed.[47] Organization was tried once again in 1904, when the National Union of Dressmakers and Milliners' Assistants was formed. But because the trade was highly seasonal, union membership fluctuated according to the availability of work. In 1906 it formed itself into a branch of the National Federation of Women Workers and conducted an organizing campaign among the Girls' Clubs of London. This campaign met with considerable initial success, although by 1909 the union again lamented its declining membership.[48]

The effort and enthusiasm of the early organizers of women's labor had not resulted in a commensurate level of success by the first decade of the twentieth century. Naturally some short-term gains were achieved, the women gained some notoriety (as with the match girls' strike of 1888), and no doubt many women felt the benefits that even some of the small unions were able to win for the working woman. Six years after its formation the WTUL announced that "the value of industrial organization among women has been fully proven by work already accomplished by this League . . . and that the extension of the work is highly desirable."[49] But the working women of London and throughout Great Britain remained generally unorganized. As Table 14 indicates, the number of women unionists in Britain in 1913 was 356,963, which was about 7 percent of the five million women in the labor force. Most of these women belonged to the textile unions, as only 99,682 belonged to unions outside the textile industry. Only in cotton-weaving was anywhere close to a majority of women workers unionized and, as a result, enjoying relatively high wages. Although the clothing industry was one of the largest employers of women in industry, only 2.6 percent of those employed in the boot and shoe trade, 1.05 percent in the hat and cap trade, and 2.74 percent in tailoring and other clothing occupations were members of trade unions in 1913. All in all, there were only 5,000 women unionists in London — about 6 percent of the female work force[50] — and only a fraction of these were among the 150,000 women employed in the clothing industry. Thus, as Tom Mann had noted in 1897, "the energy spent in attempts to organize women, whilst yielding good results in certain trades and districts, has certainly not been very encouraging on the whole."[51] Similarly, Black of the WIC told the select committee on homework in 1907 that improvement in wages for women could not come about through the organization of workers, and the WTUL *Review* noted in 1903 that "women do not seem for the most part to be alive to the need for organization."[52]

Table 14. Women in Trade Unions in Great Britain, 1913

Textile	Number of Women	Percentage of Total Number of Women Employed in the Trade
Cotton-preparing	53,317	14.94
Cotton-spinning	1,857	0.52
Cotton-weaving	155,910	43.68
Wool and worsted	7,738	2.17
Linen and jute	20,689	5.80
Silk	4,247	1.19
Hosiery and others	4,070	1.14
Textile printing, etc.	9,453	2.65
Subtotal	257,281	
Nontextile		
Boot and shoe	9,282	2.60
Hat and cap	3,750	1.05
Tailoring and other clothing	9,798	2.74
Printing	5,893	1.65
Pottery, etc.	2,600	0.73
Tobacco	2,060	0.58
Shop assistants	24,255	6.79
Other trades	8,742	2.45
General labor	23,677	6.63
Employees of public authorities	9,625	2.70
Subtotal	99,682	
Total	356,963	

Source. Labour Yearbook (London, 1916).

Gustave Doré's *London Bridge,* 1872. Every day thousands of clothing workers crossed this bridge, by omnibus, foot, or cart, to pick up work given out by firms in the central city. Because of the sweated outwork system of production, a mass of people were kept at poverty-level jobs and had to live near the center of the city where the sweating firms were located.

Men's coatmakers

Making children's overalls and pinafores

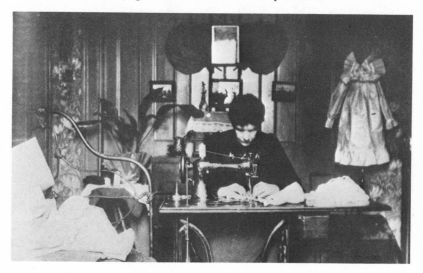

Homeworking in London, ca. 1906. Fifty years after its introduction in Britain in the 1850s, the sewing machine was still in wide use in the home for industrial production of wearing apparel. These photographs of London homeworkers were included in the *Handbook* of the Sweated Industries Exhibition of 1906. Family members and neighbors often helped in the work, which invaded the bedrooms and sitting rooms of the workers. The cut-out pieces

Baby's boot- and shoemakers

Bootmaking

of fabric were acquired from a "giver-out" of work, often a middleman or
-woman who, in turn, had acquired the pieces from a factory of some sort — or
even a wholesaler or retailer. After the finished work was returned to the
middleman or -woman, it was then given out again for completion in the
next step of the production process.

One of the most vigorous workers for the industrial rights of working women was Margaret Gladstone MacDonald, the wife of the future prime minister, Ramsay MacDonald. She was a leading member of the Women's Industrial Council, which, along with the Women's Trade Union League, pioneered the movement for greater regulation of women's work and the political-economic education of working-class women.

Lady Emilia Pattison Dilke, the second wife of Sir Charles Dilke, succeeded Emma Paterson to the leadership of the Women's Trade Union League in 1886. Although the WTUL continued its efforts to unionize women, under Dilke it pushed for increased state protection of women in industry—a campaign that saw the establishment of Britain's first modern minimum wage laws by 1909.

SPECIMENS FROM MR. PUNCH'S INDUSTRIAL EXHIBITION OF 1850.

(TO BE IMPROVED IN 1851).

The exact origins of the idea of a "sweating exhibition" are unknown, but, as this photograph of *Punch* magazine's play on the Great Exhibition of 1851 suggests, the idea existed long before the real one, sponsored by the *Daily News*, took place in 1906.

Although the weakness of these early women's unions attracted the help of men in organizing women, it also fostered male fear and prejudice against cheap and unorganized labor. This was noticeable as the "system" of cheap female labor "crept insidiously" into West End firms. The woman worker continued to incite controversy, and, as one labor newspaper lamented, "women, as a sex, despite suffragette agitations and the like, have undoubtedly allowed themselves in many trades to be used as the *willing* tools of the employers in reducing men's wages. Their standard of subsistence is lower than a man's, and their labour is cheaper as a natural consequence. Living cheaply, they work cheaply, to the impoverishment of themselves and the enrichment of their employers."[53] The writer then said that "neither sex, race or color" could be allowed to interfere with the principle of minimum wage as established by the union. The answer was still the full organization of the women workers. "Of the thousands of women employed in the trade," noted the tailor's correspondent for the *Trades and Labour Gazette,* "only a small proportion are organized, and those outside would be a dangerous menace to the men in case of a dispute."[54]

But, as in the decade before it, the London tailors' desire to organize women after 1900 was hampered by acrimonious disputes between the national and local unions. As some women lamented in 1905, the tailors were again making a determined effort to broaden their membership, but the split in the union had a detrimental effect. The movement was racked with floor fights and lawsuits. One London Trades Council member noted that there had been "a series of undercurrents in this affair not known to anybody outside the trade."[55] London branches refused to pay levies of the national AST, protested the superannuation benefits, and quarreled with the executive council over the centralization of union power. Macdonald, as secretary of the London Trades Council, presided over numerous disputes between the AST and the London Tailors and Tailoresses Society. The trades council, to the chagrin of the AST, refused membership to the AST, claiming that it no longer had a branch in London. The AST retorted that the Trades Union Congress (the federation of trade unions) and the Labour party in "clear and unmistakable language" recognized the AST and not the London union as the legitimate representative of the trade. At one point the AST succeeded in getting the council to pass a resolution condemning the actions of Macdonald himself. The London tailors continued to emphasize open membership and

"trade" membership rather than benefits membership and prided themselves on their militancy. They were adamant that log wages not be
tampered with and were appalled that the AST was willing to "emascu-
late the log." Any deviation from log prices, they claimed, could only
be treated with industrial action. They saw the log "slipping from their
grasp" and were dissatisfied with the "rigid and undemocratic" constitution (i.e., central control) of the national union, and, therefore, they
were ready and willing to fight strenuously against the "insidious
encroachments" the employers were anxious to make.[56] However
favorable were the intentions of the London men toward the women
tailors, the intraunion struggles lessened their ability to organize
women workers effectively.

Women in the boot and shoe trade

Women's unionism in the London boot and shoe industry also faced
male and female apathy and schism within the union movement, but
here there were no periodic bursts of success. As early as 1877 the
London boot- and shoemakers reported that even though they had
altered their entrance requirements so that women could be admitted
to their union, the women had no interest and not one woman had
joined the union. Four years later the WTUL undertook the formation of a woman's boot and shoe union, the Boot Machinists, Fitters,
Binders and Tackers Union. The new group attracted few members
and apparently did not exist very long after its inception.[57] No more
successful was a drive for the organization that came with the great
strike and lockout of 1895. In an effort to organize the women, the
local men's union relaxed its rules once again to allow female memberships (at one-half the male rate), and several hundred women were
given strike pay in return for a promise to join the union following
the lockout. The WTUL joined the campaign, and its organizers held
meetings (most of them in Hackney, where over 900 women boot-
and shoemakers lived), provided speakers, carried out a public campaign to raise strike funds for the women, and actively recruited members through visiting workshops. The results were disappointing: only
twenty women joined the union. The WTUL placed the blame, in
part at least, on the men, claiming they neither actively recruited and
educated the women nor made them aware of their rights as workers.[58]

All of this was occurring as new machinery and labor-saving devices in boot and shoe production meant that women machinists were in great demand. The issue of women in the workshop or working at home became increasingly crucial. In 1903 the executive of the National Union of Boot and Shoe Operatives passed a resolution protesting the hiring of women in certain branches of the boot and shoe trade. "They have no right to work at so low a price," Charles Freak, the national president, lamented in 1904; "if women were paid men's wages it would not matter so much," he claimed, "but the employers don't do this."[59] The policy of the national union toward the woman worker had always been defensive — to prevent the encroachment of women into the trade by requiring its branches to report each instance of female labor being utilized, by taking its protest to the Boot and Shoe Arbitration Board, and by striking against particular firms. At the same time, however, and particularly in London, some members realized that the trade would be better off if the women were organized. Thus, while the national union carried on a rearguard battle against female labor, in London the WTUL and certain union men, including T. F. Richards, a boot and shoe worker and future Member of Parliament, began a movement to organize women. The London union worked to get its contract with employers to apply to women and eventually adopted the principle of equal pay for equal work. Nevertheless, the results were meager. Few women joined the union, and the women organizers found it necessary in 1906 to begin the campaign again. Meanwhile, the men complained that women were not interested in the union, even as some women continued to cry out for assistance from the union men.[60]

The failure of unionism among women

Because the new industrial middle classes and the sizeable mass of poor were divided into many subclasses, it is difficult to identify in terms of interests and behavior a single working class in the last third of the nineteenth century. For many groups of workers neither class consciousness nor what has come to be called labor alienation was manifest in either political or industrial action or in any understanding of how the capitalist system worked. For many members of the working class, class consciousness and alienation found expression in confused withdrawal and fatalism,[61] or in simply clinging to traditional expectations and patterns of behavior. The consequence was political immaturity. Such behavior, until recently, has generally been ignored in favor of the more exciting study of workers storming through the streets or shutting down industries. Among sweated workers only the male artisans in tailoring and shoemaking fit the picture of the modern working-class worker: they had a political consciousness, they fought for organization and control over their trade, they protested with strikes, and they were able to identify reasons for the decline in their trades. Organized tailors, for example, were able to direct their grievances somewhere — to employer, union, trade council, or political party. "Above all," claimed the London tailors, "we will not be isolated. We will work together on the shop board, where every member knows his fellow member is working with him and not underselling his labour."[62] Like their fathers and grandfathers, these artisans knew what was happening. They fought the sweating system because they knew it would destroy their craft, their unity, and their historic identity. They had, in short, a sense of the past and the future.

The frequency of strikes in London illustrates this consciousness. The London men in the national boot union made up a small percentage of that union's national membership, but they were engaged in a large percentage of the total trade disputes reported by the union. For example, in 1897 the local comprised 7 percent of the national membership but was engaged in 70 percent of the union's disputes. The ratio for other years was much the same, 4 percent of the members and 46 percent of the disputes in 1902, and 3 and 30 percent, respectively, in 1905. In other words, the percentage of the footwear trades disputes in London were usually ten times greater than the percentage of the national union's membership in London.[63] Of the nearly thirty disputes in the London footwear industry between 1889 and 1898, the largest percentage (60) pertained to wages, and most involved, either as primary or secondary issues, worker dissatisfaction with the organization of work, the pace of work, or the location of employment. One of the disputes of the longest duration (1889–92) grew out of the workers' demand that all London employers end outwork by providing workshops for all employees. Other disputes took place over the introduction of machinery, the subdivision of labor, and the use of boy labor.[64]

Similarly, in the tailoring industry for the period 1889 to 1898, a large percentage (76) of the disputes involved wage questions, either as demands for wage increases (42 percent) or as a protest against wage reductions (33 percent). The second most frequent type of dispute related to the organization of work, mainly workers' dissatisfaction with outwork and subcontract systems of production (38 percent). Other disputes occurred over employment of female labor, unhealthy workshops, the subdivision of labor, or problems arising from the mechanization of outwork. Two strikes by mantlemakers, for example, were to force the employer to supply the materials (i.e., thread, silk, and trimmings) used in production and thereby relieve the worker of the responsibility of obtaining these materials as part of her employment.[65]

The tailors and shoemakers were the exception, not the rule. Among the bulk of the workers in the sweated trades, expression of political or industrial consciousness was much less common. Although the lives of women in the sweated trades were changed by industrialization, it was not the same kind of change felt by their husbands and brothers. More than anything else, outwork, by encouraging women to hold onto traditional values and to remain isolated from political or industrial activism, contributed to the powerlessness of women in society. Nothing better illustrates this powerlessness than the failure of trade unionism among the female sweated workers.

Working women failed to unionize for a variety of reasons. Certainly two reasons were apathy and intermittent opposition of male workers. Where available, male support of women's unionism was the "strongest . . . possible factor in successful organization";[66] but it was often lacking. The "illconcealed jealousy and selfishness of male workers" were partly due to the men's conviction that women workers drove down wages and partly due to sexism. "To organize is to recognize," claimed the male unionist. Married women, noted George Howell, should stay at home and not do men's work.[67] The problem, of course, was that women were doing both. As the royal commission noted in 1892, the attitude of the men and their unions toward the cheap labor of the women was "one of uncompromising opposition." But it was more a struggle against capitalism than it was against women. To protect themselves the men had either to exclude women from the trade, as the national garment unions wanted, or to organize women to raise women's wages to a level with their own, as the London unions proposed. But, as Dilke noted in 1885, "it is a question . . . whether unionism in its early years . . . could have undertaken the additional burden of organizing the women."[68] To the women, the obvious remedy for the "helpless blacklegging" of the woman worker was to bring her into the trade union so that "no more will be heard of unfair competition." Once they were organized and wages stabilized, the women predicted, uneasiness and opposition would disappear.[69]

Some male unionists discouraged female organization. Miss Geary of the West End Tailoresses Union complained that "we have lost several members of our Society in consequence of some members of the Amalgamated Society of Tailors persuading the women that the Society could be no benefit to them, that the tailors did not approve of the Union and that it would not stand." She pleaded with the men to encourage women to join the union. "I think that if you were to say a few words to some of the tailoresses and let them see that you do approve of it, it might make a great difference."[70] Ten years later the WTUL claimed that, although the attitude of men was improving, the lack of interest in women's unionism by husbands, sons, and brothers contributed to the weakness of unionism among women.[71]

Yet the limited support that the London workers gave to women was crucial. The only female unions in the clothing trades that enjoyed any success were those that received either the aid of the men's union,[72] or those, like the Pimlico union, which emerged out of a factory system where a large number of women were brought together to work. Some London tailors consistently supported female organization. Leaders of the tailors, like Macdonald, gave regular support to the WTUL in establishing the tailoresses union. Likewise, though less effectively, the London boot- and shoemakers gave support to the female workers in their trade. But in both of these cases, the pro-women position of the local union was hampered by the anti-women policies of the national unions. In other trades, such as shirtmaking and dressmaking, where there was no factory system or male union, the failure of the women's union was insured.

Like the national unions, the Trades Union Congress (TUC) was inconsistent in its policy toward women workers; at times, it openly opposed them. In 1874 the TUC resolved to promote women's trade unionism; in 1877 it argued that women should not be allowed to compete with male labor; in 1885 it advocated equal pay for equal work and expressed a willingness to organize women. But year after year male delegates at the congress, like Henry Broadhurst of the building trades and Peter Shorrocks of the tailors, antagonized women delegates by leaving women out of petitions the TUC was to present to Parliament. Shorrocks insisted that a TUC resolution asking that workingmen be appointed factory inspectors *not* include working women. The word "women" was eventually included, but the attack was still going on in 1889, when Broadhurst tried to exclude as many women as possible from the TUC meetings. He created a scandal at the congress by trying to unseat Mary Simcox of the London Shirt-makers Society and Black of the WIC.[73]

The WTUL hoped that by holding the 1902 meeting in London, where the injustices suffered by women workers and their lack of organization were so evident, the men of the TUC might be induced "to do everything in their power to promote organization among the women in their trades."[74] But the hopes of the women went unfulfilled, and women continued to lament the dearth of women delegates within the TUC and the apathy of that body toward female workers.[75] Consequently, the women concluded that they first must organize and then look after their own interests, two lessons "imperfectly learnt as yet."[76] Several years later the WTUL announced that women were learning the "lesson of self-reliance from the painful experience and unwilling-ness of men to help them."[77] For many years, it was the WTUL and the WIC and not the TUC that were the legislative guardians of British working women.

If male apathy toward women's unionism retarded the movement, so did the apathy of working women. It was "very sorry reading," claimed the WTUL in 1898, to reflect on the attitude of the working woman toward the union movement.[78] Some women noted that this indifference was natural and traced its origin to the historic position of women within the economy and labor market; others found the root of the problem in the political system.[79] In any case women workers, many of whom were new to the trades, had neither a strong traditional artisan consciousness nor an understanding of how industrial capitalism works. Since they had less of an interest than male artisan craftsmen in protecting and preserving the old systems of production, they did not experience the same type of alienation felt by the artisans. The prospective woman unionist needed to be motivated by some sort of ideological or intellectual commitment to trade unionism. "A proper knowledge of the state of the market," claimed a woman organizer, "and the comparative value in it of her own trade . . . is essential to the interests of the worker."[80] Without this understanding of labor power and the labor market, the working woman was helpless.

Few working-class women had "either the habit of thought or the time for thinking." Margaret MacDonald lamented that working-class women often believed that "rich people are made of different stuff" than are the working class, and Mary Macarthur said in 1907 that "the greatest curse of England's workers is the spirit of class."[81] Those who did learn the rules of the game did so when they entered the factory.[82] But often working-class women who did develop a political curiosity or class consciousness were discouraged by husbands, fathers, and brothers, who objected to women belonging to anything. Agnes Flynn, the first woman member of the AST, lamented the "stupid" antifemale prejudices of male tailors.[83] As such antipathy entered the home, it contributed to and confirmed the passivity of wives, sisters, and mothers.

Indeed, no matter how grim the conditions of female labor, marriage and isolation from her fellow worker greatly disguised job alienation. Low wages, marriage, and homework tended to prevent the woman worker from combining with other women in order to improve her position. Women unionists fully recognized that marriage and the expectation of marriage were obstacles to effective organization. Women's work, noted Sidney Webb, was "merely a prelude to matrimony." Simcox, an organizer for the WTUL, warned the tailoresses of London that they would have a problem in attracting members because many women planned to marry and then leave the trade. Another woman unionist complained of the "culpable indifference" shown by working women to their own interests, "one reason for which was the belief of the younger ones that they would marry and leave the trade." In 1864 it was claimed that few women in dressmaking and millinery remained in those trades after the age of thirty, most either getting married or setting up business for themselves.[84]

Low wages, decreased further due to transportation expenses and costs of materials connected to homework, made union membership financially prohibitive and the existence of a union precarious. "Women are difficult to organize because they are badly paid," said Mary Macarthur, "and they are badly paid because they are difficult to organize." Soon after the inception of their union, the London tailoresses found it necessary to reduce the union's entrance fee from two shillings to one. Likewise, the women ropemakers voted to reduce the subscription to its union by one-half because the earnings of the women were so small. The East End tailoresses union failed because the tailoresses could not afford membership. Other women's unions, like the boot- and shoemakers union founded by the WTUL in 1895, could not hold onto its members in times of depression in the trade.[85]

Marriage and poverty were not the only obstacles to organizing women workers. Another problem was the physical isolation of women in the sweated trades. The adverse effects of decentralized production are evident: while the factory encouraged female emancipation and the movement toward political-social consciousness, the outwork system had the opposite effect. When asked why she could not combine with fellow homeworkers to improve her position, a Mrs. Holden replied, "I do not know enough of them."[86] Since it was uncommon for a machinist, shirtmaker, dressmaker, or other outworker to know other workers in the same trade, the mechanics of identifying workers and organizing meetings were enormous. For an outworker to attend a union meeting would require a free evening and an additional tram fare, items that few working women could spare. This separation and isolation of workers encouraged employer intimidation. Soon after its founding the WTUL complained that it was losing members because of the interference of employers who threatened their workers with dismissal. Later Amie Hicks found that unionists were frequently discharged and blacklisted, and that East End tailoresses would not join the union because they were afraid to strike. Outworkers in Shoreditch reported in 1908 that they tried striking, "but someone always gets intimidated and they have to go back."[87] As a result, many unionist women, like Gertrude Tuckwell, came to the conclusion that organization of outworkers was impossible.[88]

Part of the problem was that the system of mechanized outwork gave birth to a sizeable force of women workers who subcontracted others; the women themselves became contractors who sought survival or fortune speculating in the labor of fellow workers. Sweating was, in a real sense, a system of co-exploitation, pauperizing one segment of the working class while making little capitalists of another. Though outwork was occasionally defended on the grounds that by using his or her own machines the worker had a "better opportunity of doing a little business on his own account" and hence a "better prospect of becoming their own employers,"[89] it tended to exacerbate an intraclass struggle and thus fragment the lower working classes. This is a large part of the history of women's work. "Hard she is on us like nails," said one shirtmaker of her neighbor, who farmed out a large number of shirts from a City firm to her neighbors, "always trying to get the work done for 1/2d. less than anyone else." Hard, too, was the blousemaker who employed thirteen girls in a small workroom for as little as 2s. per week.[90]

This, then, was the problem. The structure of industry in the clothing trades precluded the possibility of a modern working-class consciousness among its women workers. As in preindustrial society, the isolated condition of so many workers made combination next to impossible and political consciousness improbable. As long as employment was casual, wages low, work performed in isolation from fellow workers, and their labor a threat to male workers, both apathy and failure would mark the organizational efforts within the women's labor movement, and the political awakening and labor revolt among industrial women would be postponed.

Sweated work and the Jewish labor movement

Also weakening the labor movement in the sweated clothing trades was the problem of Jewish labor. As mentioned earlier, Jewish immigrants had an important impact on the history of working-class London, for they brought with them many of the innovations, such as the subdivision of labor, which were to form the basis of the new ready-made clothing industry. With their immigration, much clothing production moved from Russia and Poland to Great Britain, providing many new jobs and an enlarged export trade for Britain.

Many British workers regarded the immigrant Jews (like the Irish) as a threat to the English worker. "We would suggest," reported the northeast London branch of the National Union of Boot and Shoe Operatives, "that the government do something quickly to stop the alien pauper element from landing on our shores." The London Clickers Union also protested the entrance of alien-pauper Jews into London. One critic of open immigration claimed that the continued influx of the "half civilized foreigner" would only drag down the standard of living of the English people. Another London "social reformer" complained that the aliens were "swarming in upon us like plagues of Locusts — seizing upon work which ought to be kept for

our own people."[91] Occasionally the antialien issue emerged in East
End political campaigns.[92] In 1895 the president of the Board of Trade
told a number of English workers that he sympathized with them because it was clear that in some districts of London Jews were certainly displacing them: "It is a startling fact that though the population of St. George-in-the East, and Whitechapel has for the last 13
years remained practically stationary, 20 percent of the whole population of St. George-in-the East and Whitechapel has been displaced
by foreign labor."[93] Likewise, on three occasions (1892, 1894, and
1895), the TUC, "in view of the injury done to a large number of
trades and trade unions," passed proposals recommending the restriction of immigration. The resolution of 1895 was proposed by boot-
and shoemakers who objected to the "pauper greeners" who came to
London and elsewhere "and take the work, which means the bread,
out of our own members hands who walk about and starve, whilst
these people are doing the work at less than half the amount our state-
ments provide."[94] English workers resented the immigrants not only
because they flooded the job market but also because, so the English
workers believed, the immigrants were the principal cause of the sweating system. On numerous occasions boot and shoe workers complained
that the Board of Arbitration, which had been set up by employers
and employees, was a farce because employers, whenever they wished
to avoid an unwelcome decision by the board, could merely quit the
board and "get as many boots spoiled in Whitechapel as they like"
by nonunion Jewish workers.[95]

But not all English workers were in agreement as to what should
be done, nor was condemnation of the Jewish worker universal among
workers. In 1894 the London Trades Council refused to pass a resolution, proposed by north London boot- and shoemakers, that called
for government restriction of foreign unskilled labor. Although two
years later the council favored limiting Jewish immigration, some
members believed a proposed government bill to restrict immigration was not strong enough and others approved of the bill as it was.[96]
Social Democrats (SDF) and members of the Socialist League worked
for harmony between English and Jewish workers, particularly in
London, which was a SDF stronghold and where the trades council
was under SDF control. Many realized that the charges against the
immigrant workers were not always valid, for Jewish workers fought
sweating as fiercely as did the English. In March 1891, for example,

1,700 Jewish boot and shoe workers, with the radical Jewish newspaper *Arbeter Fraint* behind them, joined 10,000 of their English comrades in a two-month strike designed to obtain higher wages and to
force all employers to provide work space for all employees, thus
eliminating the sweating dens. Although this "workshop on premises"
clause was later broken, the strikers did win wage advances and the
recognition that outworking should no longer be allowed. But conflicts still existed between Jewish and English strikers. The Jews wanted
the employers to provide workshops at once because they rightly sus-
pected that every clause in the agreement would be broken as soon
as the busy season was over. But the Jews were "forced back into line"
by the English workers. To make matters worse, at the height of the
strike Jewish workers complained that some English workers were re-
fusing to work with them.[97]

This show of power and unity between Jewish and English workers
was short-lived. By the mid-1890s complaints of Jewish blacklegging
were again coming from both Jewish and English quarters. This
regression was a result of a new wave of immigration in 1891–92,
which brought in thousands of greeners, as the new Jewish workers
were called, desperate to find work in an already depressed labor
market and in a city where the quality of immigrant life was harsher
than it had been a decade earlier.[98] Antialien sentiment swept through
the boot and shoe trade again. Labor conditions would be improved,
the union reported, "if our Polish friends would only act in conformity
with the rules of arbitration." Jewish accommodation with the sweating system was the reason that nearly all of the boot and shoe manufacturers of London withdrew from the wage agreement between the
union and the Manufacturers Association. "No sooner do we have
a dispute with an employer, than [the immigrant Jews] are on the
job to do the work at a less price, at home." "We hope," announced
the officers of the London branch of the National Union of Boot and
Shoe Operatives, that something will be done to stop the "alien invasion" because "the old evil of sweating . . . is becoming worse and
worse." The unions charged that the Jewish worker not only tolerated
sweating, but he also fostered it by doing outdoor work and by working under the system of subdivided labor. Employers dismissed workers
who refused to work under the team system and replaced them with
Jewish workers who would. Wage scales broke down because nonunion Jews agreed to work for less. And Jews, Charles Freak, presi-

dent of the boot and shoe union, told the president of the Board of
Trade, "were a means of maintaining the sweating system" by working longer hours for lower wages, and under circumstances which
would be "intolerable to Englishmen."[99]

English unionists claimed that the Jewish immigrant was difficult,
if not impossible, to organize. Efforts to organize the Jews often
resulted in failure and confirmed old prejudices. For example, soon
after London bootmakers organized one Jewish workshop in 1895,
the Jewish unionists bolted from the union in the middle of a strike
and returned to work for the employer against whom the union had
struck. Why bother, claimed the union

> to fight the battle of a lot of Polish Jews who were not members and never
> would be — who do not know what cleanliness is, much less manliness
> and morality; and who are very much convinced that if these Polish and
> Russian Jews want us to fight their cause for them in the future, they
> will have to show us first that they possess the ordinary virtues attributed
> to human beings, and that the majority possess a trade card.[100]

In 1892 the Royal Commission on Labour had found that the English
worker did not and, in many cases, would not work with foreigners.[101]
The Jews resented this sort of condemnation and reacted angrily to
anti-immigration sentiment, too, as their response to the TUC
immigration restriction resolutions of 1894 and 1895 shows. Jewish
workers in London held a mass meeting to condemn the resolution
in 1894; in 1895, when the TUC passed a similar resolution, eleven
Jewish unions issued one of the most scathing denunciations of intraclass warfare in the literature of the English labor movement. The
Jewish worker, these unions claimed, was being used as the scape-
goat for the lack of employment; the real enemy of the English worker
was not his fellow worker, but the "capitalist class." "To punish the
alien worker for the Sin of the native capitalist is like the man who
struck the boy because he was not strong enough to strike his father."[102]
Fourteen years later Jewish workers were still complaining of anti-
immigrant attitudes on the part of English workers.[103]

A turning point for the boot and shoe workers came in 1904, when
its national union hired two full-time organizers in an attempt to bring
the immigrants into the union. From this time on, the once bitter
and sarcastic attitude of the boot- and shoemakers became cooperative and affable. The London branch began to report that they were
"making some headway with our East End friends," who were "be-

ginning to realize that only by belonging to the union can they help themselves." A new Jewish branch of the London Metro union was formed, and organizational meetings were held. Apologies and explanations were made. The Jewish worker, noted the *Monthly Report,* must recognize that up until the beginning of strained relations between Jew and Gentile in the early 1890s, no one had "worked harder for the poor Jewish laster and finisher than Charles Freak," whom Jewish workers had labeled an anti-Semite.[104]

Thereafter, with the aid of prominent Jews such as Rudolf Rocker, the anarchist and editor of the *Arbeter Fraint,* the Metro branch of the union held frequent organizational meetings in the East End. Rocker's success in stimulating trade union consciousness among East End workers was considerable, and his anarchist Workers' Friend Club on Jubilee Street in the East End became a center for a lively Jewish working-class movement. "There are among [the Jewish workers]," the London branch reported, "many earnest men who thoroughly detest the wretched conditions under which boot and shoe manufacture is carried on in the East End."[105]

But organizational efforts were hampered by intraunion conflicts among the English unionists. The relations between the London Metro branch, which was heavily socialist in outlook, and the more conservative national executive were never very amiable. The London union and the national differed as to the most desirable union structure in London — one great industrial union that would encompass all boot and shoe workers (desired by the Londoners) or an "amalgamation" in which branch unions would be able to retain their craft identity (desired by the executive).[106]

Jewish workers in the tailoring trade faced similar problems. Although London tailors resented immigrant Jewish labor, they did not develop the same intense animosity toward them as did the boot- and shoemakers. Indeed, although some modern scholars have claimed that the English unions were closed to Jews,[107] as early as 1867 the London tailors recognized that the solution to the problems of cheap labor and the encroachment of new production methods was the organization of all workers, including Jews. Consequently, the tailors organized an East End Jewish branch in Whitechapel, which supported the West End tailors' strike of 1867. Most Jewish tailors were outworkers, however, and organization was difficult, and so membership remained limited: only thirty-four of 4,184 tailors in the district joined the union. The union often expressed disappointment that more foreign tailors did not join the East End branch, but after its reorganization in 1872 more Jewish tailors did join.[108]

The first tailors' union founded by Jews was formed in 1874, but it lasted only a few weeks. In 1876 the socialist-anarchist Aron Lieberman, leader of the Hebrew Socialist Union, founded the Jewish Tailors Union, one of many Jewish socialist endeavors intended to improve working conditions. It was from Lieberman that the Jewish radicals, particularly the anarchists, developed their devotion to trade unionism. Henceforth, unionism was the core of the small but active Jewish radical movement.[109] Lieberman's east London union was refounded in 1883, but by 1888 it had only a small membership. Lewis Lyons, a Social Democrat, founded the Working Tailors Association in 1884 with the intent of bringing all sweating victims — small masters as well as workers — together. Later he founded a short-lived but lively newspaper, the *Anti-Sweater*. By the 1890s there were some fifteen small Jewish tailoring unions in east London, the two most prominent being the Independent Tailors, Machinists and Pressers and the International Tailors, Machinists, and Pressers Union, the latter formed in 1890 by Lyons.[110]

Although recruitment of Jewish workers did not prove very successful, it was an established policy of both the Jewish radicals and the English tailors. Unfortunately, this pro-Jewish stance got the Londoners, especially James Macdonald, into trouble with the national AST. Even though the AST national conference (at Liverpool in 1891) passed Macdonald's resolution inviting Jewish unions to participate in its conferences, the national union never fully agreed with Macdonald that the union's only avenue to survival was to open its membership. Macdonald claimed that conflict between workers would continue to exist until all workers came to accept a standard rate of wages, either one enforced by the union or one legislated by the state.[111]

The Jewish union movement received a boost in 1889. A strike of 10,000 East End tailors from the three Jewish tailoring unions, the Machinists, the Pressers, and the AST broke out in August and was led by two Jewish workers, Lyons and Woolf Wess, a member of William Morris's Socialist League and "one of the few immigrant radicals who were equally at home in both Jewish and Gentile Socialist and Anarchist circles."[112] The strikers demanded a reduction of hours from eighteen to twelve, meals off the work premises, union rates, and no government contract outworking. The strike, called the Great Strike of London Tailors and Sweaters' Victims, received support from the dockers, the West End tailors, the Social Democratic Federation, the Socialist League, and, partly to check the Jewish socialist and anarchist influences, from Lord Rothschild and Sir Samuel Montague, Member of Parliament, both of the Anglo-Jewish community. The workers won a twelve-hour day with restrictions on overtime. The *Arbeter Fraint* noted that, although "it is true that all these victories mean a minor amelioration in the economic burdens of the working masses, . . . the workers are learning unity in action, and are moving step by step towards their self-realization as a class."[113]

This unity was expressed again in 1891, when the Jewish tailors joined over 10,000 West End tailors in a strike. But this time Jewish-English relations suffered. Soon after the East End tailors joined the strike, the West End tailors reached a temporary settlement and went back to work. As a result, the Jewish end of the strike collapsed, leaving many Jews to feel betrayed by the English tailors. Their funds were exhausted, and they received no support from the English union. Macdonald and Lyons tried to mollify the bitterness of the Jewish workers who returned to their sweatshops with their old grievances unresolved. The outcome of the strike was, to many, evidence of racial prejudice and an absence of labor solidarity.[114]

Although it has frequently been noted that the English tailors were unable and, at times, unwilling to work with immigrant Jewish labor, the events of 1889–91 convinced the West End English tailors that cooperation was possible. At last, it was reported, the Jewish were "falling into line" with the rest of organized labor in respecting the principles of unionism.[115] A Federation of East London Labor Unions had been founded by the Jewish radicals in 1890, and Macdonald had already begun a campaign to organize Jewish tailors. In 1892 both of the English tailors unions worked with Lyons and other Jews to reorganize the Jewish branch of the union (it became the London Jewish Tailors Federation). Everyone discovered that, contrary to their past experience when the results of organizational efforts had been "almost nil," many Jews were ready to join the ranks of the English union.[116] Charles Mowbray, a union organizer and a Jewish anarchist, quickly signed up more than 140 Jewish workers, many of whom left the smaller Jewish unions because, they claimed, the English union (affiliated with the AST) had better leadership. Lyons not only worked with the new Jewish Tailors Federation but was also involved in frequent provincial campaigns to exterminate sweating. The tailors' federation quickly adopted one of the most rigid antihomework policies of any London union: no homeworkers were allowed in the union and no union members were allowed to engage in homework. T. A. Flynn, the general secretary of the national AST, told the English tailors that "at last our Jewish fellow workers have determined to take up their position in our ranks and work with us for the common good."[117]

In the long run, conflict among the Jewish unionists was more damaging to Jewish unionism than was the conflict between English and Jewish workers. Typical of this internal fighting is the career of Lyons, who became the head of the International Tailors Union. Lyons himself admitted that Jewish workers were poor unionists because they could not get along with one another. In 1888 he became involved in a personal struggle with David Schloss, a social investigator and union organizer, over the formation and control of the Working Tailors Association. Schloss accused Lyons of embezzling union funds. Then Lyons, a Social Democrat, became embroiled in a bitter struggle with members of the rival anarchist movement, particularly with S. Yanovsky, then editor of *Arbeter Fraint*. Again Lyons was accused of misuse of union funds. But it was really Lyons's belief in cooperation between the small master and his worker(s) and his friendly appeals to Anglo-Jewish community leaders that the anarchists regarded as abominable. "How long will you allow yourselves and your union to come to such shame, by letting this man [Lyons] lead you by the nose?" asked Yanovsky. The union men finally took Yanovsky's advice and expelled Lyons, amid physical violence, from the International Tailors Union in December 1891. Thereafter he spent some time in jail, but he became president of the union again in 1894. He later acted as the Jewish tailors representative at the TUC, and he used the TUC to voice the grievances of Jewish workers. He helped found the London Tailors Federation in 1893 and carried on an intense campaign against the antiunion and antiworker stance of Chief Rabbi Herman Adler, who saw in the radicalism of the unions a threat to the religious values of the Jewish community as well as a threat to the hard-won respectability of upper-class Jews.[118]

The fight between Lyons and Yanovsky led the anarchists to form their own union, the Independent Tailors, Machinists, and Pressers Union in 1893, which fought with Lyons and his union. When the London Trades Council opened its membership to the Jewish tailors in 1894, Lyons and the International, to the chagrin of the Independent, were recognized as the legitimate representative of the Jewish tailors and Lyons himself became a member of the council's executive committee. Thereafter, the London Trades Council became a battlefield in the war between the Jewish unions. Although the Independent and the International unions eventually merged in 1898, the trades council still continued to investigate and settle disputes between rival Jewish unions.[119]

Around 1900, largely as a result of the increased influx of eastern European Jews into London, the anti-immigrant sentiment among many English workers surfaced again. The 1903 Royal Commission on Alien Immigration served as a forum for those who regarded Jewish labor as a threat to their jobs and who wanted legislative limits on alien immigration. The effect of this opposition was to unify the Jewish community, particularly the Jewish trade unions, and to force them once again to think of themselves as separate from the English labor movement. Following the lead of the Independent and the International and under the leadership of Joseph Finn, a Jewish mantlemaker and member of the Social Democratic Federation, several mantlemakers' unions merged to form the United Ladies Tailors and Mantlemakers Union in 1901. This union was the most successful of all of the independent Jewish unions in London. By 1906 the English tailors were once again busy recruiting Jewish workers. Two new branches were added to the original English branch in the East End, and 10,000 new members were recruited in 1906.[120]

Although the relations between the Jewish and English workers were never very good, those between Jewish and women workers were worse. In many respects immigrant workers saw the women workers in the same way as they were viewed by the Englishmen: the source of the sweating system. The real labor competition, Finn claimed, was not Jews but the English women "who are actually taking the bread out of our mouths by working for half the price." Who is displacing whom, asked Finn, "the English or the Jew?"[121] Jewish unions complained to the AST that their members were suffering from unemployment because of the invasion of women, who worked for 25 percent less than men, into the various sectors of the trade. The *Journal* of the AST reported that "amongst many of the men belonging to the ready made trade in the East End the opinion seems to prevail that women workers are in some cases ousting them, and in others encroaching upon work hitherto done almost entirely by men."[122] To the Jewish workers, the solution was to organize the women.

In summary, then, it appears that, although a significant degree of prejudice against Jewish workers permeated the British labor movement (as did antifemale prejudice), it did not altogether prevent the evolution of labor organization. English workers, especially the tailors, were periodically active in organizing immigrant workers. Even the boot and shoe workers, the most stubborn on the subject of alien labor, were aware of the necessity of cooperation within the ranks of labor and recruited Jewish workers. Jews and Englishmen — like the Social Democrats Macdonald, Lyons, and Wess and the anarchists Rocker and Yanovsky — recognized that the problems relative to immigrant labor were industrial, not racial. The blacklegging Jew was as much despised by the Jewish unionist as by the English one. Although anti-Semitism was a part of British life in the late nineteenth and early twentieth centuries, the attitudes of English workers toward Jews have probably been overemphasized. Certainly the trade union literature contains no evidence that the English worker regarded the Jews from the racist perspective then current in parts of Europe at that time. Economic conditions in London and throughout Great Britain dictated that cooperation between Jewish and English unionists was the rule rather than the exception.[123]

Injurious to the Jewish labor movement, however, was the squabbling between the Jewish laborites and the leaders of the Jewish community. It was the bourgeois Jewish leaders and not the English workers who proved to be the greatest enemies of the Jewish labor movement. Time and again the unionists tried to get rabbis to recognize the evils of the sweating system and to support a war against sweating by recognizing the principle of unionism. But the religious leaders refused, and, because of their enormous hold on the traditionally minded worker, few workers questioned the rabbis' condemnation of the trade union movement. The militant atheism of anarchist labor leaders like Lieberman and Rocker caused the respectable Anglo-Jewish community, "sensitive to their recently acquired acceptance as bona fide citizens,"[124] to fear and suspect not only unions but also the aliens. To these people who saw rapid anglicization of the immigrant as necessary to deter anti-Semitism, the aliens meant ugly publicity for the Jewish community and the continual feeding of a dangerous Jewish radicalism. No one, English unionist or capitalist sweater, was attacked as repeatedly by the Jewish anarchist-socialists as were the rabbis.[125]

Gender and racial prejudice were thus two factors that contributed to labor disunity and weakness among garment workers. There were other factors equally important, however, including conflict among the English male workers themselves and, most especially, the way the industry was organized. The sweating system of production (which isolated and divided Englishmen as much as women and Jews) inhibited labor unity and promoted weakness.

NOTES

1. Women's Trade Union League (WTUL), *Annual Report of 1899–1900,* 21.

2. Eric Hobsbawm, "The Nineteenth Century Labour Market," in Ruth Glass et al., *London: Aspects of Change* (London, 1964), 13.

3. *The Tailor,* 20 Oct. 1866, 23–26; 27 Oct. 1866, 25; 3 Nov. 1866, 34; 10 Nov. 1866, 71; 2 Feb. 1867, 165.

4. Ibid., 20 Oct. 1866, 25; 17 Nov. 1866, 77.

5. *Tailor and Cutter,* 17 Jan. 1873, 181–82; *The Tailor,* 16 Feb. 1867, 299.

6. This cooperation was due to the influence of Peter Shorrocks, secretary of the AST, and Green. *Report of the Conference of Deputies of the Amalgamated Society of Tailors, 1866* (Manchester, 1866), 12, and the *First Yearly Report of the Amalgamated Society of Tailors, March 1867* (Manchester, 1867), 5; *The Tailor,* 12 Jan. 1867, 211.

7. The strike history is found in *Tailor and Cutter,* 27 Apr. 1867, 41; 18 May 1867, 86; 4 May 1867, 54; 25 May 1867, 100; 25 May 1866, 98; 20 July 1867, 209. The ending to the strike was part of an anti-union public reaction that followed the Sheffield "outrages" of that year, during which unionists had been implicated in violent attacks on nonunionists in Sheffield.

8. Ibid., 8 June 1867, 129.

9. The quote is from ibid., 14 June 1872, 414–15; this part of the strike history is found in ibid., 7 Sept. 1867, 295; 23 Nov. 1867, 52–53; 14 Dec. 1867, 77; 18 Jan. 1868, 91.

10. Ibid., 17 May 1872, 366; 19 July 1872, 482–86.

11. Ibid., 16 Mar. 1867, 361; 3 Apr. 1869, 66.

12. P.P., "The Royal Commission on the Factory and Workshop Acts,"

1876, Minutes, vol. xxx.1, Qs 2717, 2744. Paterson's interest in women's unionism grew out of her ties with the Women's Suffrage Association, of which she was secretary, and the Working Men's Club and Institute Union, of which her husband, Thomas Paterson, a cabinetmaker, was secretary. Her understanding of the women's labor movement came from firsthand observations of men's unionism in London and the women's union movement in America. Prior to 1889 the league was known as the Women's Protective and Provident League. For a brief account of Paterson's life, see *Dictionary of Labour Biography,* s.v., "Paterson, Emma."

13. Trades Union Congress, *Women in the Trade Union Movement* (London, 1955), 45; *Women's Union Journal,* July 1889, 54.

14. *Women's Union Journal,* Mar. 1866, 3; Feb. 1876, 1–2. The chief complaint of the society, which was made up of homeworkers, was that wages were declining — which they blamed, in part, on the "great influx of young girls" into the trade. Because of unionism the wages of the male workers increased. Ibid., Nov. 1876, 67–68. For the Pimlico factory, see ibid., Apr. 1880, 43, 91–92.

15. Ibid., May 1877, 25. See also *Women's Industrial Review,* 19 May 1877.

16. *Women's Union Journal,* July 1888, 5. The East End Branch (the East London Tailoresses Society) was started with the aid of David Schloss, a bootmaker who eventually became secretary to the Jewish Board of Guardians. Schloss served as treasurer of the new union.

17. Ibid., Nov. 1879, 103–4; see also *Workman's Times,* 17 Feb. 1894, 3.

18. *Workman's Times,* 17 Feb. 1894, 3.

19. Ibid., 2 Apr. 1892, 5; 22 Oct. 1892, 4; and *Women's Union Journal,* Dec. 1881, 120.

20. *Workman's Times,* 9 Dec. 1893, 2; 17 Feb. 1894, 3. The position of the Master Tailors Association is found in ibid., 5 Aug. 1893, 3. Agnes Flynn, the daughter of the general secretary of the national AST, challenged the union rules by joining the Manchester branch in 1892; the national executive did not expel her. See Agnes Flynn, "Trade Unionism in the Garment Industry: Recollections of Half a Century," *Tailor and Garment Worker,* 2 (Mar. 1933), 5–9, and 2 (Apr. 1933), 5–6.

21. Sidney and Beatrice Webb, *History of Trade Unionism* (London, 1911), 388; *Women's Union Journal,* Jan. 1890, 1; *Women's Trade Union Review,* Oct. 1906, 1. The WTUL had backed the match girls, calling for a boycott of Bryant and May and organizing a public subscription for the striking women. "The impetus and encouragement" given to the cause of female organization, reported the league, "have been very great indeed." The match girls' strike "inspired hope" and the "triumphant formation of the dockers' union showed that the capacity for trade unionism was not necessarily confined to the skilled and educated. Greatly inspired, the league resolved that it would

"use every means in its power to promote the extension of unionism" among women (*Women's Union Journal,* July 1889, 54; Oct. 1890, 87).

22. *Women's Union Journal,* Oct. 1890, 87.

23. Emilia Dilke, "Trade Unionism for Women," *North American Review* (n.d.), reprinted by the WTUL. See also *People's Press,* 1 Nov. 1890, 13.

24. Paterson died in 1886, and Dilke became the new president of the WTUL.

25. *Women's Trade Union Review,* Jan. 1905, 17.

26. WTUL, *Annual Report of 1895,* 1.

27. One union wrote to the league: "Please send an organizer to this town as our amalgamated society decided that if the women here cannot be organized they must be exterminated." Trades Union Congress, *Women in the Trade Union Movement,* 60.

28. *Women's Union Journal,* July 1890, 7.

29. Ibid., Jan. 1889, 1; July 1890, 53.

30. WTUL, *Annual Report of 1894,* 5.

31. *Women's Trade Union Review,* Oct. 1894, 3.

32. Ibid., Jan. 1892, 6–7; June 1892, 7.

33. *Women's Union Journal,* Oct. 1889, 77. Oddly, the WIC and its forerunner, the Women's Trade Union Association, are seldom mentioned in present-day accounts of the women's trade union movement.

34. "What has already been done," in WIC, *Annual Report of 1906–7.*

35. Macdonald was a staunch member of the socialist Social Democratic Federation and, unlike its leader, H. M. Hyndman, had great faith in the worker coming to socialism by way of trade unionism. He was never reluctant to express his belief that the principles of class warfare and the socialization of the means of production should be adopted by every worker.

36. "Interview with James Macdonald," *Workman's Times,* 14 Nov. 1891, and "James Macdonald," Sec. A, vol. 14, item 77 of the Webb Collection, British Library of Economic and Political Science, London. Macdonald had proposed a censure of the executive of the AST for withholding strike funds that the London men claimed were due to them. The funds had been used as strike pay for the London tailoresses. The censure was rejected by the conference.

37. Apr. 1896, 64.

38. "James Macdonald," news clipping, Sec. A, vol. 14, item 77, Webb Collection; *Workman's Times,* 28 Nov. 1891, 8; 6 Feb. 1892, 5; 7 Apr. 1893, 2; *Trades and Labour Gazette,* Aug. 1908, 4.

39. *Workman's Times,* 3 June 1893, 3.

40. *Women's Trade Union Review,* July 1891, 6; *Women's Union Journal,* Mar. 1880, 36; *Workman's Times,* 4 June 1891, 5; WTUL, *Annual Report of 1894,*

5, and *Annual Report of 1892.* See also P.P., "Report on Strikes and Lockouts for 1891," 1893, vol. lxxxiii, pt. 1, p. 146, and WTUL, *Annual Report of 1904,* 5.

41. AST, *Journal,* July 1898, 60; Feb. 1900, 20; Sept. 1901, 11. For example, see ibid., Sept. 1898, 74. London Trades Council, *London Trades Council, Minutes and Papers, 1862–1909,* 6 Dec. 1894. Prior to this time there had been criticism that the council had been unresponsive to the needs of unorganized labor. One woman noted that "it seems unfair that women workers have no representative yet" on the executive board and that "from some of their discussions there seems to be an impression that their function is only to act for the organized trades." *Workman's Times,* 22 Oct. 1892, 4. Amie Hicks, a member of the WIC, became the first woman member of the executive. For the opening of the tailors' union to women, see *Workman's Times,* 27 Jan. 1894, 6.

42. *Women's Trade Union Review,* July 1903, 4; *Trades and Labour Gazette,* Feb. 1904, 12; WTUL, *Annual Report of 1904,* 4–5. A letter from Elvery to Macarthur conveys the enthusiasm of the women tailors: "I feel I am just bursting to tell you what great success I had in organizing yesterday. Thirty six have given me their names. I cannot find words to express my feelings. Fancy, 36, and very few with a query. I visited 13 shops and could have gone on until I almost dropped—but closing time came. I have never talked so much in all my life, really you don't know what you can do till you try. It was tiring work, but encouraging" (*Women's Trade Union Review,* Apr. 1904, 33).

43. *Women's Union Journal,* Jan. 1880, 1–2; Jan. 1881, 1. *Workman's Times,* 12 Sept. 1890, 8. WTUL, *Annual Report of 1896,* 4.

44. WTUL, *Annual Report of 1895.*

45. P.P., "Royal Commission on Labour," Fifth Report, 1894, vol. xxxv, p. 542; *Women's Union Journal,* Mar. 1880, 36; May 1890, 37. This is one of the few instances of corruption within the female labor movement.

46. *Women's Union Journal,* Apr. 1888, 27.

47. *Workman's Times,* 18 June 1892, 5.

48. National Federation of Women Workers, *Annual Report of 1908, Annual Report of 1909;* WTUL, *Annual Report of 1904,* 6, *Annual Report of 1905,* 4, *Annual Report of 1906,* 4.

49. *Women's Union Journal,* July 1880, 69.

50. This was an estimate made by Margaret MacDonald in 1907. See P.P., "Royal Commission on the Poor Laws and the Relief of Distress," vol. xxxxviii, Appendix ix, p. 230.

51. Tom Mann, "Women's Organizations," *Women's Trade Union Review,* Jan. 1897, 12.

52. Black's observation may be found in P.P., "Select Committee on Home Work," 1907, vol. vi, Q2879, and that of the *Review* in *Women's Trade Union Review,* July 1903, 4.

53. *Trades and Labour Gazette,* July 1907, 8.

54. Ibid., Feb. 1906, 8.

55. WTUL, *Annual Report of 1905.* On one occasion members of the AST burst into a London Tailors and Tailoresses Union meeting; the disrupters were led by an AST official "who strutted up the floor evidently in a state of wild excitement." *Trades and Labour Gazette,* Feb. 1906, 8. See also ibid., July 1905, 4.

56. The details of this AST–London Tailors rift are found in ibid., Mar. 1906, 21; July 1909, 8; Sept. 1907, 5; Oct. 1907, 3–6; Dec. 1907, 4; and *London Trades Council, Minutes and Papers,* "Delegates Meeting," 11 July 1907. Other quarrels among the tailors are found in AST, *Journal,* Dec. 1898, 108; Nov. 1899, 143; Apr. 1900, 53; May 1901, 11. In one case, the AST took the London union to court (*Madden vs. Rhodes,* 1905) rather than use the London Trades Council as an arbitrator.

57. *Women's Union Journal,* Oct. 1877, 66; Oct. 1880, 33; Jan. 1881, 6.

58. *Women's Trade Union Review,* Apr. 1895, 17–18; July 1895, 11; WTUL, *Annual Report of 1895,* 4.

59. NUBSO *Monthly Report,* June 1903, 1–2; Mar. 1904, 105; July 1909, 266; Aug. 1909, 380.

60. Ibid., Sept. 1906, 306; Nov. 1906, 363; Sept. 1908, 314; Jan. 1909, 12–13. *Leicester Post,* 13 June 1908, as found in item 504-L, Tuckwell News Clippings Collection, Gertrude Tuckwell Collection, Trades Union Congress Library, London.

61. For a discussion of the withdrawal and fatalism of the working class, see Standish Meacham, *A Life Apart: The English Working Class, 1890–1914* (London, 1977), ch. 7.

62. *Workman's Times,* 27 Aug. 1892, 1.

63. Calculated from NUBSO *Monthly Report,* Jan.–Dec. 1897, 1902, and 1905.

64. P.P., "Reports on Strikes and Lockouts, 1889," 1890, vol. lxviii; "Report, 1890," 1890–91, vol. lxxxviii; "Report, 1891," 1893–94, vol. lxxxiii, p. 43; "Report, 1894," 1895, vol. xcii, pp. 90–93; "Report, 1895," 1896, vol. lxxx, p. 114; "Report, 1896," 1897, vol. lxxiv, p. 76; "Report, 1898," 1899, vol. xcii, p. 68.

65. Ibid. The 1891 report noted that "workshops are still a bone of contention . . . as they are badly lighted, worse ventilated and the sanitary aspect is bad." "Report, 1891," 1893–94, vol. lxxxiii, p. 192.

66. *Women's Trade Union Review,* Apr. 1898, 2.

67. The "illconcealed" phrase were the words of a male supporter of the

WTUL in the *Women's Union Journal,* May 1882, 39; *Women's Trade Union Review,* Oct. 1897, 7. Howell expressed this idea in a speech before the WTUL. One female unionist responded as follows: "We often heard that women must not do men's work, but we never heard anyone say men must not do women's work [laughter]. And men would go on wearing a thimble to the end of the chapter." *Women's Union Journal,* July 1890, 51.

68. The royal commission observation is noted in P.P., "Royal Commission on Labour," Fifth Report, 1894, vol. xxxv, p. 479; Dilke's comment is in *Labour Leader,* 5 Jan. 1895. See also Emilia Dilke, *Women's Work* (London, 1895).

69. From a speech by Mary Macarthur, cited in the *Manchester Dispatch,* 10 Nov. 1908, item 458, Gertrude Tuckwell Collection.

70. *Women's Union Journal,* May 1881, 46. Geary may have made an impression on the men because several months later David Schloss reported that he was encouraged by the "sympathy and desire" on the part of the tailors to help their female co-workers and that "the tailors had certainly shown that they did care about helping the women employed in their trade." Ibid., Dec. 1881, 120.

71. *Women's Trade Union Review,* July 1891, 17–18. On the other hand, women tended to be critical of the men who assumed the leadership of the women's unions. "The women have not been encouraged to take leading parts in the administration of their organizations," wrote one observer, and "since they are rarely secretaries, or officers . . . they lose interest [and] fail on payments." Katherine G. Busbey, "Women's Trade Union Movement in Great Britain," *Bulletin of the Bureau of Labor,* 83 (Washington, D.C., 1909), 17.

72. The same was true for a number of other unions. An upholstresses union, "in spite of many years of devoted work on the part of its secretary, Miss Mearns," gradually dwindled away and had to be reorganized by the male union in 1899. Thereafter it existed as a branch of that union. WTUL, *Annual Report of 1894,* 5, *Annual Report of 1898; Women's Trade Union Review,* July 1899, 3.

73. For the account of these disputes see the *Women's Union Journal,* Oct. 1880, 114; Oct. 1889, 75–76. One London representative to the TUC–Edinburgh was "astonished" at the opinion of some men wanting to protect themselves from women "because that was just an echo cry of the upper classes, that they must protect themselves against the working classes." *Women's Union Journal,* Oct. 1879, 90.

74. *Trades and Labour Gazette,* Sept. 1902, 9.

75. *Women's Trade Union Review,* Oct. 1906, 8–9; *Trades and Labour Gazette,* Oct. 1902, 10. Emilia Dilke attended every TUC from 1889 to her death in 1904, but never as a delegate.

76. *Women's Trade Union Review,* Oct. 1906, 8–9.

77. Ibid., 10.

78. Ibid., Apr. 1898, 2. The issue of women's labor consciousness was frequently discussed. One man wrote to the newspaper *Justice* (9 June 1894, 5) that "men are far less indifferent to the sufferings of women than women are to those of men. There is never any lack of men to help women, the difficulty is to get women to help themselves."

79. See, for example, Hutchins, *Women in Modern Industry,* 55–58, and Francis Swiney, "Women's Industries," *Westminster Review,* Apr. 1909, 392. Swiney wrote, "We find that in those countries where women are electors, legislation dealing with all the evils from which we suffer has followed upon the women's vote."

80. *People's Press,* 1 Nov. 1890, 5.

81. Clementina Black, *Married Women's Work* (London, 1915), 3n1; James Ramsay MacDonald, *Margaret MacDonald* (New York, 1924), 57, and a speech by Mary Macarthur on wages, reported in the *Chicago Tribune,* 17 Mar. 1907, 5.

82. For example, Rosina Whyatt, a domestic servant and daughter of a Somerset farmworker, knew nothing about unions or the woman's suffrage movement and did not acquire any sort of political consciousness until she entered the factory and discovered the intellectual and political support of her working sisters. See John Burnett, ed., *Annals of Labour* (Bloomington, Ind., 1974), 127. Amie Hicks acquired her knowledge of unionism working in a ropemaking factory in New Zealand. Emma Paterson learned about unionism through her job with a men's union. For testimony that the factory radicalized women and taught them lessons in political citizenship and social emancipation, see the discussion in R. M. Hartwell, "Interpretations of the Industrial Revolution in England," in S. B. Clough et al., *The European Past: Reappraisals in History from the Renaissance through Waterloo,* 2 (New York, 1964), 219.

83. Flynn, "Trade Unionism," *Tailor and Garment Worker,* Mar. 1933, 5–9; Apr. 1933, 5–7.

84. *Women's Trade Union Review,* Oct. 1891, 5; *Women's Union Journal,* May 1877, 26, and July 1888, 51; and P.P., "Children's Employment Commission," Second Report, 1864, vol. xxii, p. xlv.

85. Macarthur is quoted in Mary Agnes Hamilton, *Women at Work* (London, 1941), 12. See also Macarthur's testimony in P.P., "Select Committee on Home Work," 1907, vol. vi, Qs2694–95; 1908, vol. viii, Qs 2245–48. *Women's Union Journal,* Mar. 1878, 13; July 1890, 40; *Workman's Times,* 30 Apr. 1892, 5; *Women's Trade Union Review,* July 1895, 11, and Apr. 1895, 17–18; WTUL, *Annual Report of 1895,* 4.

86. P.P., "The Select Committee on Home Work," 1908, vol. viii, Q3629.

See also P.P., "The Select Committee on the Sweating System," First Report, 1888, vol. xx, Q1648, 1689.

87. P.P., "Royal Commission on Labour," 1891, vol. ci, Qs8225–27; *Women's Union Journal,* July 1876, 37; *Workman's Times,* 5 Mar. 1892, 5; Women's Industrial Council, *Home Industries of Women in London* (London, 1908), 45.

88. Tuckwell's statement is found in P.P., "Select Committee on Home Work," 1907, vol. vi, Q 2333. For other examples of intimidation by employers, see the testimony of Michael Daly, organizing secretary for the AST, ibid., Q 3415, and Richard Goddard, assistant factory inspector, London, ibid., Q 1572. See also Dilke, "Trade Unionism for Women," Gertrude Tuckwell Collection; *Women's Trade Union Review,* Oct. 1906, 5. Further views by Dilke can be found in *People's Press,* 1 Nov. 1890, 13; *Workman's Times,* 13 Apr. 1891, 4; 5 Mar. 1892, 5.

89. *Tailor and Cutter,* 13 Sept. 1872, 580. See also V. DeVesselitsky, *The Homeworker and Her Outlook* (London, 1916), 8–9.

90. Women's Industrial Council, *Home Industries of London* (London, 1897), 17, and 1908 survey, 59.

91. P.P., "Royal Commission on Labour," 1893–94, vol. xxxvi, p. 297; *Workman's Times,* 7 July 1891, 7; W. H. Wilkins, *The Alien Invasion* (London, 1892), cited in a review in the *Charity Organization Review,* May 1895; the "social reformer," Father Bernard, is cited in the *Weekly Dispatch,* 19 Jan. 1908, item 225, Gertrude Tuckwell Collection. Others associated the Jewish immigrant with the deterioration of the physical and intellectual habits of their community. See, for example, *The Report of the Medical Officer of Health, Bethnal Green, 1893* (London, 1894), 6: "A majority of these undesirable immigrants are of an extremely low type both of physical and intellectual development, dirty in their habits, and totally ignorant of the laws of health."

92. For a discussion of such political campaigns, see William Fishman, *East End Jewish Radicals, 1875–1914* (London, 1975), ch. 3 and 246–52.

93. NUBSO *Monthly Report,* Sept. 1895, 10, for the statement by Ritchie, president of the Board of Trade.

94. Ibid., 6, 9, 10.

95. Ibid., Sept. 1897, 7. This is the main reason the Jewish unions distrusted arbitration under the Arbitration Act of 1895. To them it was merely a means to delay a settlement long enough for the sweating masters to get their work done by nonunion labor. Others denied the claim that Jewish labor was the source of sweating. See *Women's Trade Union Review,* July 1905, 31, and the article on sweating by Constance Smith in *Women's Trade Union Review,* July 1906.

96. *London Trades Council-Minutes,* 13 Feb. 1896, 22 Aug. 1894.

97. Fishman, *East End Radicals,* 189.

98. Ibid., 213.

99. NUBSO *Monthly Report,* Aug. 1894, 7; Dec. 1897, 2, 8; Mar. 1901, 7; Mar. 1903, 14. See also ibid., June 1895, 9, and Aug. 1901, 8. Freak is quoted in ibid., Sept. 1895, 9.

100. Ibid., Mar. 1895, 9–10.

101. P.P., "The Royal Commission on Labour," 1893–94, vol. xxxvi, p. 511.

102. These TUC resolutions, calling on the government to halt the entry of alien paupers into Britain, were repetitions of the 1892 resolution. Joseph Finn, *A Voice from the Aliens — About the Anti-Alien Resolution of the Cardiff Trades Union Congress* (London, 1895?).

103. *Trades and Labour Gazette,* Dec. 1909, 8.

104. NUBSO *Monthly Report,* Nov. 1904, 325, and May 1904, 140. This was reprinted from *Footwear* in the NUBSO *Monthly Report,* Feb. 1904, 74. The article blamed East End Yiddish newspapers for falsely accusing Freak of being anti-Semitic.

105. NUBSO *Monthly Report,* Sept. 1905, 278, and Oct. 1905, 308.

106. The national executive wanted the Clickers to rejoin the NUBSO as a separate London branch, while the Metro branch wanted the Clickers to join its branch. Ibid., Oct. 1905, 308, and Apr. 1904, 125.

107. For example, see Lloyd P. Gartner, *The Jewish Immigrant in England, 1870–1914* (London, 1960), 57.

108. *The Tailor,* 26 Jan. 1867, 256; 20 July 1867, 209; 27 Oct. 1866, 41; *Tailor and Cutter,* 15 July 1872, 37.

109. Fishman, *East End Radicals,* ch. 4.

110. Actually a Jewish union (the Tailors Mutual Association) had existed since 1870, although it was largely a masters' and journeymen's society. The following is a partial list of Jewish clothing workers' unions in the 1890s: Independent Tailors, Machinists and Pressers; United Ladies Tailors and Mantle Makers; Amalgamated Mantle Makers; International Mantle Makers Union; Jewish National Tailors, Machinists and Pressers; United Tailors Trade Protection Society; Hebrew Branch of the AST; International Journeymen Tailors, Machinists and Pressers; Military and Uniform Tailors and Tailoresses; Jewish Vest Makers; Trousers Makers Union; London Pressers and Underpressers Union; London Garment Workers Machinists Society; United Cap Makers; International Furrier Union. Shirley Lerner, "History of the United Clothing Workers Union" (Ph.D. diss., University of London, 1956), 98.

111. "Report of the Liverpool Conference, Amalgamated Society of Tailors," 20 Aug. 1891, item 77, Webb Collection; *Workman's Times,* 26 Mar. 1892, 5. Macdonald's attitude toward Jewish immigrant labor was no doubt

influenced by his membership in the Social Democratic Federation, which opposed any sort of limits on alien immigration.

112. Fishman, *East End Radicals,* 172.

113. Ibid., 179.

114. This was the attitude of the *Workman's Times,* 26 June 1891. For additional accounts of the strike see ibid., 3 Mar. 1891, 4, and 5 June 1891.

115. Ibid., 29 June 1891, 1.

116. Ibid., 24 Sept. 1892, 1.

117. Flynn is quoted in ibid., 9 Dec. 1893, 2. The remainder of this paragraph is from ibid., 30 Jan. 1892, and 5 Mar. 1892, 5. New Jewish unions frequently sprang up to challenge the AST. See ibid., 26 Nov. 1894, 2; 15 Oct. 1892, 2; 7 Sept. 1891, 7.

118. For an account of Lyons's activities and his troubles, see P.P., "Select Committee on Sweating," First Report, 1888, vol. xx, Qs10723–30; Fishman, *East End Radicals,* 202–9; *Workman's Times,* 5 Aug. 1893, 3, and 15 Oct. 1892. Physical fights at the union's meetings were not uncommon. See, for example, *Workman's Times,* 2 Oct. 1891, 4, and 23 Oct. 1891.

119. The Independent tailors claimed that Lyons called their union a "bogus union" and threatened to "smash" it. This battle between Lyons and other unions culminated, eventually, in Lyons and his International withdrawing from the London Trades Council. *London Trades Council-Minutes,* 4 Oct. 1894, 25 June 1896, 9 July 1896, 10 Sept. 1896, 5 Nov. 1896, 3 Mar. 1898.

120. Lerner, "United Clothing Workers Union," 103. Lerner places considerable emphasis on the thesis that widespread anti-Semitism forced the Jewish unions to unite. Ibid., 99–101. For the growth of the AST among Jewish workers at this time see *London Trades Council-Minutes,* July 1906, "Executive Minutes," and *Trades and Labour Gazette,* Mar. 1909, 3, which states that the original Jewish branch of the AST was still independent in 1909.

121. Finn, *Voice from the Aliens.* See also *Labour Leader,* 30 Nov. 1895, 3.

122. AST, *Journal,* Feb. 1901, 25, and Sept. 1899, 119–20.

123. For example, see the discussion as recorded in *London Trades Council, Minutes,* 25 June 1903, "Executive Meeting." Especially from the 1890s on, there are more documented examples of cooperation than of mutual antipathy. See, for example, *Workman's Times,* 27 Jan. 1894, which describes 2,000 Jewish and Gentile clothing workers joined together in protest of a lockout. For the opposing view, see "Discussion of Shirley Lerner's Paper," *Urban History Newsletter,* 12 (1970), 19, and Fishman, *East End Radicals.*

124. Fishman, *East End Radicals,* 112, 156–57, 164, 204–5.

125. For an account of a confrontation between the chief rabbi's representatives and Leiberman, see ibid., 118.

CHAPTER 5

Workshops for Workers

IN 1875 ONE-QUARTER OF ALL the work spaces used by the members of the British tailors union were rooms in attics or basements; three-quarters of the work spaces used by these workers were little workshops set up in houses. The average worker labored in a space of 210 cubic feet, far below the 1,000 cubic feet of work space that the union claimed was necessary for good health.[1] As shown previously, most nonunion workers in tailoring and other clothing trades, particularly women, labored in equally cramped and unhealthy outwork spaces, often their kitchens or bedrooms. One solution, of course, was to use industrial action or legislation to require employers to provide acceptable work space for each employee. Not surprisingly, then, unions sought adequate workshops for workers while employers boasted, though not always truthfully, that their work was done "only on the premises." The investigation of the House of Lords, in 1888–89, into the sweating system provided a major impetus for at least some employers—including local and central government—to consider the ill effects of the outwork production. "The Sweating Commission," noted one employer, "induced a good many of us to feel that we ought to put our houses in order, and a resolution was passed then that all the work in London should be done indoors, in the factories."[2]

Although the unions failed to master the problems arising from an excess supply of labor (Chapter 4), they enjoyed partial—albeit short-lived—success in forcing some employers to establish clean and regulated workshops for their workers. As one worker put it, aside from the regulation of the supply and price of labor, the "logical outcome of unionism amongst workers is the provision of workshop accommodation."[3] This chapter traces labor's attempt to obtain regulated workshop space for all workers.

The work-on-premises movement

Establishment of workshops was one of the goals of the tailors when they formed their "amalgamated" union in 1866, and one of their first resolutions pertained to workshops, stating "that this conference recommends to employers the necessity of providing proper workshops for their workmen; and we consider that a good workshop should allow 1,000 cubic feet of breathing space to each man — should have side lights — lime washed walls — proper ventilation, and should also be provided with proper sanitary conveniences, and a supply of water; and should, in no case, be below the level of the ground on any side." As a corollary, the union passed a resolution calling for the limitation of outwork, declaring "that this Amalgamated will use its best endeavours to limit, as much as possible, out-door working; and where it cannot be avoided, will endeavour *to procure* a higher price to outworkers to counterbalance their extra expenses, so as to some extent do away with the necessity of working longer hours than those who work in shops."[4]

The peculiar circumstances of their trade made tailors and other clothing workers believe that outworking should be attacked through both industrial action and state regulation. As early as 1867 some tailors advocated a law to compel all employers to provide suitable workshops for their employees. The tailors had turned to the state because, they believed, action through outworker unity was too difficult to achieve "since the workmen have no opportunity of seeing each other, comparing notes, or conferring upon means by which their condition might be improved."[5] Nearly thirty years later the London Trades Council resolved that the state make employers responsible for the sanitary conditions of all places — including the home — in which their work was carried on. Not only would the onus for protection be with the employer, but also he would be discouraged from using his workers' homes as workshops.[6] Some branches of the AST did not allow outwork by their members, but in London the system was entrenched and the union was too weak to effect its abolition.

Nevertheless, the London workers occasionally waged wars against employers of outworkers and the outworkers themselves. The most noteworthy occurred in the late 1880s and early 1890s. In 1889 East End tailors had struck to end the putting out of work by government contractors. In 1890 the tailors passed a resolution stating that "we respectfully ask the manufacturers . . . to provide workshops and abolish the intervention of middlemen" and struck once again for the establishment of healthy and proper workshops. Both times the tailors were unsuccessful, but another strike occurred in 1891. This time the East London workers were more explicit in their demands: they insisted on the establishment of workshops by May 23, 1891. When the demand was not met, they struck again. However, at the same time that these East End workers went on strike, the West End and City tailors were going back to work after their employers had given them provisional guarantees that workshops would be improved and provided for all workers. Because the two strikes were not coordinated, the East End tailors stood alone and ultimately failed. After three weeks they returned to their old outwork system.[7]

While outworking remained entrenched in the East End, it was slowly phased out in the West End during 1892 as employers provided workshops for workers. This was the year the issue of outworking became national. The Liverpool tailors precipitated the crisis, demanding certain tailoring be done only on workshop premises. Consequently, the MTA of Great Britain (the employers) came to the defense of the Liverpool masters and organized a lockout in Liverpool, which eventually expanded to include much of England.

The MTA persuaded the London masters to join the lockout and threw the tailoring industry of London into a war over outworking. It was a curious struggle in London. Neither the masters nor the unions were well organized or in agreement as to objectives, but both vied for the support of the outworkers, who, obviously, were even less organized. The employers made it clear they wanted the outwork system preserved. George Allen, the secretary of the MTA, expressed frequent and persistent support of outworking and was viewed by the unions as the arch-enemy of organized labor. Allen and the tailors association organized outworkers in a campaign for the preservation of outwork. This campaign included the circulation of letters supposedly signed by workers:

> To Journeymen Tailors, outdoor workers
> working at home in THEIR OWN WORKROOM.
>
> Fellow workmen. Beware of the present
> movement in the country of men in shops
> which is intended to force us to go and

work indoors, or wipe us out
altogether.

The author signed himself AN OUTDOOR TAILOR, NOT A SWEATER.[8]

It is impossible to say who felt more threatened, the outworkers or the masters. Allen was anxious to convince the London masters that the outworker was "far and away the best" tailor. In a secret meeting he told the master tailors of the West End that the outworker was more docile, obedient, and would work for less — not mentioning that he could easily contract the labor of family and neighbors. The master tailors wrote on their doors, "We shall send out just as much as we please to be done where and how we please." Outworking, to the MTA, was a "right" of all workers.[9]

On the other hand, the unions and most of the workers saw outworking as an evil rather than a "right." The *Workman's Times* called for an end to outwork, which it described as the "moral cesspool of English social life" and the enemy of unionism. The tailoring correspondent of the paper argued that the claim by some outworkers that they were not subject to irregularity of work was foolish. Clothing should be produced only in the workshop, she claimed, and workers should not be allowed to take work "into every little dirty den of their own" to work for starvation wages. "The sooner steps are taken to counteract the senile, selfish, apathy of the past," she argued, "the better it will be for all concerned." "We will not turn our homes into factories to enrich our employers," another unionist added.[10]

The outworkers themselves could not agree on the value of outworking. Some felt that cooperation with the work-on-premises movement would result in unemployment. Others, and these would appear to have been the majority, welcomed the elimination of the system. "A large meeting" of outworkers took place at the Tailors Club, where they repudiated "with scorn and indignation" the master tailors' claims that protection of the outwork system was in the interest of the worker. These outworkers maintained that the masters were using outwork as "an insidious device to create and intensify dissension within our ranks" and to bypass the agreed upon wage rates for the trade. Still others, however, were not as willing to join the union in its condemnation of the system. "A handful of outworkers," claimed the *Workman's Times*, "have taken serious objection" to the criticisms of outwork by the tailors unions. Too often when outworkers were asked if they would not be better off in a workshop, the invariable answer was something to the effect that "it has always been like this, ever since we can remember." Particularly among Jewish workers and married women workers did support for outwork prevail. The lack of unanimity produced warfare between outworkers and unionists in the West End. Union men picketed firms (which went on with putting work out), raided the outwork dens, and stopped workers on the streets to inspect their bundles.[11]

The outcome of the 1892 lockout was inconsequential. Allen and the MTA failed to get all of the London masters to join the lockout, and in a sense, the London working tailors could claim victory. But that the London tailors did not follow the lead of the Liverpool tailors in making demands for the abolition of outwork demonstrates how well entrenched outwork was in London. Despite the willingness of a few employers to provide workshops, tailoring in London remained strongly tied to outwork. Not only were many masters opposed to ending the system, but also a large number of workers feared that the demise of the system would result in the elimination of their jobs.

Nevertheless, the work-on-premises demands soon resurfaced. In 1893 the London tailors passed a resolution calling for employers to provide "adequate sanitary workshops for all the people they employ." Two years later the Ladies Tailors and Mantle Makers Union struck for the abolition of the outworking "middleman" system.[12] As outwork continued, the tailors persisted in complaining of the "considerable amount of homework" in the West End and of employers who, after unsuccessful attempts to cut wages, closed down their shops and put the work "out of doors." Consequently, the *Journal* of the AST noted, the system of outwork was growing.[13] Again, physical confrontation between outworker and unionist was common, as in 1903, when the *Trades and Labour Gazette* reported on a series of raids conducted by unionists into the sweating district of Soho: "A considerable number of cut-out garments, supposed to be strike work, were seized. Assaults are said to have been committed, and house property damaged. Five men have been arrested in connection with the raids, and detectives, piloted by uncanny looking men of the Jewish persuasion, are haunting the neighborhoods in search of others."[14] Six years later London tailors still complained that some tailors had to provide their own workshop accommodations.[15] The work-on-premises movement by the tailors had failed.

The work-on-premises movement in footwear

Between 1887 and 1890 the boot- and shoemakers of London forced their employers to provide workshops for their workers. Outworking was rapidly diminishing. This movement had begun in the East End with Jewish boot and shoe workers in 1887 and by 1890 had spread to the English boot and shoe districts, where the workers received assurance from their employers that workshops would be provided. Resolving to end outwork, the National Union of Boot and Shoe Operatives announced in 1890 that henceforth all labor was to be done in the factory or workshop, a move welcomed by workers as bringing an end to overtime, scamping, drinking, and gambling.[16] This work-on-premises movement was supported by the national arbitration board of the industry, which insisted that the workshop agreement between workers and employers be upheld. Although victory was partly due to favorable trade conditions (the boom of 1890), it was the direct result of an agreement between union and employers' association and worked out through a board of arbitration. As one factory inspector reported in 1891, the workers had succeeded in preventing overcrowding and homework.[17] By 1892, because of the work-on-premises movement, the London boot- and shoemakers had been able to "break through this awful system of sweating."[18] A solid blow had been struck against overcrowding and homework.

But success was short-lived and elusive. By late 1891 workers were conducting protest marches to the homes of scab workers who had disregarded the agreement. These anti-homework marches became regular Sunday spectacles, complete with a band playing the traditional funeral dirge and with a crowd sometimes as large as 1,500. By 1892, when the economy of London was in a state of depression (the worst since 1867 for the boot and shoe trades), the employers had reverted to the outwork system. What usually happened was that the employer would break from the employers' association, reduce wages, and return to the practice of giving out work. As one unionist stated:

In London, especially, we find it most trying and difficult to maintain this new method [of indoor work], our officials being hardly pressed, efforts being daily made to break through it, and scores of men having to be stopped at the expense of the Union, as these sweaters offer to do the work at such prices that tempt numbers of Jewish employers to try to break away from it; besides this, there is such a quantity of this pauper labour in London willing to work all hours merely for sustenance.[19]

In effect, because of the economic advantages of outworking, there was a large increase in the number of outwork workshops, with all of the conditions of the previous decade. "There is a growing disposition and intention of large manufacturers in the clothing trade to encourage work done by outworkers," Mr. Lakeman, the factory inspector, reported in 1894.[20] In 1908 about 75 percent of boot and shoe employees carried on their trade in their homes.[21] In some cases the union would strike against the firm that broke the indoor work agreement, but most often the strike would be unsuccessful and the men would either be replaced or return to work under the old conditions. "On Sundays it is no exaggeration to say," reported the London boot-and shoemakers, "that . . . furniture makers, bootmakers, and other trades, are busy taking home the sweated work from morn till night." Homeworking, they reported, was as prevalent as ever.[22] Employers, despite the protest of the board of arbitration as well as the union, continued to claim that they had a right to have work done indoors or outdoors. In June 1896 the union published a list of fifteen London firms that had recently gone to giving work out, "therefore violating the rules of the Board [of arbitration], and making it impossible for our members to work thereon."[23] Time and again the union lamented the contravention of the outwork agreement. And time and again, if the union protested, the employers would merely quit the employers' association and claim exemption from the agreement, although the board of arbitration ruled that if the firm was a member of the board when it broke the agreement it was in violation of the agreement.[24]

By 1907 the work-on-premises movement was underway again. This time the English and the Jewish boot and shoe unions cooperated in their efforts to get the principal violators of the indoor work agreement (the Jewish employers and Jewish workers) to adhere to the principle of indoor work only. The workers, led by T. F. Richards, received the support of the employers' association as well. But although the battle against "Dirty Home Sweating" successfully struck against the outworking firms and received a guarantee that workshops would be provided, by the fall of 1908 the union was complaining again that certain firms had broken the agreement and numerous workers, mainly Jews, were taking work out.[25] It is difficult to say why the work-on-premises movement in the boot and shoe and tailoring trades failed. One obvious reason was the weakness of the employers' association in forcing its members to adhere to the indoor agreements. Likewise, the outworking system was, in part, a result of union strength. As the unions became more aggressive, employers reacted by putting the work out to more docile hands. The demands of the boot and shoe operatives, for example, on the issues of machinery and production changes encouraged employers to put the work out,[26] just as wage demands of the unions encouraged outwork. As the president of the MTA claimed, union demands were forcing the employer to "turn his key in his workshop and say for the future I will get all my work made out."[27]

In actuality, however, the work-on-premises movement did not fail because of union strength but because the unions were weak and unable to change the system, particularly in times of recession and with a glut of immigrant workers available. Outworking could not be eliminated until the trade was thoroughly organized, and the trade could never be thoroughly organized until outworking was eliminated. Ironically, then, the work-on-premises movement was strong enough only to cause a reaction on the part of their employers — which came in the form of outwork and not in the form of cost-cutting factory methods.

NOTES

1. *Tailor and Cutter,* 11 Feb. 1875, 201–2. This is based on a survey by the AST. Twenty percent of those surveyed had only 100 cubic feet of workspace.

2. P.P., "Royal Commission on Labour," First Report — Evidence, Group C, 1892, vol. xxxvi, pt. 2, p. 102. Still in 1906 outworking was a common London scene, as Black noted: "As I went home yesterday I passed in Cheapside a little girl carrying a large bundle of tailoring. In all probability she was going to a good City tailor, whose customers, no doubt, thought that their clothing was made upon that tailor's premises." National Anti-Sweating League, *Report of a Conference on a Minimum Wage* (London, 1907), 43.

3. *Workman's Times,* 7 May 1892, 4.

4. Amalgamated Society of Tailors, *Report of the Conference of Deputies* (Manchester, 1866), 14, 17.

5. *The Tailor,* 9 Mar. 1867, 342.

6. *London Trades Council, Minutes-Delegates Meeting,* 28 Feb. 1895.

7. P.P., "Report on Strikes and Lockouts for 1891," 1893–94, vol. iii, pt. 1, pp. 281–82; *People's Press,* 14 June 1890, 11. A brief discussion of this work-on-premises movement is in P.P., "Report of the Chief Inspector of Factories and Workshops, 1889–90," 1890–91, vol. xix, pp. 9–12.

8. *Workman's Times,* 13 Aug. 1892, 5; 27 Aug. 1892, 1; 3 Sept. 1892, 1.

9. Allen is quoted in ibid., 30 July 1892, 4. See, too, ibid., 25 June 1892, 7; 13 Aug. 1892, 5; 27 Aug. 1892, 1.

10. Ibid., 6 Feb. 1892, 5; 24 Sept. 1892, 1; 15 Oct. 1892, 1.

11. Ibid., 23 Apr. 1892, 5; 30 Apr. 1892, 5; 7 May 1892, 4; 27 Aug. 1892, 1; 10 Sept. 1892, 1; 24 Sept. 1892, 1.

12. Ibid., 13 May 1893, 3; P.P., "Report on Strikes and Lockouts for 1895," 1896, vol. lxxx, pt. 1, pp. 96–97.

13. AST, *Journal,* Mar. 1899, Sept. 1899.

14. Apr. 1903, 12.

15. Ibid., Aug. 1909, 5. Workers' demands for an end to outworking are not difficult to document. The committee that drew up the Factory bill of 1895 heard proposals by the AST that the law require compulsory factory work in the tailoring trade. The same proposal was periodically proposed by the tailors at the TUC.

16. *Workman's Times,* 7 Oct. 1890, 1.

17. P.P., "Royal Commission on Labour," Third Report, 1893–94, vol. xxxiv, Q 33189.

18. P.P., "Report of the Chief Inspector of Factories and Workshops for 1901," 1902, vol. xii, pp. 9–10.

19. P.P., "Royal Commission on Labour," Second Report—Evidence, Group C, 1892, vol. xxxvi, pt. 2, p. 102; also *Workman's Times,* 4 Sept. 1891, 1, 4; 29 Oct. 1892, 1.

20. P.P., "Report of the Chief Inspector of Factories and Workshops for 1894," 1895, vol. xix, pp. 48, 51; see also NUBSO *Monthly Report,* Apr. 1900, 8–9.

21. P.P., "Report of the Chief Inspector of Factories and Workshops for 1908," 1909, vol. xxi, p. xxxiii.

22. NUBSO *Monthly Report,* Aug. 1902, 7; Sept. 1902, 2; July 1895, 11.

23. Ibid., June 1896, 8.

24. Ibid., Feb. 1900; also ibid., Aug. 1896; Feb. 1899, 4; May 1899, 4; Aug. 1899; Apr. 1900, 8–9; Nov. 1901, 2; Sept. 1906, 296; Feb. 1906; Mar. 1906, 102; Mar. 1907; Oct. 1909, 446.

25. Ibid., Mar. 1908, 119; Apr. 1908, 149; May 1908, 166; June 1908, 198; Aug. 1908, 320; Oct. 1909, 446.

26. Alan Fox, *A History of the National Union of Boot and Shoe Operatives, 1874–1957* (Oxford, 1958), 93. Conversely, Booth noted, the demands to end outworking encouraged the employment of machinery. Charles Booth, *Life and Labour of the People in London* (London, 1902–3), ser. 2, 3: 19.

27. P.P., "Royal Commission on Labour," Second Report, Group C, 1892, vol. xxxvi, Q 14193; see also P.P., "Report of the Select Committee on Home Work," 1907, vol. vi, Qs3444, 3452, 3363–68.

CHAPTER 6

The State and the Sweating System

IT BECAME PAINFULLY APPARENT in the 1880s to the British public that the benefits of industrial society were unevenly spread; some groups gained great wealth, others remained untouched, and still others saw what little they had being eroded. This paradox of poverty amid wealth is partly a result of that mysterious economic crisis called the "Great Depression," which lasted from about 1873 to the mid-1890s; it meant a shrinking British share in the world market, a slowdown in economic growth, an upturn in unemployment in certain sectors, and the decline of certain older traditional industries. All of this was capped by a slump in British agriculture. It must, however, be kept in mind that at the same time the urban working class found real wages going up.[1] These movements caused the middle class to ask a series of questions — not just about economic growth but about poverty and job dislocation. This so-called discovery of poverty led to a redefinition of liberalism and of social policy — what Beatrice Webb called "the humanitarian upsurge of the eighties." Social reform became important as the Victorians began to reconsider the relationship between the state and the individual. The upper middle class became determined to use state intervention to combat the evils of sweating. The decade of the 1880s was a watershed in British social theory.[2]

As an army of middle-class social investigators tramped into every street and alley of every industrial city, the discovery of the sweatshop played an important role in this revolution in social policy. For the London public the results were particularly disturbing. In 1883 there appeared a penny pamphlet entitled *The Bitter Cry of Outcast London,* a polemic on the poverty of life experienced by a large number of Londoners. This work led to a series of investigations, the first of which was a report in 1884 on working conditions in the sweated clothing trades in the East End of London by the Women's Trade Union League (WTUL). The report, which "caused a great sensation," was followed by surveys of working conditions in East London by David Schloss for the Jewish Board of Guardians, by John Burnett for the Board of Trade, and by Factory Inspector Lakeman for the Home Office. A Royal Commission on the Housing of the Working Class was appointed in 1884, and two years later Charles Booth began his monumental study of poverty and labor in London.[3]

With the aid of Beatrice Potter (later Webb), George Duckworth, and others, Booth carried out an extensive investigation into the working conditions in many of London's industries in order to determine the reasons for the inordinate amount of casual employment, unemployment, and poverty in London. His initial investigations were published in two volumes in 1889–91 and later expanded into a seventeen-volume work. Booth found about one-third of the population of London living in poverty. One result of this and the earlier investigations was the creation, by the request and later the leadership of Lord Dunraven, of the House of Lords committee on sweating in 1888. The committee at first was charged with investigating sweating in East London, but, following a report by the WTUL that the evil existed in areas outside of London, the scope of the investigation was extended to include all of England, Ireland, and Wales. This chapter examines how an emerging public consciousness of the problem of sweating was translated into government action.

Government reform and workshop labor

The impact of the state on the sweating system is complex. Ostensibly, legislation regulating working conditions, hours of labor, and the like was important in homogenizing and unifying the labor force and in fostering the growth of the factory system. But the history of sweating points to an entirely different conclusion: the state — quite unwittingly — actually fostered and encouraged the growth of sweated labor.

The first state regulation of nonfactory labor was the Workshop Act of 1867,[4] which pertained to women, children, and young persons who worked on premises other than the home that employed *less* than fifty persons. Premises employing *fifty or more* persons were regarded as factories and were subject to the Factory Acts. The Workshop Act regulated the hours and intervals of work of protected persons employed in workshops, provided for certain educational obligations on the part of the employers, and mandated that sanitary conditions of the workshops conform to the Sanitary Act of 1866. The most controversial aspect of the act was that its enforcement was given over to the local medical officers of the vestry and district councils.

The enforcement provisions, as it turned out, were wholly inadequate. To start with, enforcement varied according to the whims of local government. Some of London's vestries performed their duties better than others, but for the most part the local officials paid slight if any regard to the Workshop Act.[5] Not only were local authorities financially and otherwise unwilling and unprepared to expand and reorganize their medical and sanitary departments as necessitated by the new law, but their refusal to enforce the law was supported and encouraged by employers and workers. The medical officer of the vestry of Bethnal Green in East London reported that child labor and illegal work hours were so common in his district that it was impossible to enforce the 1867 act "because it would limit the work of many impoverished workers and probably cause a riot." He added that to carry out the act would "necessitate the employment of 20 inspectors," which the vestry obviously did not have nor was likely to appoint.[6] Nearly thirty years later another Bethnal Green medical officer, looking back on the situation faced by his predecessor in 1868, came to a similar conclusion: The 1867 act did not work because the Bethnal Green Council was determined "not to meddle with trade matters in its parishes" and the act expected too much without providing the machinery necessary to carry it out.[7] In short, the act failed because there was no way by which the central authorities, either the Home Office or the Office of Factory Inspectors, could exercise any check on local officials.

An amending act in 1871 attempted to correct this situation by placing the inspection of workshops, except for some sanitary provisions that were left to the local authorities, in the hands of the factory inspectors. But this system of dual control was also ineffective. The factory inspectors, who had put considerable pressure on the government to end the system of local inspection, soon realized that inspection of workshops under their direction was nearly as impossible as it had been under the local inspectors, even though their staff was increased.[8]

On balance, then, the extension of regulation to workshop labor was not effective in regulating the nonfactory labor market either after 1867 or after 1871. In fact, considerable evidence exists to show that the reform of 1867, initially intended to bring uniformity and standardization to the labor market and industry, was counterproductive and self-defeating. The Royal Commission on Factory and Workshop Acts in 1876 found many employers and workers who believed that the law fostered the growth of the least-regulated and least-desirable mode of industrial organization, namely workshop production. This was largely because the Factory Act was more stringent than the Workshop Act. For example, the Factory Act was regarded as a hardship by London's clothing manufacturers because it eliminated the traditional system of overtime during the busy seasons. The result was that many London dressmaking factories closed and the work was put out.[9] In contrast, the Workshop Act was more lax than the Factory Act with regard to the employment of children and the hours of labor. It was difficult under the Workshop Act to prevent illegal overwork because the period in which work could be undertaken was longer than the hours allowed to work. In addition, the Workshop Act provided for no minimum penalty for offenses and required no register, abstracts, or notices, all of which were mandated of factory occupiers.[10]

The definition of a factory at fifty or more persons was arbitrary. Manufacturers kept their labor force below fifty workers in order to evade the more stringent law. The commission reported that "some manufacturers will sometimes purposely keep down the number of their workpeople to 48 or 49 in order to escape the Factory Act," while other firms would "farm out work among the smaller workshops" for the same reason.[11] Factories that adhered to the costly provisions of the law lost orders to workshops that were not required to have inspection. As Inspector Baker reported, these factories lost their workers as well: "Workers may be employed long hours in a workshop without much fear of detection." Therefore, factory operators had "their best hands drafted away from their factories one by one, to the higher wages of workshops, because they can work longer hours."[12]

Women complained that state regulation had caused a reduction

in their employment in regulated industries, thereby forcing them
into unregulated, overcrowded, and underpaid work. In effect, where
the law equalized work conditions, either men would be preferred
to women, or the work would be given out to unregulated labor. In
either case women were the losers. Some women feared that state
regulation might drive them from the labor market altogether.[13]

It is not surprising then that the commission of 1876, in recognizing
that "the regulations under the Workshop Act are very much fewer
and less binding than under the Factory Act," concluded that "the
imperfection of the law thus produces an aggravation of the evil which
it was intended to alleviate," namely, undesirable working conditions
and wages.[14] The commissioners followed the lead of the factory
inspectors and recommended not only that the "fifty hands" definition of a factory be abolished but also that workshops be placed under
the same regulations as factories.[15]

The commission's report led to the Factory and Workshop Consolidated Act of 1878, which sought to eliminate some of the inequities
of the 1867 acts. This act changed the legal definition of a factory
from a workplace with fifty persons to any workplace with motive
power; all other places were to be considered workshops. While this
provision corrected a major defect in the older laws, the disparity
between factory and workshop regulations remained and continued
to fragment the labor market. In fact, the act of 1878 was retrogres-
sive in terms of nonfactory labor. First, it exempted from the act all
workshops, including domestic shops, that employed only female labor.
Second, the act left inspection to be shared by local and state inspectors, and enforcement was rendered even less effective because the
factory inspectors were henceforth required to obtain a written warrant
from the secretary of state or a justice of the peace before entering
a home workshop, a requirement that they found extremely frus-
trating.[16] Also the act allowed workshops, but not factories, considerable elasticity in the arrangement of work hours for protected
persons, and it exempted workshop owners from registration and certification of children's ages and physical fitness. Evasion of regulation
continued to be easy and widespread. Characteristic was a London
firm that had two premises, one a factory without child workers because the firm wanted to avoid the registration and certification clause
pertaining to children, and another, a workshop with child workers
because workshops were exempt from that part of the law. Finally,

the act allowed a considerable number of overtime exemptions for workshops, thereby allowing thousands of workshop employers in London's seasonal trades to evade the law legally. As a result, unhealthy conditions and overtime were the rule rather than the exception in the case of workshop labor.[17]

At the same time the act of 1878 strengthened the factory regulations, causing workers and others to complain that the increased disparity between the factory and workshop laws contributed to the movement of industry and labor away from centralized factory production.[18] The consensus of the witnesses before the select committee on sweating was that the nonfactory system of production was growing, partly because of the nature of the law. Skilled artisans complained that unskilled outwork labor was invading their industries, putting them out of work, and lowering the status of their trades.[19]

It would, no doubt, be unfair and an exaggeration to attribute the growth of the workshop labor market solely to the inequities of state intervention. Certainly other factors, such as production changes, market demands for "cheap clothes and nasty," and pressure to cut production costs, were of equal or even greater importance in influencing the structure of the labor market and the character of production. But there is little doubt that the impact of government reform was an unwelcome reality for many late Victorian and Edwardian working people. Many London workers, for example, complained that employers evaded factory acts by shifting work to unregulated premises. They lamented that the law that "is intended to benefit us as a trade, at all events, has the direct opposite effect and simply protects the middleman as a sweater." The home was becoming a dirty workshop, and factories were closing because greater profits could be made with nonfactory labor. One factory inspector claimed that the trend toward centralization of labor had been reversed because the law encouraged workshop production.[20]

Nothing is more indicative of the failure of workshop regulation than the system of enforcement and inspection. Inspection was virtually nonexistent. As the select committee on sweating in 1888 concluded, the system was "harmful."[21] In theory, inspection was divided between local authorities, who were responsible for the sanitary inspection of workshops as set forth by the Factory and Workshop Act and the Public Health Acts of 1875 and 1891, and factory inspectors, who were responsible for enforcement of provisions relative to working conditions and hours of labor of protected persons. In practice, local inspection did not work, not only because of the apathy of the local councils and their officers but also because of the absence of a system of registration and the limited medical and sanitary staff of the local councils. Similarly, inspection by the factory inspectors was thwarted by the ambiguity and weakness of the law. The law allowed the factory inspectors to inspect only workshops employing children and/or young persons, thereby placing the greater part of workshop labor outside the inspectors' authority; and, as noted above, the need for a warrant made inspection of home workshops a practical impossibility. A random survey of East London workshops by three London inspectors in 1884 revealed that of 1,478 workshops, inspectors had full jurisdiction over only 367, partial jurisdiction over an additional 387, and no jurisdiction whatever over 724.[22]

Demands that workshops be inspected and regulations enforced came from many quarters: factory inspectors, local health authorities, workers, unions, and government commissions. One London unionist, Lewis Lyons, made workshop regulation the chief aim of his anti-sweating campaign.[23] Likewise, the Trades Union Congress and the London Trades Council repeatedly pleaded for more inspectors and better inspection, as did working-class newspapers such as the *People's Press* and the *Workman's Times*. The *People's Press* noted in 1890 that there was scarcely one workshop in London's tailoring industry that conformed to the requirements of the workshop regulations.[24] Thus, a female worker claimed that after sixteen years in various workshops in London she had neither seen nor heard of an inspector coming to a workshop where she was working, and neither had she seen the abstract of the act, which the law required be put up in every shop.[25]

Workshop reform and the growth of outwork

The revelation of sweating in the 1880s — by way of the House of Lords' committee and the various private investigations — and a women's trade union revival, which sought state intervention in the sweating crisis, encouraged an attack by the state on illicit sweatshops. Two amending acts were passed, one in 1891 and the other in 1895. The Factory and Workshop Act of 1891 established a system for the mandatory registration of all new workshops and provided that the secretary of state could require employers to keep a register of their outworkers. The act of 1895 rejuvenated the system of local inspection by clarifying the duties of the local authorities and made them, for the first time, answerable to the secretary of state for the sanitary inspection of workshops.[26] The Factory and Workshop Act of 1901 further strengthened the system of local inspection and made the employer of outwork labor responsible for the sanitary conditions of the outwork premises. In the decade following 1891 enforcement of workshop regulation was turned over to the local authorities, but this time considerable power was given to them, a clearer definition of duties was provided, and provisions for redress were listed, should the local authority fail in its responsibilities. As a result, many of the medical officers of health of the vestry and district councils (after 1900, the borough councils) slowly, but often with vigor and thoroughness, remodeled their health and sanitary departments in order to administer the law.[27] Many vestries had for the first time effective regulation of their workshops.

Vestries varied in their responses to the acts. As a consequence of the act of 1891, the medical officer of St. Pancras vestry appointed its first male and female inspectors of factories and workshops in 1895. Similarly, the local medical officer of Paddington succeeded in getting the vestry to appoint two workshop inspectors in 1894; in response to the 1901 act he reorganized the vestry's health department, appointed a female workshop inspector, and established the vestry's first system of workshop and outworker registration. But Paddington did little workshop inspection until well after 1901. On the other hand, the Islington vestry was one of the first to undertake systematic inspection of its many outwork and clothing workshops by appointing an inspector of outwork in 1894 and male and female workshop inspectors the following year. As early as 1896 Islington inspectors made nearly 6,000 inspections of workshops, resulting in some 200 defects being corrected. Workshop inspection in Islington was considered so progressive by its medical officer who reported that the borough was in the fortunate position of "having anticipated" the requirements of the 1901 act.[28] Poplar, another district with a large workshop labor force, began outwork registration and inspection in 1893 and workshop inspection a few years later. Kensington began workshop inspection in 1892–93 by doubling its inspection staff from four to eight.

Other vestries did not perform as well. In St. Marylebone, one of London's chief centers for the dressmaking trade, the local medical officer pleaded almost every year, unsuccessfully, for a larger staff in order for the vestry to comply with the workshop acts. St. Marylebone had a reputation for overcrowding and was notorious for its negligence in enforcing the acts. Although a female workshop inspector was appointed in 1899, the borough's medical officials continued to complain to the vestry that it was impossible to inspect each workshop even once a year. Prior to 1901, enforcement in Bethnal Green was almost nonexistent. For ten years after the 1891 act the vestry's medical officer tried to get the vestry to appoint three additional inspectors to handle the growing number of small workshops. The vestry's sanitary committee repeatedly refused to prosecute violators of the workshop acts, even when urged to by its health officer, and inspection remained erratic.[29]

Just as the disparity between factory and workshop regulations led to the growth of workshops, effective workshop regulation resulted in the expansion of outworking. The reports of the local medical officers of health illustrate a general shift from workshop production to outwork production in the period 1902-7. Four out of nine boroughs in which clothing trades were centered experienced a decrease in the number of workshops; all nine experienced a growth in the number of outworkers (Table 15). To be sure, part of this increase was merely statistical, as collection and reporting of data became more efficient. However, since data on both outwork and workshops suffered somewhat equally from the vicissitudes of collection, we can conclude that outwork production was growing at a considerably faster rate than previously. Most important, the decline in workshop production is most evident in boroughs where the factory and workshop acts were rigorously enforced. It is not known what happened to the work formerly done in these disappearing shops, even though it is known that the ratio of outworkers to workshops tended to grow faster in the districts in which workshops were declining. Whether or not the work was put out to outworkers depended on the specific trade. Dressmaking, for example, was a workshop trade in which employers were more likely to move to a borough where enforcement was less strict rather than to remain and give work out. Industries in Kensington tended to move out, while in Hackney the industries of shoemaking and tailoring were more prone to remain and put the work out. In

Table 15. Workshop Inspection-Enforcement and Workshop Growth in Nine Wearing-Apparel Trades Boroughs, 1902–9

Borough	Inspection-Enforce-ment Frequency*	Growth in Number of Workshops+	Growth in Number of Outworkers†
Poplar	4.99	– 15.5	+ 93.3
Hackney	3.24	– 36.6	+ 417.0
Islington	3.15	– 13.0	+ 124.5
Kensington	2.97	– 8.8	+ 25.8
Bethnal Green	2.67	+ 1,019**	+ 243.0
Paddington	2.14	+ 11.4	+ 341.0
Stepney	1.63	+ 37.1	+ 93.3
St. Pancras	1.18	+ 61.4	+ 439.0
St. Marylebone	0.65	+ 72.2	+ 219.0

*This figure is the number of inspections per workshop plus the average number of defects found per workshop per year.

+ This figure is the number of workshops in 1909 as a percentage of the number of workshops in 1902.

†This figure is the number of outworkers in 1909 as a percentage of the number of outworkers in 1902. Much of this growth is statistical, not real. The statistics on outworkers were haphazardly gathered in some boroughs. Many outworkers went undetected, and some were counted twice (owing to the fact that the outwork lists were sent in twice a year). The totals on which these percentages are based are probably somewhat low, since the list totals have been halved, not allowing for casual workers who are on one list and not another. See Appendix A.

**The large increase here is deceiving. Bethnal Green reported only 174 workshops in 1902, which is no doubt too low. The growth between 1904 and 1909 was 57 percent, which is more realistic.

Source. London County Council, *The Reports of the Chief Medical Officer of Health,* 9 vols. (London, 1902–9), and *The Reports of the Medical Officers of Health of the Borough Councils of Poplar, Hackney, Islington, Kensington, Bethnal Green, Paddington, Stepney, St. Pancras, and St. Marylebone* (London, 1902–9).

any case, the most striking aspect revealed in Table 15 is the correlation between effective workshop regulation and the shift away from workshop production. Some employers preferred to move, close their shops, or change the makeup of their labor force rather than to adhere to the reform acts. For example, authorities in Poplar were so anxious to see workshop reform carried out that they personally made recommendations to the Home Office for the improvement of workshop inspection and its administration. Poplar's workshop inspection staff increased from four in 1895 to nine in 1901, with the result that by 1901 the district was inspecting its workshops on an average of three times a year at a time when other districts could hardly make one inspection a year. Some workshops were inspected every month. Through its efficient outwork inspection, unregistered workshops were discovered and compelled to recognize the workshop laws. In 1903, for example, a total of eighty-eight new workshops were found and registered as a direct result of outwork inspection.[30] Poplar also experienced a leveling off and decline of the number of workshops after 1902–3 and a steady rise in outworkers. Poplar's medical officers of health claimed that increasing outwork production and decreasing workshop production were due to some workshop employers closing their shops and putting their work out to homeworkers in order to evade the workshop and public health acts; others escaped the law by firing protected laborers. In both cases the result was an increase in work done in unregulated premises.[31]

Similar trends occurred in Hackney, where the combination of a heavy influx of foreign, mainly Jewish, labor in the 1890s and of the more stringent workshop regulations of the 1890s led the local medical officer to crack down on crowded and unsanitary workshops. Up to this point one inspector, a woman, handled the entire system of workshop inspection. The staff was enlarged in 1903, a workshop register was carefully revised, and inspections increased considerably. Like Poplar inspectors, those of Hackney uncovered numerous unregistered workshops and made their owners conform to the sanitary and work provisions of the law.[32] The number of workshops in Hackney reached a peak of 1,727 in 1901 and thereafter declined precipitously to about 60 percent of that figure by 1904 where it remained for the next five years. Conversely, the outwork labor force increased steadily until it reached a peak (of 4,322) in 1906–7. These growth patterns are particularly surprising because the boot and shoe industry was supposedly undergoing a rapid conversion to machine-factory production.[33] Like the Poplar officials, Hackney officials noted that the factory and workshop laws were forcing labor into the least regulated labor market, namely outwork. The law was a hardship to workshop owners because so many of these shops were either converted houses or parts of existing houses, thus making it difficult to comply with the legal requirements, especially those on sanitary facilities. The law "will fall so heavily on the owners of small workshops and businesses as to cause them to close rather than to go to the heavy outlay of building additional conveniences." Three years later one inspector reported large numbers of workshop occupiers moving from the borough or quitting the business.[34]

No borough had a better reputation for regulation of workshops than did Kensington, about half of whose workshops were in the dress-making trade. The Kensington Borough Council led the way in inspection of workshops when it appointed two women workshop inspectors in 1893. The statistics show that workshops in general and dressmaking shops in particular declined between 1902 and 1909, the period during which the 1902 act was being efficiently enforced. Although Kensington officials attributed the decline in dressmaking workshops to a depression in the trade, it is more likely that the decline was due to employers' dislike of the workshop regulations, especially in light of the fact that while the regulated trade declined the unregulated male-tailoring workshop trade increased in Kensington by 40 percent between 1903 and 1907. In addition, the dressmaking trade grew by 33 and 21 percent, respectively, in St. Marylebone and Paddington, which were notorious for their nonenforcement of the workshop laws.[35] It would appear, therefore, that government interference was significant in determining the growth patterns of this trade.

Local officials were not the only ones to testify to the pressures which the factory and workshop acts exerted on the labor market and the structure of industry. Businessmen frequently complained that state requirements, such as overtime notices or certificates of fitness, were a hardship and "source of great annoyance."[36] This apprehension was characteristically expressed by Arthur Chamberlain, brother of the colonial secretary, when he said, "If only we could have a free hand; if only the manufacturer could carry on his business free from local boards and bye laws, free from sanitary inspectors, free from smoke inspectors, free from chemical inspectors, free from School Board inspectors, free from Home Office inspectors, what enormous economies could be effected."[37] London businessmen obtained such economies by closing their shops and putting out the work.

London workers had long complained of the "large and continued increase of out-door working," which they regarded as a tool used by the employers to depress wages and divide the workers, thereby making labor organization impossible.[38] Boot and shoe workers nearly monthly complained that their work was being put out to outwork labor.[39] As we have seen, the WTUL, the WIC, and clothing trades unions in London pushed for years to control outwork either by organizing the outworkers or by having outwork prohibited altogether. Shoemakers claimed that employers who abided by the factory and workshop acts were "heavily handicapped" by the unscrupulous ones who did not and who were therefore able to undercut them in the market. Not infrequently, workers were discharged because of "alterations required by the sanitary inspector."[40] The shoemakers of London reported that "we are almost afraid to interfere with some of the indoor workshops . . . as it is likely to cause the workers to be forced to work outdoors in their homes if the Factory Act regulations are insisted upon."[41] Another common practice in London was to move the workshop to a district where inspection did not exist or where it could be temporarily avoided. Whitechapel slippermakers reported that "it had become the habit of small employers to move, and then open new workshops without notifying the inspector."[42]

Although sweating and its evils are traditionally associated with East London, the Select Committee on Home Work in 1907–8 heard numerous complaints that in the West End, particularly Soho, factories and workshops stood empty because manufacturers had returned to the outwork system in order to relieve themselves of the burden of factory inspection. The committee heard numerous complaints that the factory and workshop acts were an economic burden in an age when cost cutting was the key to economic survival, especially in London, where the means of expansion were limited. Protection of labor, it was argued, was equivalent to an increase in the cost of labor. Over one-third of the witnesses called before the select committee specifically stated that homework was expanding because of the attempt to escape the factory and workshop acts. The witnesses claimed that homework relieved the employer of the "irksomeness attached to factory inspection." The law had driven the worker "out of the workshop into private homes."[43] Michael Daley of the Amalgamated Society of Tailors and Tailoresses union pressed upon the committee the importance of regulating homework as well as workshops because workshop regulation had "driven the worker out of workshops into private homes."[44] Typical of the testimony before the committee was that of Rose Squire, a London factory and workshop inspector:

Q. Is it not so that a great many obligations have been thrown upon employers within the factory, and almost every year more and more, which do not apply to work done in the home?

A. That is so.

Q. Where you find an increase, do you not attribute that to any specific cause as apart from the nature of the particular trade?

A. I think it may be true that the requirements of the Factory Acts and of the other Acts, and so on, may press somewhat harder on an occupier in a certain industry and he will therefore provide himself with a large number of workers outside.

Q. I suppose a certain class of factory owner to save building large factories and being under the Factory Acts is very glad to put work out into homes?

A. Yes, I think that is so, and in some trades, I suppose, the outwork is increasing.[45]

It is clear that the labor market and industrial structure were shaped, in part, by the factory and workshop reforms. Because workshop regulation was so ineffective, the gap between workshop and factory conditions and wages widened, and production tended to drift from the factory to the workshop. The factory and workshop acts were intended to equalize conditions of labor, but in practice they often resulted in the stratification of labor and the decentralization of production. Their effect on unionization was negative, for they encouraged the growth of the most dispersed and isolated sector of the labor market.

In the late 1890s and into the 1900s, workshop regulation was enforced in some boroughs with some efficiency, and the gap between factory and workshop conditions began to close. Effective local enforcement of the workshop acts proved to be the most dramatic event in the regulation of nonfactory labor in London since the origin of workshop regulation in 1867. It was then that production tended to drift into the only remaining sector of unregulated labor. The increase in outwork in London after the mid-1890s must be associated with the assumption of regulatory power by the local vestry and later borough councils. Outwork production was not merely a remnant of the old domestic system, but rather a result, in part, of state intervention in the economy. One of the chief lessons of the previous forty years of government factory and workshop reform was that uneven and disparate measures tend to generate growth in the least regulated sectors of the labor market and to stratify working classes. Sweated industries were being fostered by the state.

Attitudes of women toward state regulation

The uneven and disparate nature of the factory and workshop acts reinforced a traditional working-class fear and distrust of the govern-

ment. As Henry Pelling in a recent study has argued, state intervention was "by no means welcomed by members of the working class
. . . [and] was indeed undertaken over the critical hostility of . . .
perhaps most of them."[46] But this statement is only partially true for
women workers in the sweated trades, who seldom argued that government reform was entirely harmful. Many of them recognized that a
great improvement in factory working conditions occurred as a result
of the twelve years of labor legislation between 1864 and 1876. Working
women had mixed attitudes, and some, like those who testified before
the Royal Commission on Factory and Workshop Acts, were uncertain
about governmental interference in certain areas of women's labor.
These women expressed fear that further extension of the law would
be detrimental to women workers, just as past legislation, by placing
regulations on female labor, made their labor less desirable to
employers and thus drove them from certain industries into "a few
trades which . . . would become overcrowded and underpaid." In
short, the law forced women from the workshop to home workrooms
with a reduction of wages.[47] But Emma Paterson noted that, although
the WTUL opposed legal interference with the labor of women, working women "generally" did not oppose such action. Paterson presided
over a conference of working women in 1875, which dealt with the
subject of government labor regulation. It concluded that "it is undesirable that any special restrictions be placed on the work of married
women," especially in the form of reduction of hours if it was accompanied by a reduction of wages. However, the women workers did
ask that overtime work in certain seasonal trades be abolished, that
the interval between meals be shortened, and that women inspectors
be appointed for the sanitary inspection of workshops employing
women. Paterson claimed that working people were against legislating the hours of labor, even though the excessive hours of labor was
their primary grievance.[48] The secretary of the London Working
Dressmakers, Milliners, and Mantle Makers Association told the commission that the women did not desire governmental interference with
outworking and were not in favor of legislating shorter hours unless
weekly wages remained the same. They were, however, in favor of
better inspection of workshops and in the appointment of women workshop inspectors.[49] Reporting on the same meeting of the working
women, the secretary of the Commission on Labour similarly concluded
that "none would accept shorter hours, if combined with reduction

of wages, but they all advocate regulation in order that both work and wages may become more steady."[50]

These views reflect the anti-government interference policy of the WTUL in its early years — a hostility more ingrained in the league's leaders than in its rank and file. The leaders of the league who favored legislative protection were in the minority. The WTUL had even invited Professor and Mrs. Henry Fawcett, both advocates of the laissez faire school, to represent the WTUL in the debates of Parliament by opposing the factory bill of 1876. In turn, Mrs. Fawcett told the WTUL that it must "protest most gravely against further legislative interference with women's labor . . . as any honest work, however hard and physically trying, was surely preferable to starvation."[51]

Various reasons existed for the WTUL's opposition to state interference. One is that Paterson and the league "fell under the influence of certain confused women of the middle class,"[52] who were advocating self-sufficiency and self-help. Then, too, and perhaps more important, Paterson feared state reform because in certain cases it was prejudicial to the interests of working women. Legislation that regulated only women's and children's labor placed a premium on male labor, which was left unregulated. Some women claimed that if the Shop Hours Act were passed, it would certainly lead to the discharge of women and their replacement by men who were not regulated by the act. "Gifts of legislation of this kind," stated the treasurer of the East London Tailoresses Union, "seemed to be like the famous horse given to the Trojans."[53] As Emilia Dilke observed a number of years later, Paterson saw legislation as a last resort, believing women could get all they wanted through trade unionism.[54] Indeed, Paterson thought that "the time had come when no fresh legislation should be sought for in the work of women . . . [since] women were beginning to show a disposition to protect themselves . . . by combination . . . as men had done."[55] This attitude reflects the optimism and vitality of the WTUL in its infancy. It was under this initial spell of excitement that Paterson spoke against legislative action at the Trades Union Congress at Newcastle in 1876, protesting the proposed restriction of female employment to a twelve-hour period. The following year at Leicester she took a similar stance, claiming that women felt that factory legislation "interfered with and curtailed their means of obtaining a livelihood by honest work."[56] This statement put the women at odds with male unionists such as Henry Broadhurst, who claimed that women unionists could never succeed unless they used the government to put some restrictions on "those who would work their mothers and sisters like dogs or slaves."[57] But the WTUL generally believed that women could solve their problems through combination and that "the time was passing when women needed legislative protection more than men." Hence, its members resolved that "any legislative interference in work of adults is becoming less and less necessary."[58] Five years later Miss Wilkinson, a member of the WTUL, noted that "as women became more ready and able to protect themselves by uniting in societies, the legislation would gradually become effete and would fall away."[59] A WTUL editorial noted that legislation "weakens the self-reliance of workwomen by seeking to do for them that which the experience of men's unions has shown can be better done by means of trade organizations."[60]

However, Paterson and the WTUL were neither fully representative of working-class attitudes, nor did their opinions last long. Most working women tended to be ignorant about government regulations and did not understand that laws existed to protect them. One girl pitied her employer because, she believed, he was forced by the factory act to work his employees overtime.[61] On the other hand, some informed working women were more in favor of governmental interference than were the union leaders, although fear of reprisals caused them to remain silent. For example, Miss A., a dressmaker from the West End, told investigators that government legislation was desired and welcomed by working women, although it was a subject that the women spoke of only among themselves and never to anyone else.[62] In 1877, as a consequence of the WTUL's protests against government interference at the Trades Union Congresses in 1876 and 1877, Factory Inspector Henderson surveyed London working women and reported that he had "found the limitations imposed upon their hours of work most cordially approved of, and the greatest anxiety and positive alarm entertained at the prospect of any relaxation which would expose them to the irregular and uncertain hours of work." The inspector then said that dressmakers and milliners expressed "a strong desire" for "further restrictions."[63]

The hesitancy of the women unionists on the issue of state regulation ended in the late 1880s, as the WTUL adopted a strong pro-state intervention policy. This conversion to state regulation was a result of several factors, not the least of which was the union revival and the socialist enthusiasm of the 1880s, the failure of the women's union movement, and the lessening reliance of the middle class on laissez faire thinking. The unionists and the socialists now considered state regulation to be not only workable but also necessary. The London match girls' and dockers' strikes, the public revelations of the chronic problems of poverty and casual labor, and the spread of socialist ideas inspired an aggressive and activist WTUL stance.[64] But equally persuasive in pushing women toward state intervention was the failure of unions to organize the sweated trades. The WTUL and the WIC were convinced, as was the Royal Commission on Labour, that the chief hope of the woman worker was not in trade unionism but in the "extention of collective action by the state." For the women the principle that "the state has a right to interfere with the labor of women and children . . . has been conceded."[65] The old school of economics, noted Gertrude Tuckwell of the WTUL, was gone, and women must realize that their fear of state intervention was "groundless."[66]

Under Dilke, who succeeded Paterson as president of the WTUL in 1889 and who had shared some of her predecessor's concern that laws treating women differently than men might be harmful, the WTUL in the 1890s became a staunch proponent of government legislation. Meanwhile, the WIC had been founded to promote the welfare of women workers through government reform legislation. By 1900 both organizations were devoting much of their energy to lobbying for increased regulation of labor and industry. For example, in an effort to upgrade the system of inspection of women's work, the WTUL succeeded in 1893 in getting a woman appointed as a factory and workshop inspector,[67] and by 1898 it had a minimum wage proposal before the House of Commons. The WIC brought about child labor reform legislation, educated local candidates on matters affecting women workers, proposed legislation to protect women workers, and even succeeded, with working women like Amie Hicks presenting its case, to convert the Women's National Liberal Federation in 1899 to the idea of state regulation of homework.[68] Behind all of this was the argument that working women were in favor of legislative restrictions and that existing legislation was beneficial.[69] In a joint effort with the British Association (largely a collaboration between A. L. Bowley and Margaret MacDonald) the WIC issued a series of reports on the helpful effects of legislation on working women.[70] At the same time the WIC used its Girls Clubs to educate young workers as to these benefits and to inform them of their rights under these laws.

The WTUL also promoted government regulation. In the summer of 1895 it solicited over 100,000 letters, telegrams, and resolutions from women asking for increased protection under the law. Tuckwell, with the support of Adolphe Smith and James Macdonald, then led the WTUL in a campaign to strengthen the factory and workshop acts. The WTUL issued a pamphlet on overtime, and through lectures and petitions it laid the views of women workers before various trade union councils, the London County Council, middle-class groups, and influential individuals. In this effort the WTUL claimed to be acting in the interest of the working woman and carrying out her wishes. "We have made inquiries among hundreds of nonunionists," stated a WTUL organizer in 1897, "and have found that their voice is unanimous" on the subject of increased legal coverage.[71] All of this went on amid the warnings of some old-line unionists like George Howell that women depend too much on law and not enough on mutual support.[72]

The WTUL also established an Industrial Law Committee to teach women workers, health visitors, teachers, and others the merits and operation of industrial law. It served as a clearinghouse for workers' complaints on breaches of the law; it informed factory inspectors of these breaches, and, to protect the worker from an employer's retaliation, it set up an indemnity fund for women and girls dismissed from their jobs for giving evidence to an inspector.[73] A few years later this committee founded the Labour Law Association, whose object was "the dissemination of knowledge of what the Factory Acts were, how they came about, and what had been their effects . . . on working women."[74] In 1901 the association published *The Case for the Factory Acts*, whose authors, Beatrice Webb, Clementina Black, and Gertrude Tuckwell, proposed that the state "enforce on all employers a minimum of humane order as the inviolable starting point of competition."[75] Thus, as the title of the book made clear, the battle strategy was narrowing as women looked to the state to guarantee the industrial rights of women workers.

The WTUL and the WIC campaign for public acceptance of state intervention on behalf of working women was successful, but it is difficult to determine how much this effort brought working women to view the state as friend and protector. Factory inspectors frequently reported that workers were thankful for the benefits of legislation, one inspector noting that he had "certainly been astonished by the spontaneous heartfelt expressions of gratitude and thankfulness from young laundresses" for increased regulation of labor. He continued, "I have not found yet among workers a trace of the antipathy to regulations which has been rather widely thought to exist."[76] Many women "expressed their gratification" to the inspectors "that the number of days on which overtime is allowed will be decreased in the new year."[77] Other inspectors reported not only that workers were thankful but also that they participated in enforcement procedures.[78] Whereas formerly some women helped to deceive the inspectors, by the late 1890s women were more and more confident of the inspectorate system—especially of women inspectors—and were willing to register complaints. Out of 400 complaints in 1897, 122 came from workers' organizations and trade unions, 159 from workers or friends of workers, and twenty from public officials. The WTUL received between fifty and sixty complaints each week. The WTUL investigated each case and then reported it to the chief woman inspector of factories and workshops.[79]

But to suggest that all of these actions and responses represent a mass conversion of working women to government intervention or the idea of a welfare state is misleading. Only the small groups of women who were the leaders and the few they were able to touch entered the political arena. A new awareness developed among working women, but it was at a dishearteningly slow pace. The majority of working women, unless prodded, ignored politics and, if asked, would probably have responded as did one sweated worker who, when asked if she thought the House of Lords' inquiry would do any good, replied, "No. You might as well get me to give an opinion on politics as them Lords give an opinion on sweating."[80]

NOTES

1. By 1873 the economy was no longer setting growth records, unemployment was rising, and a relative decline in exports and profits was taken as a sign that the economy was in trouble. Modern historians have revised the view that the economy was in a depression—but only to a point. Although agreeing with H. L. Beales ("The Great Depression in Industry and Trade,"

Economic History Review, 2d ser., 5 [1934–35]: 65–75) that the era was not
a depression in the modern sense of the term, historians today believe that
from about 1873 until the mid-1890s Britain went through a period of economic deceleration, marked by a decline in the rate of economic growth,
a loss in her share of world trade and productivity, and a steady fall in prices.
This period was also marked up to the mid-1890s by rising real income.
One of the arguments frequently set forth is that British innovation in technology and entrepreneurship lagged behind that of the United States and
Germany. See David Landes, *The Unbound Prometheus* (Cambridge, 1970),
336–58, and John Saville, "Some Retarding Factors in the British Economy before 1914," *Yorkshire Bulletin of Economic and Social Research,* 13 (May
1961), 52–54. See also E. H. Phelps Brown and S. J. Handfield-Jones, "The
Climacteric of the 1890s: A Study in the Expanding Economy," *Oxford Economic Papers,* 4 (1952), 286–89.

2. For a discussion of this see E. P. Hennock, "Poverty and Social Theory
in England: The Experience of the Eighteen Eighties," *Social History,* 1 (Jan.
1976).

3. The WTUL report was written by Adolphe Smith and appeared in
The Lancet, 5 Mar. 1884, and was reprinted in the *Jewish Chronicle,* 9 May
1884. The investigation by Schloss was printed in the *Charity Organization
Review,* Jan. 1888, 1–12, and Burnett's report may be found as the "Report
to the Board of Trade on the Sweating System in the East End of London"
in the Appendix of the House of Lords' Sweating Commission reports, P.P.,
1888, vol. 21, pp. 569–89.

4. Few studies have touched on the relationship between the factory and
workshop acts and the changes in the industrial and labor structure. Standard
works, such as May E. Abraham and A. L. Davis, *The Law Relating to Factories and Workshops* (London, 1902), and B. E. Hutchins and E. Harrison,
A History of Factory Legislation (London, 1903), are helpful but do not go
beyond explaining the evolution of the law. Somewhat more analytical studies
are Frank Tillyard's *The Worker and the State* (London, 1936), and Tien Kai
Djang's *Factory Inspection in Great Britain* (London, 1942). Neil Smelser's classic
study, *Social Change in the Industrial Revolution* (Chicago, 1960), discusses the
relationship between the factory and the changing structure of the family.
No study has considered the impact of nonfactory legislation on the family
or the industrial structure.

5. *Tailor and Cutter,* Apr. 1868, 211. Typical of this neglect was the vestry
of Paddington, whose records show that little or no attention was paid to
workshop inspection until the mid-1890s, even though Paddington was a
major center for the workshop clothing industry. It is not until 1894 that
the Paddington medical officer mentions workshop inspection, and then he

laments that his staff was too small for any periodic and systematic inspection. *The Report on the Health of Paddington for the Quarter Ending September, 1894* (London, 1894), 11.

6. The medical officer felt the act was unfair because its enforcement provisions were difficult and ambiguous and because it imposed a social hardship on the community, forcing employers to turn their live-in (i.e., resident) employees out into the streets and replace them with day workers in order to evade the law. P.P., "Report of the Chief Inspector of Factories and Workshops for the Year 1867–68," 1869, vol. xv, pp. 13, 52.

7. *The Report of the Medical Officer of Health, Bethnal Green, 1895* (London, 1896).

8. P.P., "Report of the Chief Inspector of Factories and Workshops for the Year 1872," 1873, vol. xix, p. 12. The staff was enlarged and reorganized from four districts with thirty-nine inspectors to thirty-nine districts with a staff of fifty-four.

9. *The Report of the Chief Inspector of Factories and Workshops for 1868* (London, 1869), 8–9. That state regulation caused the expansion of the unregulated labor market was not new in the history of industrialization. Andrew Ure noted such a result in the 1830s. See Philip A. M. Taylor, *The Industrial Revolution in Britain* (Lexington, Mass., 1970), 13.

10. For example, it was impossible to determine at 8:30 P.M. whether a boy was working longer than the maximum 10½ hours unless one knew the precise hour at which he began his labor. P.P., "Royal Commission on the Factory and Workshop Acts, 1876," 1876, vol. xxix, pp. xv–xvi, xxv.

11. Ibid., pp. xv–xvi.

12. P.P., "Report of the Chief Inspector of Factories and Workshops for 1872," 1872, vol. xvi, p. 76.

13. P.P., "Royal Commission on the Factory and Workshop Acts, 1876," 1876, vol. xvi, Qs435–37, 6654, 6648, 2811.

14. Ibid., vol. xxix, pp. xiv–xvi.

15. Ibid., vol. xxix, p. xvii.

16. P.P., "Select Committee on the Sweating System," 1888, vol. xx, Q8252.

17. See P.P., "Report of the Chief Inspector of Factories and Workshops for 1894," 1895, vol. xix.1, pp. 29–30; and P.P., "Select Committee on the Sweating System," 1888, vol. xxi, Q16476, 16516, 1786–88, 8351–62.

18. Ibid., Q 8308, 7925.

19. These were cabinetmakers and tailors. Ibid., vol. xxi, Qs3801, 3883–88, 1946.

20. Ibid., vol. xx, Qs1495–1503, 5047, 5118, 3266, 8089, 1776, 1952, 7975, 8252, 8125–30, 1229, 709–11, and vol. xxi, Q 16706.

21. Ibid., P.P., Fifth Report, 1890, vol. xvii, p. xlii.

22. P.P., "Report of the Chief Inspector of Factories and Workshops for 1884," 1884–85, vol. xv, 93, pp. 21–36.

23. Lyons was president of the International Tailors, Machinists, and Pressers Union and publisher of the short-lived (1886–87) *Anti-Sweater* newspaper. See the *Anti-Sweater,* July 1886, 2. For similar views of eighty-five other unions, see the P.P., "Report of the Royal Commission on Labour," 1892, vol. xxxv, pp. xii–xiv.

24. *People's Press,* 23 Aug. 1890, 13. See also *Workman's Times,* 2 Feb. 1892, 5; 2 June 1892, 5.

25. *Charity Organization Review,* 15 Sept. 1885, 375.

26. The sanitary regulations that they were required to enforce were: (1) each workshop must have 250 cubic feet per person (the standard amount); (2) ventilation must be provided for any workshop where gas, vapor, or impurity is generated and inhaled by the worker to an injurious extent; (3) sanitary conveniences must be adequate; (4) a register of workshop and outwork laborers must be kept; (5) a reasonable temperature must be maintained in each workshop; (6) no outwork can be allowed in a diseased premise; (7) reports must be made to the factory inspector as to what action was taken with regard to complaints forwarded by the inspector to the local officials. The return of inspection powers to local authorities was one of the recommendations of the Royal Commission on Labour.

27. Some labor organizations opposed the transfer of power to local officials and greeted local enforcement with gloom. See *The London Trades Council Minutes and Records, Delegates Meeting,* 13 Feb. 1896, Executive Meeting, 20 June 1901.

28. This paragraph is based on the following sources: *The Report of the Medical Officer of Health of Islington for 1896* (London, 1897) and *for 1901* (London, 1902), 184–85; *The Report of the Medical Officer of St. Pancras for 1892* (London, 1893), 37–38, and *for 1895* (London, 1896), 50–53; *The Report on Vital Statistics and Sanitary Work for Paddington for 1894* (London, 1895), 11; *for 1895* (London, 1896), 158; *for 1900* (London, 1901), 87; *for 1901* (London, 1902), 59; and *for 1902* (London, 1903), 53; *The Report of the Medical Officer of Health for Poplar for 1893* (London, 1894), 78; and T. O. Dudfield, *Women's Place in Sanitary Administration* (London, 1904), 2–3.

29. For St. Marylebone see *The Report of the Medical Officer of St. Marylebone for 1895* (London, 1896), 21; *for 1896* (London, 1897), 16; *for 1907* (London, 1908); and *for 1908* (London, 1909), 424. For an example of St. Marylebone's infamous reputation with regard to workshop conditions and inspection, see the *Charity Organization Review,* 1 (Jan. 1885), 6, 17. In Bethnal Green registers were set up, and some inspection was undertaken, but the office of female inspector was short-lived. *The Report of the Medical Officer of*

Bethnal Green for 1891 (London, 1892), 28; *for 1894* (London, 1895), 31; *for 1897* (London, 1898), 40, 53; and *for 1901* (London, 1902), 25.

30. *The Report of the Medical Officer of Poplar for 1894* (London, 1895); *for 1901* (London, 1902); *for 1903* (London, 1904), 94; *for 1904* (London, 1905), 226; and *for 1903* (London, 1904), 189.

31. *The Report of the Medical Officer of Poplar for 1903* (London, 1904), 189; *for 1904* (London, 1905), 226; and *for 1905* (London, 1906), 235.

32. *The Report on the Sanitary Conditions of the Borough of Hackney for 1901* (London, 1902), 33; *for 1904* (London, 1905), 68–72; and *for 1909* (London, 1910), 79.

33. The trend away from factory production in the Hackney boot and shoe industry is noted in P.P., "Royal Commission on the Poor Laws and Relief of Distress, 1909," 1909, vol. xliv, Appendix. Alan Fox, in his *A History of the National Union of Boot and Shoe Operatives, 1874–1957* (Oxford, 1958), makes little mention of outwork production after the mid-1890s.

34. *The Report on the Sanitary Conditions of the Borough of Hackney for 1902* (London, 1903), 59–60.

35. *The Report of the Medical Officer of Health of South Kensington, 1902–1909* (London, 1903–10), 9 vols.; *The Report of the Medical Officer of Health of Paddington, 1902–1909* (London, 1903–10).

36. See, for example, the article by T. Fallows, "The Perplexing Factory Acts," *Drapers Record,* 1 Aug. 1908.

37. Cited in *Trades and Labour Gazette,* July 1901, 8.

38. *The Tailor,* 20 Oct. 1866, 25; *Tailor and Cutter,* 17 May 1872, 366–67. The same complaints were expressed thirty years later; see AST *Journal,* Jan. 1900, 11.

39. For example, see NUBSO *Monthly Report,* Oct. 1895, 11–13; Mar. 1896, 11; June 1896, 8; Aug. 1896, 8; May 1899, 4; Apr. 1900, 8–9; Nov. 1901, 2.

40. Ibid., Sept. 1902, 2; Oct. 1905, 308.

41. Ibid., Dec. 1906, 381.

42. Ibid., Oct. 1909, 468.

43. P.P., "Report of the Select Committee on Home Work," First Report, 1907, vol. vi, Qs1020–22, 1032, 1113, 1116, 1121, 1716, 1894, 2502, 2769, 3141, 3427–29, 3578, 3582, 3771–74, 4289.

44. Ibid., Q 3771.

45. Ibid., Qs1032, 1113–16.

46. *Popular Politics and Society in Late Victorian Britain* (London, 1968), 2. Pelling argues that the aversion the worker felt toward state intervention had its roots in a long list of government reform policies in the nineteenth century, ranging from the New Poor Law of 1834 and Peel's police force to the working-class housing acts and the education acts. Except to claim

that the eight-hour bill "never received the full support from the working
class" (5), he makes little or no mention of state intervention into the most
important aspect of life for the Victorian worker, his job. For a similar view
see Standish Meacham, "The Sense of an Impending Clash: English Working
Class Unrest before the First World War," *American History Review,* 77 (Dec.
1972), 1352–53, 1361.

47. P.P., "Royal Commission on the Factory Acts, Report, vol. I," 1876,
vol. xxix.l, Qs6654, 6648, 2811.

48. Ibid., Qs2700–2769; ibid., 1876, vol. xxix.l, Appendix C, "Report
of Adjourned Conference," by Emma Paterson, 1 May 1875, p. 193; ibid.,
"Report, vol. II," 1876, vol. xxx.l. The league never gave more than tacit
support to the eight-hour bill.

49. Ibid., Qs2776, 2781, 2778.

50. "Notes on the discussion taken by the Secretary," ibid., "Report, vol.
I," Appendix C, p. 193.

51. *Women's Union Journal,* Jan. 1878, 1; Mrs. Fawcett's speech to the
annual meeting of the league is found in *Women's Union Journal,* July 1881, 68.

52. Trades Union Congress, *Women in the Trade Union Movement* (London,
1955), 46. A Women's Rights party existed at this time in Birmingham and
claimed that regulation of female labor was merely a way for men to get
the women out of the labor market. See Edward Cadbury et al., *Women's
Work and Wages* (Chicago, 1907), 24.

53. "Second Annual Meeting of the East London Tailoresses Union,"
Women's Union Journal, Dec. 1881, 119. Thirteen years later the London
tailoresses were complaining that the factory and workshop acts discrimi-
nated against women workers by putting a premium on male labor because
it allowed men to work overtime, whereas women could not. *Workman's Times,*
3 Mar. 1894, 5.

54. *People's Press,* 1 Nov. 1890, 13.

55. *Women's Union Journal,* Oct. 1876, 60.

56. Ibid., and P.P., "Report of the Chief Inspector of Factories and Workshops for 1877," 1878, vol. xx, p. 11.

57. *Women's Union Journal,* Nov. 1877, 72.

58. Ibid., Dec. 1876, 78.

59. Ibid., July 1881, 70.

60. Ibid., Sept. 1881, 79.

61. See Clara Collet's report in P.P., "Report on the Employment of
Women and Girls," 1894, vol. lxxxii.l, p. 13, and P.P., "Royal Commission
on the Factory Acts," 1876, vol. xxx.l, Q 2769.

62. P.P., "Children's Employment Commission," First Report, 1863, vol.
xviii.

63. P.P., "Report of the Chief Inspector of Factories and Workshops for 1877," 1878, vol. xx, pp. 12, 13–14; see also *Women's Union Journal*, Sept. 1881, 79. Several years earlier, however, another inspector expressed a contrary opinion—that the workers did not want any further government legislation pertaining to them. P.P., "Royal Commission on the Factory Acts," 1876, vol. xx.l.

64. For evidence of this aggressiveness, see *Women's Union Journal*, July 1880, 54; Oct. 1889, 77; Jan. 1890, 3; July 1890, 49; *Women's Union Review*, Apr. 1891, 1; Jan. 1892, 6–7.

65. *Women's Union Review*, Apr. 1891, 1; July 1894, 3.

66. Gertrude Tuckwell, cited in the *Redditch Indicator*, 20 Jan. 1909, item 21, and WTUL, *Restriction, or Increased Opportunity* (a leaflet), item 301, both in the Gertrude Tuckwell Collection, Trades Union Congress Library, London.

67. The first woman inspector of factories and workshops was May Abraham (later Mrs. H. J. Tennant). She was Dilke's secretary and a labor organizer for the WTUL. Women inspectors, whether factory and workshop or local sanitary, reduced the prejudice of working-class women against state interference. See, for example, *Women's Industrial News*, Sept. 1901, 254.

68. In 1897 Mrs. F. C. Hogg carried on a WIC investigation into child labor, which led to an ad hoc Wage-Earning Children Committee, which, in turn, led to a Home Office and Board of Education Committee to study proposals to strengthen the power of local education authorities with regard to child labor. The WIC campaign was carried on by A. J. Mundella, former president of the Board of Trade. Out of the committee's work came, in 1902, a government bill regulating employment of children, the Employment of Children Act of 1903. *Women's Industrial News*, June 1899, 110; Sept. 1900, 194; Mar. 1901, 222; July 1914, 262–63. The Women's Liberal Federation resolution to support the legal regulation of homework is discussed in ibid., June 1899, 119.

69. For example, see "A Working Woman's Opinion on Factory Legislation," ibid., Dec. 1899, 151.

70. The reports are discussed in ibid., Dec. 1903, 411–12.

71. *Women's Trade Union Review*, Apr. 1897, 10. The women wanted (1) the abolition of overtime, (2) the strengthening of the outworker protection clauses, (3) the retention of the dangerous trades clause, and (4) the inclusion of laundries under the Factory and Workshop Act. Ibid., July 1895, 28. About this time the league addressed the London Trades Council on the necessity of workingwomen to demonstrate in favor of a proposed factory bill. *London Trades Council, Minutes*, 10 May 1894.

72. *Women's Union Journal*, July 1890, 51.

73. "The Industrial Law Committee," *The Guardian,* 30 Apr. 1909, item 11, Gertrude Tuckwell Collection.

74. Introduction by Mrs. Humphrey Ward to Beatrice Webb, ed., *The Case for Factory Acts* (London, 1902), viii.

75. Ibid., 18. Some women tied the issue of protection to suffrage and found that as long as women had no voting rights legislative protection was farcical, dangerous, hypocritical, and paternalistic. Claiming to be writing from a "socialist view," the women's correspondent for the *Labour Leader* (27 Oct. 1894, 6) wrote, "I most emphatically protest against any legislation which further interferes with the rights of women, so long at least, as women are debarred from having any say in the matter of such legislation." Further legislation, she claimed, would merely "add a bit more to the patchy and tinkering of social conditions which is so proverbial of the Liberal Party." But the socialist Independent Labor party proposed further government regulation of married women's work. The discussion continues in the *Labour Leader,* Apr., Sept. 1895.

76. P.P., "Report of the Chief Inspector of Factories and Workshops for 1895," 1896, vol. xix, pp. 122–23.

77. P.P., "Report of the Chief Inspector of Factories and Workshops for 1896," 1897, vol. xvii, pp. 92–94, 106.

78. P.P., "Report of the Chief Inspector of Factories and Workshops for 1895," 1896, vol. xix, p. 14.

79. A report by Mary Macarthur in the *Daily Express,* 20 Nov. 1907, item 225, Gertrude Tuckwell Collection. See also P.P., "Report of the Chief Inspector of Factories and Workshops for 1901," 1902, vol. xii, p. 166.

80. [Margaret Eloise Harkness], *Toilers in London* (London, 1889), 314–15.

CHAPTER 7

The Way of Escape

FOR THE WORKING CLASS the idea of a state-legislated minimum wage was not altogether new. Many workers in the early nineteenth century were accustomed to state regulation of wages through apprenticeship laws and had memory of wages being set by local magistrates.[1] In 1830, for example, Parliament still regulated the wages of workers in the London silk industry just as it had, a few decades earlier, regulated the wages of tailors. But somewhere about the middle of the century British workers discarded their ancient ideas of fair wages and work and then, playing the rules of the game (as E. J. Hobsbawm calls it), demanded the highest price for the least work and worked to create a scarcity of labor. These workers cast aside both the principle of "a fair day's work and wage" and that of a minimal standard of comfort; by the 1870s workers had adopted the capitalist rule book and were demanding what the traffic would bear. As Sidney and Beatrice Webb noted, workers adopted the "intellectual position of the employers" by accepting the capitalist theory that wages must fluctuate accordingly to prices and profits. Whereas the Webbs found this unwise, Hobsbawm finds it a matter of getting smart.[2] For the workers in the sweated trades the traffic did not bear much.

In the last quarter of the century this trend was somewhat reversed, as labor developed a new interest in the idea of an enforced minimum wage, particularly in those sectors of the labor market where wage protection through unionism was weak or impossible.[3] One of the early proponents of this idea was the laborite Lloyd Jones, who argued in 1874 that "the first thing . . . those who manage trade societies should settle is a minimum wage, which they should regard as a point below which they should never go, unless under pressure of absolutely uncontrollable circumstances." Such a minimum, Jones claimed, should be "one as will secure sufficiency of food and some degree of personal and home comfort to the worker . . . to shield the recipient from the degradation of a workhouse, or from the horrors of hunger in his home."[4] In effect, Jones returned to the ancient concept of "a fair day's wage for a fair day's work," that is, of setting wages according to a certain standard of comfort needed by the individual. This argument jumped backward over the theory of Thomas Malthus and David Ricardo's so-called iron law of wages, which denied the possibility of a minimum standard of life above the subsistence level, to the argument of Adam Smith that wages are to be related to the efficiency of the worker and that the efficient worker is worth such wages as will keep him at a sufficient level of comfort.

Legislative proposals

The initiative for government regulation of wages and conditions in sweated work came in the 1890s from the two women's industrial rights groups, the Women's Trade Union League (WTUL) and the Women's Industrial Council (WIC). Up to this time most reformers cautiously avoided the subject of regulation of sweated work because it was largely outwork, and controlling outwork meant enforcement problems and philosophical problems of invasion of the home by the state. Some reformers even feared that reform might add to the problems of poor working women by legislating away their jobs.

It was a WIC investigation in 1896 under the leadership of Edith Hogg and Margaret Gladstone (who later that year married Ramsay MacDonald) that made homework the major legislative concern of the WIC. Hogg and MacDonald, with a number of working-class women, investigated conditions in homework trades in which women were employed. Hence, shortly after the Royal Commission on Labour had recommended that homework *not* be covered by state legislation, Hogg's account of women homeworkers in fur-pulling work, written in graphic detail and published in the journal *Nineteenth Century,* pointed to the opposite conclusion — the need for state regulation.[5] The women then extended the investigation to include thirty-five home industries in London, an ambitious project that was repeated ten years later.[6] Encouraged by the interest sparked by the homework investigation and Hogg's article, the WIC sponsored a conference on homework in November 1897.[7] The conference gave responsibility for proposing legislative reform to the WIC Legal and Statistical Committee, of which Margaret McDonald was chair.

About this same time MacDonald visited the United States to explore the idea given her by a working-class woman, Amie Hicks, that a system of licensing and inspection of the dwelling places of homeworkers, similar to that used in Massachusetts, was the best way to improve the conditions of British homeworkers.[8] The result of this was MacDonald's bill for Better Regulation of Home Work, which proposed that in order to control conditions of sanitation and overcrowding and to prohibit children under thirteen from taking part in home industries, all homeworkers should be licensed by factory inspectors. The bill was first presented in the House of Commons in July 1899 (by Colonel Denny) and again, to no avail, but with support from, among others, John Burns and Winston Churchill, in every session until 1909.[9] With his election to the Commons in 1906, Ramsay MacDonald became the chief spokesman for the bill and watched closely the administration of the factory and workshop acts, particularly the provisions that applied to homeworkers.[10]

Most important in the movement toward government regulation, however, was women's interest in minimum wage legislation, which went back to the 1880s, when East London tailoresses asked the London County Council for a government enforced minimum wage.[11] The first minimum wage bill, a Wages Board bill, was introduced in the House of Commons in 1898 and in each session for the next decade by Sir Charles Dilke, the Liberal-imperialist.[12] The bill was suggested by the WTUL, of which Dilke's second wife, Emilia Pattison Dilke, was president. The bill proposed that the secretary of state, on the recommendation of employers or workers, appoint a board, consisting of an equal number of workers and employers, to set the minimum rates of wages for certain industries. Although this bill did not get beyond a second reading in the House, it attracted the attention of people interested in sweated labor. Here was a possible solution. Would it work? On this question the proponents of the bill had an advantage because wage boards had existed in the state of Victoria in Australia since 1896, and, apparently, the system had worked well.

The Australian experiment with wage boards was enormously appealing, even though they had existed for only a short time when the WTUL suggested that experiment be tried in Britain. A short time later the Amalgamated Society of Tailors (AST) also called for the creation of trade boards as "the way to abolish homework" and force production into the factories.[13] Many others — trade unionists and labor and liberal politicians — added to this call, finding that the most appealing result of the Australian wage boards was the growth of factory production and a corresponding decline in outworking. Sweating in Australia had disappeared.

The WIC, on the other hand, was divided on the proposal. Clementina Black, its president, led the majority of the members in support of the proposal, and throughout the long campaign for the bill she was one of its most active proponents. Black promoted it in her book, *Sweated Industries,* and in her testimony before the Select Committee on Home Work, she called it "the next step" in the advance of industrial rights for women and children.[14] B. L. Hutchins, editor of the WIC monthly *News* and co-author of *A History of Factory Legislation,* wrote in support of the bill, as did another WIC member, Beatrice Webb.[15] But the WIC never took an official position on the bill, partly because of the MacDonald licensing plan. Margaret MacDonald had gone to Australia to study the wage boards system and returned convinced that wage boards were not a practical solution to the problem of low wages. As a result, she and her husband continued to push for their licensing bill. It appears that the support of Black and other WIC members outweighed the MacDonalds' aid to the opposition, although the MacDonald bill helped to prepare the way for the public interest that culminated in the passage of the Trades Boards Act.

The campaign for government intervention

Meanwhile, the WTUL and the WIC organized an efficient and aggressive public relations campaign for legislative protection for homeworkers through the state wage board system, although the MacDonald licensing plan was still being discussed. Mary Macarthur, the general secretary of the WTUL and an advocate of the wage board plan, persuaded A. G. Gardiner, the editor of the liberal *Daily News,* to sponsor a Sweated Industries Exhibition in London in 1906. Such an exhibition had already been held successfully in Berlin. George Shann became the managing secretary of the London exhibition; the organizer was Richard Mudie-Smith.[16] The WTUL and the WIC,

led by MacDonald and Macarthur, organized the workers and collected the merchandise to be displayed at the exhibition.

The *Daily News*'s Sweated Industries Exhibition was opened by
Princess Henry of Battenburg on 2 June 1906 in Queen's Hall,
Langham Place, in London's West End. It was so successful that it
was extended for two extra weeks. Forty-five trades, representing the
familiar clothing trades as well as lesser known sweated industries like
tennis-ball making, furniture-making, saddlery, hosiery-making, and
cigarette-making, were depicted; workers were present to perform their
tasks. The faces and workrooms of society's least fortunate were
brought to the front steps of the Edwardian upper classes. "It was a
new thing to realize," claimed the *Women's Trade Union Review*, "how
deeply the canker of sweating had eaten into the national life." The
exhibition "illustrated with equal force the dictum that home work
is the main cause of sweating."[17] The first series of lectures at the exhibition was given by Gertrude Tuckwell, who spoke on the hours and
wages of women; she was followed by Macarthur, who spoke on "trade
unionism for women." Keir Hardie and the bishop of Hereford also
gave presentations.

"What can we do? What can we do?" asked the princess of Wales,
as she passed through the exhibition.[18] Others asked the same question. Members of the House of Commons told of the profound impression that the exhibition had on them and asked the government
to extend protection to outworkers. MacDonald hoped that the exhibition would help push her proposal of licensing home workshops.
And, it appears, that the exhibition did influence some manufacturers
to abolish outworking; as one observer noted, a sweated industries
exhibition in a town "instantly means that two or three manufacturers
stop giving out work."[19]

The immediate outcome of the exhibition was the formation of the
National Anti-Sweating League, an upper-middle-class organization
that did much of the promotion for the Trade Boards Act of 1909.
The moving force behind the league was Tuckwell. With Gardiner
as chairman of its executive committee, and George Cadbury, the
chocolate manufacturer and major stockholder of the *Daily News,* as
its president, Tuckwell led the league into a five-year program of
meetings, lectures, and additional exhibitions, two of which were held
in 1908. League branches were established in Liverpool, Manchester,
Oxford, Leicester, and Bristol. The league attracted the support of

some of Britain's best-known literary and political figures, and it became a fashionable organization: not infrequently the league reported
that its speakers lectured to audiences "that expressed the very out-
flow of wealth and quintessence of fashion."[20] It established its headquarters at 34 Mecklenburg Square (the headquarters of the WTUL)
and by 1909 claimed 1,050 members and a list of sixteen publica-
tions on sweating.[21]

The first activity of the Anti-Sweating League was to organize a
Conference on a Minimum Wage. Hundreds of people, mainly
workers and women, came together to call for a new kind of guarantee from the state. This Guildhall conference was opened on 24 Octo-
ber 1906 by the lord mayor of London and chaired by Sir Charles
Dilke. One day was devoted to lectures and discussions on the anti-
sweating legislation in Australia and New Zealand, where, it was
noted, state intervention in the form of wage boards and industrial
arbitration had proven effective in eliminating unfair working conditions. The conference also heard Sidney Webb argue that a minimum
wage was nothing more than intelligent economics and that its ultimate effect would be to improve the organization of industry and increase the efficiency of labor. Webb claimed that sweated industries
were parasitic because their workers could survive only by turning
to private or public aid. Sweated industries, in short, were subsidized
by charity. Tuckwell spoke on the problems of wages in the non-
unionized industries, arguing that competition was disastrous not only
for the sweated worker but also a constant threat to the organized
and skilled worker as well. Black placed the case of child labor before
the conference, pointing out that a minimum wage law was impera-
tive to alleviate the sweating of children. "Even if there were no other
reason in favor of a minimum wage," she claimed, "it would help
release children" from the toil of sweated labor. Her argument was
that the minimum wage, by raising the wages of adult workers, would
eliminate the dependency of many workers on the wages of their
children and would disincline employers to use child labor because
it would cease to be cheap.[22]

The unorthodox economist, J. A. Hobson, argued against the complaint that a minimum wage would result in increased production
costs and a loss of jobs, particularly for women. He claimed that wage
increases would not result in fewer jobs because higher wages were
more economical: among the formerly weak and "dispirited" sweated

workers, industrial efficiency would increase at a greater rate than wages. Besides, he said, even if wages rose faster than production, the difference could be made up from "surplus profits" and from greater economy resulting from technological and entrepreneurial improvements.[23]

The conference ended on a curious note. A number of delegates threw the meeting into a last moment frenzy by insisting that the conference's minimum wage resolution include an amendment advocating "the complete suppression of 'outwork.' " These delegates argued that outworking was the crux of the problem of sweating and that as long as it continued to exist there would be sweating. In fact, some feared that outworkers would sabotage the minimum wage proposal because enforcement and inspection could never be made to apply to the outworker. In the opinion of one tailor, "a move in the direction of a minimum wage was the compulsory workshop." However, the leader of the conference refused to accept the amendments and had it not been for the judicious intervention of Macarthur, the conference might well have ended in disaster. Macarthur convinced the dissident members that the conference was arranged to deal with only one phase of the problem, that of wages, and she appealed to them to pass the resolution, which they did. Then, taking cognizance of the strong belief among the delegates that outwork could not be divorced from the issue of the minimum wage, the conference went on to call for the abolition of outwork in all industries.[24] Nevertheless, the conference emphasis on a minimum wage set the tone for the war on sweating for the next decade. As in Australia, outworking would disappear, the proponents of the minimum wage declared, as soon as the wage boards went into effect. As two of the participants of the conference wrote the following year, the best remedy for the sweated trades was a national minimum wage.[25]

The Sweated Industries Exhibition and the Guildhall conference led to a major government investigation. On the eve of the exhibition, Member of Parliament James O'Grady proposed that the government appoint a royal commission to investigate the trades covered by the exhibition.[26] The London Trades Council, noting the revived interest in sweating and homework that resulted from the exhibition, also called for a national investigation of homework.[27] Parliamentary members MacDonald and Hardie introduced separate bills for the regulation of homework, and the Dilke wage board bill was reintroduced by Ernest Lamb. A new wage board bill — called the Sweated Industries bill — was reworked by the Guildhall conference and the WTUL and was introduced by the chairman of the Parliamentary Labour party, Arthur Henderson. The first response of the Liberal government was to avoid the subject, and it was months before the government took action. In June 1907 it set up a select committee of twenty-one members to investigate the conditions of labor in home-work industries and to consider proposals to license outworkers and establish wage boards. Included on the committee were a number of members of the Anti-Sweating League: Lamb, Henderson, Leo Chiozza Money, a liberal and Fabian, and Charles Trevelyan, the wealthy liberal who would eventually join the Labour party.[28]

The Select Committee on Home Work, as it was called, interviewed nineteen persons in 1907 and thirty-five persons in 1908. Although women were not allowed to sit on the committee,[29] more than half of the witnesses were women, and one, Macarthur, gave detailed testimony before both sessions of the committee. From the beginning the cutting edge of the investigation was clear: homework was the most widespread form of sweating. The question was how to eliminate sweating: by abolishing outwork through minimum wage boards or by regulating it through licensing and inspection? The witnesses were, for the most part, in favor of the minimum wage plan. Through a national minimum wage outwork would no longer be profitable, and the employer would seek his profits in the workshop and factory. Most of the witnesses, including employers, welcomed a movement of production from home to workshop.[30] But this predicted shift caused some consternation as to what would happen to the inefficient immobile homeworker who was unable to take up factory or workshop labor. What about poor wives and widows who could get no other work? A member of the National Home Workers' League, an organization formed to lobby against the wage board plan, protested that "every interference with homeworkers causes manufacturers to build factories, so that they will not have the bother of home-work any longer." A sanitary inspector told the committee that suppression of homework would be cruel because of the unemployment it would produce. But when the committee questioned these skeptics, most of them conceded that a wage board would mean improvement for the worker. Other homeworkers, brought before the committee by Macarthur, decried the absence of equal wage for equal work and welcomed a system that would force their employers to "time an article, state how long the article would take to make and give . . . a certain wage of so much an hour."[31]

It was largely the concern of whether homeworkers could continue to earn for their families that led MacDonald to oppose the wage board plan. She had a close and affectionate friendship with many working women and believed that wage boards would make it difficult for the homeworker to work in a shrinking industry and thus "she will have every inducement to evade the law which is passed in order to help her." She wrote to Black that she and her husband were certain that wage boards would "be harmful and a setback to reform." "One cannot have it both ways," she claimed; the wage boards cannot increase factory work and protect the homeworker at the same time. What was going to happen, she predicted, was that the homeworker would come to "regard the law as an enemy."[32] Part of her opposition was based on personal observation of the Australian experiment, which proponents of the plan claimed had eliminated sweating. "The English-woman fighting for money to buy bread for her children will be as clever as the boot or furniture maker of Victoria [Australia] in evading the law which to her will symbolize the loss of her trade." Besides, she argued, the minimum would become the standard wage, and thus lower many workers' incomes to the lowest level; and, she added, the minimum wage would be impossible to enforce.[33]

MacDonald's opposition grew from her fear that the wage board would palliate and not remedy the problem of women's work; it would put the public to sleep and cause it to "turn away in despair from legislative proposals which might be more practicable, and we shall be further back instead of further forward on the path to reform."[34] To the MacDonalds, what was needed was the reorganization of industry on a collective basis. "We are diverting our energies," she claimed, "from the direct fight for socialism in order to advocate a palliative which . . . would be not only ineffective, but in some cases possibly harmful." Child labor should be abolished through stronger education acts, she claimed, and many of the present homeworkers—old people, the sick, widows, and mothers—should not be working at all but finding relief through state-funded old age pensions, insurance, and the like.[35]

The MacDonalds had their own plan. Their bill for the Better Regulation of Home Work required that in order to get work the outworker must show a license, which would prove that certain sanitary conditions were adhered to in the home. This licensing plan was not consistent with their previous stands on factory and workshop legislation. No one was more aware of the ineffectiveness of the existing state inspection system than they were; year after year Ramsay MacDonald called the attention of the government to the inadequacy of such inspection. Yet they advocated a system of licensing of home workshops that would require a large and efficient inspection system, a plan, the MacDonalds' opponents charged, that put the onus on the worker and that would benefit only the consumer. As it was, many outworkers were already paying, in the form of work-related expenses, for the improved sanitary conditions requested by law.[36]

The issue of wage boards isolated the MacDonalds, temporarily at least, from the women's labor movement. A minority in the WIC, led by MacDonald, opposed the bill. Neither Ramsay nor Margaret MacDonald participated in the Guildhall conference and the disagreement between Margaret MacDonald and Black over the position of the WIC caused the MacDonalds to resign from that organization in 1909.

However, the wage board plan was supported by nearly everybody else. The Select Committee on Home Work recommended that it be applied to women homeworkers only in its second report, as did the Fair Wages Committee of the House of Commons. The regulation of wages, the homework committee claimed, went "to the root of the matter of sweated homeworking: Your committee are of the opinion that it is quite as legitimate to establish by legislation a *minimum standard of remuneration* as it is to establish such a standard of sanitation, cleanliness, ventilation, air, space and hours of work."[37]

The trade boards act of 1909

In December 1908 a WTUL delegation met with Prime Minister Herbert H. Asquith to ask him to bring forth a government-sponsored wage boards bill. The meeting, which had been arranged by Sir Charles Dilke and the archbishop of Canterbury, ended with Asquith's promise to introduce the bill.[38] In his opening the 1909 session of Parliament, King Edward VII announced that "a bill will be introduced for the constitution of Trade Boards in certain branches of industry in which the evils known as 'sweating' prevail." This bill—

the Trade Boards bill it was called—was introduced in the Commons in March 1909 by Winston Churchill, president of the Board of Trade. Churchill had convinced Asquith to let him "play" with the proposal. But the bill Churchill first presented to the House was unsatisfactory to the WTUL, so he amended it according to the old WTUL-Dilke proposal, which had, in fact, been reworked by Henderson to conform to the Anti-Sweating League–Guildhall conference recommendations (namely, that the boards be set up for wholesale tailoring, lace-making, cardboard box-making, and chain-making).[39] The bill was debated twice, first on 28 April 1909 after its second reading and on 16 July at its third reading. The debate on the bill was remarkable for the absence of party spirit and party politics. Opposition was slight and centered on a fear that the bill would damage the country's ability to compete with cheap (that is, sweated) goods produced abroad. For this reason a protectionist amendment, which would prohibit the importation of sweated foreign goods, was proposed to be attached to the bill. However, the amendment was withdrawn after Churchill convinced the proponents that such an amendment was unnecessary as other countries, particularly Germany and Austria, were taking similar measures to curtail sweating. The bill passed in the House on 16 July 1909.[40]

Can it be said, then, that this first minimum wage act was largely an invention of the Liberal government? How much was the victory a product of Churchill's hand or a product of the so-called administrative revolution carried out by reform-minded civil servants? No doubt Churchill "showed more courage" in support of the bill than did Herbert Gladstone, the home secretary at the time, and this "determined attack," as Churchill's son wrote, "proved a notable first attempt to introduce the idea of a National Minimum into British labour legislation."[41] However, the suggestion that Churchill was the leader of this attack on sweating is an exaggeration. His original scheme for a bill covering one-third of the employed most likely would have been thrown out by his own party, and it was Henderson, then chairman of the Parliamentary Labour party, who convinced Churchill to adopt the Anti-Sweating League bill. No doubt Churchill saw this as an experiment worth trying—like the Beveridge labor exchange idea he was to embrace later that year.

Neither is there evidence to suggest that the plan was the brain-child of civil servants. George Askwith, who was the labor conciliator for the labor department, wrote and spoke in favor of the wage board plan and was perhaps the most persuasive witness to come before the Select Committee on Home Work. The initiative, however, did not lie with Askwith or with any government department. Although Askwith probably encouraged Churchill to sponsor the plan, the plan did not evolve from Askwith's work at Churchill's Board of Trade.[42] Indeed, until Gladstone refused the select committee's recommendation that his Home Office establish wage boards, most observers thought the boards would be set up under him and not Churchill. But Gladstone was not enthusiastic about the plan. In the case of wage boards, it appears that the government and civil service waited on events.

A current assessment that the act received little support from labor is misleading.[43] It is difficult to imagine the act passing over the objections of labor. Indeed, some labor voices chided unionists, particularly the better-off skilled male workers, for their lack of interest in the plan,[44] and, while it is true that the Trades Union Congress and the Labour Representation Committee were never overly enthusiastic about it, the Parliamentary Labour party, particularly George Barnes and Henderson, played an important role in promoting the bill. "It is impossible," claimed the WTUL, "not to pay a tribute of gratitude to Mr. Henderson and the Labour Party for the constant care and attention by which the Bill has been carried to a successful issue."[45] Other sectors of the labor movement campaigned for the principle of a state-enforced minimum wage, although the claim that the plan was the result of "pressure of new ideas from below" is an exaggeration.[46] The London Trades Council, frequently the champion of the unskilled worker, supported the bill and in 1906 asked the Parliamentary committee of the Trades Union Congress to push harder for a minimum wage. In the spring following the Guildhall conference, the London Trades Council resolved "that in view of the well-known alarming extent and gravity of sweating, this Council calls upon the Government to at once introduce a Bill creating wages boards, for the establishment of a minimum wage to the sweated workers."[47] West End tailoresses, initially reluctant to support a minimum wage because they feared it would be to the advantage of only skilled workers, were convinced by Mary Elvery, their secretary, to support the plan.[48] Government clothing workers also joined the campaign. The only way to remedy the unfair system of wages in the London clothing trades, claimed the secretary of the Amalgamated Society of Government Workers, was through the establishment of wage boards that would set a fixed wage for all work.[49]

Similarly, the organizing secretary of the AST advocated wage boards as the only effective means to control the clothing industry.[50] While the Jewish Board of Deputies opposed the wage boards bill, Jewish workers favored it and were angry when the board claimed to speak on their behalf in opposition to the bill. In the spring of 1908 the Jewish tailors of East End held "a great demonstration" in support of the wage boards proposals; they were addressed by Ben Cooper of the London County Council and by members of the House of Commons, Pete Curran and G. Toulmin. Toulmin told the workers that "since Tom Hood wrote the 'song of the shirt,' they had been and still were inquiring; but now it was time they tried the [wages boards] experiment."[51] The boot- and shoemakers, through T. F. Richards, also favored the plan. Speaking to a meeting of fellow workers, Richards expressed his hope that the boot and shoe trade would come under the new wage boards system and that the system would "check" homeworking.[52]

Finally, of greatest importance in the passage of the act was the women's industrial rights movement, particularly the ten years of work by the WTUL and the WIC. Women of all classes had come together to investigate the problems of industrial outwork and to propose reform. While working-class women took part in organizing and investigating, middle- and upper-class women set up the forums — the sweating exhibition, the Anti-Sweating League, and the Guildhall conference — from which the plan was passed to the public and then to the chambers of government. Crucial in this process was the contact that the WTUL and the WIC had in high places. Both organizations had members whose husbands sat in Parliament and were members of the government. As a result, there was a flow of influence from these women on the periphery of power to its center. The WTUL Dilke-Tuckwell group illustrates this relationship. Emilia Dilke, the president of the WTUL, was the wife of Sir Charles Dilke, who introduced the WTUL's minimum wage proposal in the House of Commons. Her niece, Gertrude Tuckwell, who succeeded her at the WTUL in 1905, organized the Anti-Sweating League; her one-time secretary and WTUL union organizer, May Tennant, was married to H. J. Tennant, the Member of Parliament who guided the Trades

Boards bill through debate in the House. May Tennant pressured her brother-in-law, Prime Minister Asquith, to introduce the bill as a government measure. Equally important was Margaret Macarthur, the former shop assistant whom Dilke brought into the WTUL as general secretary in 1903. Macarthur was the inspiration for the sweating exhibition of 1906, and it was she who campaigned hardest for the bill and kept the issue of sweated labor alive in the press.[53]

There were other parliamentary friends of the WTUL and the Anti-Sweating League. Lord Dunraven had chaired the House of Lords' sweating committee twenty years earlier, and the influence of Barnes and Henderson has already been noted. Still other friends were members of the WIC: R. B. Haldane, G. P. Gooch, Sydney Buxton, and Leo Chiozza Money. Buxton and Haldane were members of Asquith's cabinet. The husbands of Margaret MacDonald and Mary Macarthur were Labour members of Parliament. Finally, the WTUL and the WIC claimed as members several influential men and women: Mrs. George Bernard Shaw, Mrs. Herbert Samuel, Mrs. J. L. Hammond, R. H. Tawney, Herbert Burrows, Mr. and Mrs. George Cadbury, the countess of Aberdeen (one time president of the WIC), and Beatrice Webb.

The trade boards act and the London sweated trades

The Trade Boards Act of 1909 established wage boards to fix a minimum hourly wage for the approximately 250,000 workers in paper box-making, chain-making, machine lace-finishing, and ready-made and wholesale bespoke tailoring. Because of its regional variations and numerous subdivisions, the tailoring trade was the most difficult of the four trades for which to establish and administer guidelines. Untouched by the act were retail bespoke tailoring, ladies' tailoring, shirtmaking, dressmaking, and mantlemaking. Although the Tailoring Board was organized in 1910, it was not until August 1912 that the thirty-one members of the board, representing workers, employers, and the public, were able to agree on exactly what subdivisions of tailoring were covered by the act and then the hourly wage rate.[54]

The first minimum wage, set by the Tailoring Board in 1912 and made obligatory in 1913, was substantially above the existing wages of many workers in that trade. The board set a minimum hourly rate

Table 16. Effect of the Trade Board Act of 1909 on Women's Weekly
Wages in the Tailoring Trade as of 1913

Pre-1913 Wage	Percentage of Work Force Receiving the Wage	Increase Necessary to Reach 1913 Minimum
under 5s.	0.2	8s. 6½d.
5s. and under 6s.	1.6	8s. 6½d. to 7s. 6½d.
6s and under 7s.	3.4	7s. 6½d. to 6s. 6½d.
7s. and under 8s.	4.8	6s. 6½d. to 5s. 6½d.
8s. and under 9s.	6.0	5s. 6½d. to 4s. 6½d:
9s. and under 10s.	7.9	4s. 6½d. to 3s. 6½d.
10s. and under 11s.	10.0	3s. 6½d. to 2s. 6½d.
11s. and under 12s.	10.5	2s. 6½d. to 1s. 6½d.
12s. and under 13s.	10.0	1s. 6½d. to 6½d.

Source. Calculated from R. H. Tawney, *Studies in the Minimum Wage, No. 2 — Tailoring* (London, 1915), 77–78.

of 6d. for men and 3¼d. for women. Since this was based on a
standard work week of fifty hours, the minimum weekly wage came
to 25s. for men and 13s. 6½d. for "ordinary" women. The board
allowed any employer to exempt up to 20 percent of his female labor
force from the minimum wage, on the grounds that women were
physically incapable of performing average work. This allowance for
"subordinary" workers enabled employers to retain less productive older
or otherwise handicapped workers and left the possibility that 20 percent of the women workers would automatically fall under the minimum.[55]

Table 16 shows how far below the 1913 minimum the various groups
of women were in 1906 and how much of a weekly wage increase
was needed to bring them up to that minimum. In comparing the
new minimum of 1913 to the earnings reported by the 1906 wage
census (Table 17) — which showed that 24.4 and 58 percent, respectively, of male and female workers received less than the 1913 minimum — we see that about a quarter of the men and, allowing for the
20 percent of subordinary workers, about a third of the women were
brought up to the minimum as a result of the Trade Boards Act of
1909, that is, if the new rates were universally adopted.

R. H. Tawney's investigation of the wages of tailoring workers
during the first fifteen months of the Tailoring Board's operation
showed that, indeed, the act did bring nearly all of the men and all
but about 20 percent of the women workers up to the new 1913 mini-

Table 17. Effect of the Trade Board Act of 1909 on Weekly Wages
in the Tailoring Trade as of 1913

Workers	Minimum Weekly Wage, 1913	Below Minimum, 1906 (%)	Below Minimum 1913 (%)
Men	25s.	24.4	0
Women	13½s.	58	20

Note. These statistics do not include homeworkers. The 20 percent of the female work force below the minimum was that portion that the Board of Trade deemed as "subordinary" and therefore not entitled to the new minimum.

Source. Calculated from R. H. Tawney, *Studies in the Minimum Wage, No. 2 — Tailoring* (London, 1915), 71–77, 82–85.

mum. Employers raised hour and piecework rates so that their workers could make the legal hourly minimum. In addition, some workers already above the minimum in 1913 benefited because employers tended to adjust the hourly rate of all workers upward after fixing the new minimum. The average increase for the lowest worker (excluding the 20 percent of subordinaries) was about 42 percent, but it is not clear if all workers enjoyed this much of an increase. In London, for instance, twenty-one of twenty-five firms had raised wages. The new minimum, however, was fixed so low that it had little effect on the already higher paid women workers in the north and was therefore beneficial mainly to women of the southeast and southwest and men in the midlands (including the low-paying centers of Bristol and Norwich).[56] As Margaret MacDonald predicted, some evasion took place. Tawney found that one out of three indoor employers visited by Trade Board investigators were required by inspectors to pay arrears to some of their workers.[57]

Other investigators also found evidence of evasion. B. L. Hutchins observed that evasion increased after the war broke out in 1914.[58] The WTUL reported, at about the same time, that certain London clothing factories were paying less than the minimum wage to a considerable number of its workers.[59] Dorothy Sells found that evasion of the minimum wage was still common as late as 1937.[60] In summation, Tawney concluded that although a large increase in wages had taken place among the poorly paid workers, the wages of women workers in tailoring were "still so low . . . that no marked or general influence upon the workers' standard of life can be expected to result from them."[61]

Note, too, that these improvements (however slight) pertained only to indoor, that is, non-homework, workers. For homeworkers the new board minimum was less beneficial. Since probably more than 58 percent of all homeworkers were below the 13s. 6½d. minimum in 1906 (homeworkers were *not* included in the 1906 wage census), it is conceivable that a larger proportion of homeworkers were thereby brought up to the minimum as a result of the act. But Tawney and his assistant, Miss de Vessilitsky, found that over half (54.4 percent) of women homeworkers were below the new minimum a year after it went into effect, which suggests that either more homeworkers were below the minimum to begin with, or that the minimum was not adopted on any widespread basis, or both. In the East End only 24 percent of those surveyed reported an increase in wages as a result of the Trade Boards minimum.[62]

A more favorable picture is drawn from a comparison of how well the Trade Board workers did as a whole compared to workers in other industries over a longer span of time. For the first two years of the war (1914–16) the Trade Board probably prevented the kind of rapid wage declines that occurred in other industries.[63] Then from about 1916 through 1919 rates rose sharply but lagged behind increases in other industries and the upward movement of prices. In the immediate postwar period of 1919–21 the Trade Board rates outstepped the cost of living and rose more rapidly than did wages in other trades and then fell less in 1921–23 when wages for most workers declined. Thus the Trade Boards were important in protecting and raising wages in the years immediately before, during, and right after World War I and then prevented the rates from falling as fast as did ordinary wages in the period of general decline up to the mid-1920s.[64] Overall, it is probable that the Trade Boards contributed to the more rapid increase in the wages of unskilled labor as compared to the wages of skilled labor that occurred after 1910. By 1928 skilled wages were up 133 percent over 1890, while those of the unskilled were up 180 percent.[65]

The establishment, by law, of higher wages in tailoring resulted in increased worker productivity and better employer organization and management of production, all of which offset the increased wages and proved that, indeed, sweated wages were not economically necessary. The fear expressed by employers that the Trade Boards Act would destroy their competitive position with foreign production was also unrealized. For one reason, since most tailoring work, even in the factories, was based on piecework wages, women worked harder when the prospect of a higher wage existed. Said one manufacturer, "The output has increased owing to the increased earning power of the lower grade worker." "The girls do 33 percent more work than before," said another.[66] Part of this work speedup, however, was not voluntary. As the law had now made employers responsible for the weekly earnings of the worker, it encouraged them to demand greater output. Tawney found that many firms, with only a minor increase in piecework rates or managerial efficiency, informed their workers—indoor and outdoor—that they had to earn no less than the minimum of 3¼ d. per hour. "Some women have spoken to us very bitterly of the manner in which they are harassed and intimidated" into speeding up production.[67] More typical, however, was the employer who combined improved worker efficiency with better management and organization to enable the worker to achieve the new minimum without sacrificing his profits. J. A. Hobson's prediction that higher wages would result in technological and entrepreneurial improvements was accurate. The technical backwardness of the clothing trades was reversed. Treadle machines were replaced with machinery driven by electricity, employees were more carefully trained (or trained for the first time), and attention was given to the efficiencies of production that had been worked out earlier in the Jewish workshops.[68]

The higher wages, the improved organization of the workshop, and the more efficient factory production placed the outworker at a disadvantage. The prediction, by Mary Macarthur, the tailors' unions, and others, that the Trade Boards would result in work being moved out of the home and sweatshop and into the factory was correct, although Margaret MacDonald's prediction that a legal minimum would place a premium on homework and thus encourage its growth cannot be substantiated.[69] De Vesselitsky and Sells found that homework in tailoring—and eventually shirtmaking and mantlemaking as these trades were brought under the act—declined somewhat more slowly than in other trades, but there was an overall shift of work into the factory. Only in custom tailoring did homework remain stationary.[70] Many employers found homework burdensome because it was difficult to fix minimum piece rates for homeworkers; as a result they tended to fix outwork rates higher than they might have in order to avoid confrontation with the inspectors. Older women and weaker workers were weeded out first, and less work was given to those outworkers who remained; few new outworkers were taken on.[71] With the exception of the boot and shoe trade, which was not covered by the Trade Boards, the Trade Boards "accomplished what was originally expected of them" — the elimination of sweated homework.[72]

Workers in the sweated clothing trades reaped two additional benefits from the Trade Boards Act. First, because wage rates were set at a level so that the worker could make a specified wage based on a fifty-hour work week (which was reduced to forty-eight hours during the war), the standard work week fell considerably below the fifty-eight to sixty hours that had been customary at the time the act was passed.[73] Second, the Trade Boards Act stimulated trade unionism in those trades in which union organization had been found to be difficult or impossible. The operation of the board meant that some sort of worker organization was needed to enable the workers to elect representatives to the board. By establishing, in effect, mandatory worker-employer arbitration of wages, the Trade Boards pointed to the advantages of a united labor front. Hence, clothing unions — particularly the small Jewish unions — were stimulated toward amalgamation, and many clothing workers joined a union for the first time. Membership in unions grew dramatically. The National Federation of Women Workers, and its parent organization, the WTUL, were able to claim that it represented a considerably larger number of women workers than before the passage of the 1909 act. In some instances a strengthened union was able to gain wage increases above the minimum rate. The Trade Boards Act of 1909 was the first notable blow against the sweating system in a long and arduous half-century battle.[74]

NOTES

1. A fixed minimum wage — subsidized from the poor rates — was the idea behind the famous Speenhamland Act of 1795.

2. Sidney and Beatrice Webb, *History of Trade Unionism* (London, 1911), 323–37; E. J. Hobsbawm, "Custom, Wages, and Work-Load in Nineteenth-Century Industry," in John Saville and Asa Briggs, *Essays in Labour History* (New York, 1967), ch. 3.

3. For example, the London Women's Machinist Society passed a resolution in 1876 calling for "a fair day's wages" and "a fair day's work." *Women's Union Journal*, Mar. 1876.

4. *The Beehive*, 18 July 1874, 1. Jones was a Manchester artisan and co-

author (with J. M. Ludlow) of *The Progress of the Working-Class, 1832–1867* (1867; reprint ed., New York, 1973).

5. Edith Hogg, "The Fur-pullers of South London," *Nineteenth Century,* Nov. 1897, 734–53.

6. Women's Industrial Council, *Home Industries of Women in London* (London, 1897), and *Home Industries of Women in London* (London, 1908).

7. *Women's Industrial News,* Dec. 1897, 7–8.

8. P.P., "Select Committee on Home Work," First Report, 1907, vol. vi, Q4302.

9. *Women's Industrial News,* June 1899, 112; Dec. 1901, 272; Great Britain, Parliament, *Parliamentary Debates* (Commons), 1901, 4th ser., 91: 1387. The *Daily Chronicle* supported the bill, as did the periodical *Echo.* See *Women's Industrial News,* Sept. 1901, 255; Dec. 1901, 273–74.

10. At the same time the WIC worked for changes in the existing factory and workshop acts. For example, two of its suggested amendments, set out in a memorandum to Home Secretary C. T. Ritchie in 1901, were incorporated in the 1901 Factory and Workshop Act. But the women were less than satisfied with the new law and continued to push for a variety of reforms. *Women's Industrial News,* June 1901, 241–42.

11. *Women's Union Journal,* 15 July 1890, 55.

12. WTUL, *Annual Report of 1899,* 11.

13. AST, *Journal,* Nov. 1899.

14. *Women's Industrial News,* June 1908, 35.

15. Hutchins's support can be found in *Women's Industrial News,* June 1908, 31–32. Sidney and Beatrice Webb (*Industrial Democracy* [London, 1897]) argued that the principle of a minimum wage was sound and practical.

16. Shann, with Edward Cadbury and M. C. Matheson, advocated a national minimum wage in their book, *Women's Work and Wages* (Chicago, 1907). Mudie-Smith had organized a successful sweated industries exhibition at the Bishopsgate Institute, in the East End, earlier that same year (in January or February). Still earlier, in 1904, the Reverend J. E. Watts-Ditchfield, vicar of Saint James the Less, Bethnal Green, organized a sweating exhibition to attract attention to sweating in Bethnal Green. It was held for two days in a hall attached to the church but attracted little attention (Richard Mudie-Smith, *Sweated Industries, Being a Handbook of the Daily News Exhibition* [London, 1906]). I am indebted to David Webb, librarian of the Bishopsgate Institute, for this information.

17. *Women's Trade Union Review,* July 1907, 7–8. See also "Select Committee on Home Work," Second Report, 1908, vol. viii, Q 554.

18. Quoted in Clementina Black, *Sweated Industries and the Minimum Wage* (London, 1907), xvi.

19. P.P., "Select Committee on Home Work," Second Report, 1908, vol. viii, Q 2729.

20. Anti-Sweating League Papers, item 224, Gertrude Tuckwell Collection, Trades Union Congress Library, London.

21. Approximately one-third of the league's members were unmarried women. James Mallon was its secretary; the other officers were: Vice-presidents — Clementina Black, Bishop Boyd Carpenter, the earl of Dunraven, the Viscount Gladstone, the Viscountess Gladstone, Keir Hardie, M. P., Lord Haversham, Canon Scott Holland, Dr. Horton, Miss Irwin (Scottish Council for Women's Trades), the earl of Lytton, the Reverend J. Scott Lidgett, William Maxwell (Scottish Wholesale Society), Honourable W. P. Reeves, Mr. and Mrs. S. Webb, H. G. Wells, and Henry Vivian. On the executive committee were George Barnes, M. P., Lord Bentinck, M. P., Herbert Burrows, the bishop of Birmingham, Mrs. M. A. Gasson, T. E. Harvey, M. P., Arthur Henderson, M. P., J. W. Hills, M. P., Mary Macarthur, L. C. Meney, M. P., Mrs. W. P. Reeves, George Shann, Mrs. George Bernard Shaw, Mrs. H. J. Tennant, Gertrude Tuckwell, F. A. G. Ware, the Reverend Watts-Ditchfield. Other members included Mrs. H. Ward, G. K. Chesterton, R. C. K. Ensor, and Charles Trevelyan.

22. *Women's Trade Union Review,* Jan. 1907, 14. That outworkers were dependent on poor law charity was often claimed but never proven. National Anti-Sweating League, *Report of Conference on a Minimum Wage* (London, 1907), 35–36. The report includes all of the speeches and debates.

23. The delegates to the conference also heard speeches by G. R. Askwith, arbitrator for the Board of Trade, who spoke on the general failure of the trade unions to establish minimum wage through arbitration; Leo Chiozza Money, who spoke on underpayment of wages and capitalist profits; and the Honourable Bernard Wise, who addressed the delegates on the failure of industrial arbitration as a remedy for sweating.

24. Ibid., 19, 47, 18, 88. The outwork amendments were proposed by Harry Quelch of the Social Democratic Federation and Pete Curran of the Labour party and the General Federation of Trade Unions. It was feared that outwork would increase as employers would seek to escape the new law. On the other hand, not all workers were convinced that the conference could succeed in its goals: see, for example, the comments of the tailors' correspondent for the *Trades and Labour Gazette,* Nov. 1906, 12.

25. Cadbury et al., *Women's Work and Wages* (Chicago, 1907), 252.

26. Great Britain, Parliament, *Parliamentary Debates,* 1906, 4th ser., 153: 561; 157: 356–57; 159.

27. London Trades Council, *Minutes and Records, Delegates Meeting,* 4 Aug. 1906.

28. The government set up a "committee" rather than a "commission." A committee is made up of members of the House and, unlike a commission, cannot include outside members.

29. This angered many women, particularly the members of the WIC. See *Women's Industrial News,* Sept. 1907, 649–50.

30. P.P., "Select Committee on Home Work," First Report, 1907, vol. vi, Miss Squire, Qs935–39; G. R. Askwith, Q 3962; Coddard, Qs1573–82; Howarth, Qs422, 451; Miss Macarthur, Qs2727; Evans, Qs3700–04; P.P., "Select Committee on Home Work," Second Report, 1908, vol. viii, Shann, Qs632, 642. The earlier Dilke proposal was, however, opposed by the Master Tailors (employers) Federation (*Master Tailor,* May 1900, 118–19). They claimed that the bill was a union attempt to oust all but trade union members from the trade.

31. P.P., "Select Committee on Home Work," 1908, vol. viii, Lawson, Q3075, "Miss B," Q2146; P.P., "Select Committee on Home Work," First Report, 1907, vol. vi, Staford, Q3119, also Qs3015–48.

32. Margaret MacDonald to the editor of the *Morning Post,* 11 Feb. 1909, item 26, to Clementina Black, 27 Nov. 1908, item 24, and draft of a speech ("Sweated Industries and Wages Boards"), item 31, all in the MacDonald Collection, London School of Economics and Political Science, London.

33. Women's Industrial Council, *The Case for and against a Legal Minimum Wage* (London, 1909), 15.

34. Ibid., 11. See also *Women's Industrial News,* Sept. 1907, 665.

35. *Labour Leader,* 17 May 1907, and Women's Industrial Council, *Case for and against a Minimum Wage,* 23–24.

36. P.P., "Select Committee on Home Work," First Report, 1907, vol. viii, Qs2219, 2846. For Macarthur's reply to Margaret MacDonald, see *Labour Leader,* 14, 21, 28 June 1908—"Socialism and the Sweater."

37. Emphasis added. P.P., "Select Committee on Home Work," First Report, 1907, vol. viii, pp. xiv, xvii.

38. National Anti-Sweating League Papers, item 224, Gertrude Tuckwell Collection.

39. Ibid., and *Women's Union Review,* July 1909, 1–2.

40. In the debate on the Sweated Industries bill in 1908, Mr. Goulding (Worcester) regarded the minimum wage proposal as acceptable because it "involved the protection of British labour, and he supported it as the forerunner of measures to protect British industry from the competition of sweated alien produce coming from abroad," and "a great step towards tariff reform." Great Britain, Parliament, *Parliamentary Debates* (Commons), 1908, 4th ser., 184: 1228–30.

41. Randolph Churchill, *Winston S. Churchill,* vol. 2: *Young Statesman, 1901–1914* (Boston, 1967), 288–90. See also Margaret Stewart and Leslie

Hunter, *The Needle Is Threaded: The History of an Industry* (London, 1964), 140–43, and *Women's Trade Union Review,* Apr. 1908, 12.

42. The *Women's Industrial News* (June 1908) reported that on 8 April Mr. Askwith, K. C., gave a most interesting lecture at the house of Mrs. Tennant, describing the working of the Arbitration Boards in fixing minimum rates and discussing the ordinary objections made against regulating wages in sweated industries. Askwith writes of his role in the minimum wage campaign in ch. 28 of his book *Industrial Problems and Disputes* (1920; reprint ed., London, 1974).

43. H. A. Clegg, Alan Fox, and A. F. Thompson, in their study of trade unionism since 1889, note that most of the pressure for the Trade Boards "came from Dilke and his friends, although MacDonald and his wife . . . also took their share in the campaign. The Parliamentary Committee was well disposed but played little part in inducing the government." As shown earlier, the authors are clearly mistaken with regard to the MacDonalds. Dilke's "friends," of course, were the women unionists. *A History of British Trade Unions since 1889,* 1 (Oxford, 1964), 403. See also Henry Pelling, *A History of British Trade Unionism,* 3d ed. (London, 1976), 129–30.

44. See, for example, the *Trades and Labour Gazette* editorial (by A. P. Hazell) of Feb. 1908 (8).

45. WTUL, *Annual Report of 1909,* 12.

46. *Trades and Labour Gazette,* May 1909, 8.

47. London Trades Council, *Minutes and Records, Delegates Meeting,* 12 July 1906; *Delegates Meeting,* 14 Mar. 1907.

48. *Trades and Labour Gazette,* Feb. 1905, 12.

49. P.P., "Select Committee on Home Work," Second Report, 1908, vol. viii, Qs2565–66.

50. Ibid., Q3350.

51. *Trades and Labour Gazette,* May 1908, 14.

52. NUBSO *Monthly Report,* Mar. 1908, 29; May 1908, 229; May 1909, 218–19.

53. For example, see the *Daily Express* for 20 Nov. 1907, which reported sweating cases uncovered by Macarthur. The WTUL *Annual Report of 1908* noted that Macarthur and Tuckwell "have spent considerable time in helping in the work of the Anti-Sweating League campaign to secure passage of the Sweated Industries Bill." Much of the Anti-Sweating League research was undertaken by the WIC investigation committee under Black.

54. R. H. Tawney, *Studies in the Minimum Wage, No. 2 — Tailoring* (London, 1915), chs. 2 and 3.

55. This was an administrative rule of the Trade Board. Each employer had to show that at least 80 percent of his workers received the minimum hourly wage. See ibid., 48–54.

56. Ibid., 64–96.

57. Ibid., 73.

58. B. L. Hutchins, *Women in Modern Industry* (London, 1915), 244–45.

59. WTUL, *Annual Report of 1914*, 9.

60. Dorothy Sells, *British Wages Boards: A Study in Industrial Democracy* (Washington, D. C., 1939), 231.

61. Tawney, *Tailoring*, 135.

62. Ibid., 202.

63. *Women's Industrial News*, July 1915, 358.

64. Sells, *Wages Boards*, 270–80.

65. Hubert Llewellyn Smith et al., *The New Survey of London Life and Labour*, 1 (London, 1934), 115.

66. Tawney, *Tailoring*, 121.

67. Ibid., 137–38, 140.

68. Ibid., 21, 137–40, 153–59.

69. P.P., "The Select Committee on Home Work," 1907, vol. viii, Macarthur, Q 2727, and MacDonald, Q 4390; see also AST *Journal*, Nov. 1899.

70. Tawney, *Tailoring*, 215–17; Sells, *Wages Boards*, 306–7.

71. Tawney, *Tailoring*, 216–17.

72. Sells, *Wages Boards*, 307. Sweated homework increased in some trades not protected by the minimum wage legislation. See *Women's Industrial News*, July 1913, 144–45, on sweating in the boot and shoe trade of North East London, where wives and husbands worked together at home.

73. Tawney, *Tailoring*, 39; Sells, *Wages Boards*, 290–91.

74. Sells, *Wages Boards*, 123, 310–17; Tawney, *Tailoring*, xi, 90–96; Lloyd P. Gartner, *The Jewish Immigrant in England, 1870–1914* (London, 1960), 139; *Women's Industrial News*, Jan. 1912, 14; Jan. 1915, 310.

CHAPTER 8

Sweating and History

THIS BOOK HAS ARGUED that sweating in the London clothing trades was a result of industrial growth, not stagnation. Many of the skilled artisan workers were being displaced not by the factory system but by a system of mechanized outwork. Unlike places where outwork declined, in London the process appears to have speeded up in the last decades of the century.[1] New machines, such as the sewing machine, cloth- and leather-cutting machines, and the veneer band saw, and new production methods, such as subdivision and subcontracting of labor, enabled unskilled clothing workers to do at home or in a small workshop what skilled workers formerly had done in factories or artisan shops. Machinery caused an increase, not a decrease, in sweating, as employers who lacked capital and space discovered that mechanized outwork allowed them to expand production without expanding facilities. Many of these sweaters were marginal employers or middlemen scarcely able to survive cutthroat competition and unable to give their workers decent wages. Decentralization meant a shift in production from the traditional manufacturing locations to nearby working-class neighborhoods, as the old centers of production, the West End and the City, became centers for giving out work, which would be done in the more distant home or the small outwork shop. To make this possible, London, particularly the East End where thousands of families were unable to survive on the father's wage, had to provide a ready mass of women who would work for starvation wages. Because the London clothing industry was based on this outwork form of production, in which employers could remain in the inner city without providing workspace for their employees, many workers were also forced to remain in the inner city. Outwork, in short, was a source of social compression. As long as it existed, the movement of the working classes to the suburbs would be retarded. Social reforms such as workmen's trains and workmen's housing were of little aid to thousands of outworkers who needed to live closer to their employment than more fortunate workers who did not need to carry their work home with them and who did not need to search constantly for work.

Moreover, it is clear that outwork was more than a preindustrial phenomenon. And it was not merely an extension of the factory system, as Karl Marx and Friedrich Engels believed. They saw outwork labor as an "outside department of the factory," available for rapid expansion of production in times of growing markets and thus attributable "chiefly to the capitalist's need of having at hand an army ready equipped to meet any increase of demand."[2] But rather than an outside department of the factory, outwork in the London clothing trades was a substitute for it.

Many factors were thought to be the chief cause of sweating. Not infrequently, workers blamed the "unhealthy craze" for cheap goods as the source of their problems. But by the end of the nineteenth century, after years of debate, agitation, and investigation, most observers believed sweating was a result of decentralized production, aggravated by uneven factory and workshop regulation and ineffective labor organization. The answer was to end outworking and force production into the factory or workshop where wages and conditions of labor could be controlled by the state and trade unions.

This is not to say that other factors, such as urban growth and fluctuations in the trade cycle, as well as administrative influences like the factory and workshop acts, did not play a significant role in the centrifugal patterns of growth. In addition to the technological innovations that welcomed less skilled labor in the trades and the putting out of production, the factory and workshop acts had an important role. Had the state not intervened, the movement out of the factory and workshop and into the sweating rooms would probably have proceeded far more slowly and might, in certain boroughs, not have taken place at all. However, economic and urban changes affected work and industry in London, and administrative action by the state was capable of accelerating, retarding, or, at times, even reversing the patterns of economic growth. Where state regulation was uneven, sweated labor grew faster; when legislation was effective, particularly in the case of the minimum wage legislation, production moved from the home to the factory and large workshop. In those boroughs where all work premises were uniformly regulated, the trend away from centralized production was abated. Hence, it appears that in industries such as the London clothing trades noneconomic variables such as state intervention were strong enough to determine patterns of growth.

The victims of sweating were defenseless. The sweating system goes far to explain why the women's movement was able to recruit only a few of the millions of women of the working class. In the process of urban and political socialization nothing is quite as important as work. As long as the sweating system isolated women in their homes or tiny workshops beyond the reach of labor organizations, most of them remained politically backward and powerless. Instead of uniting workers, the sweating system threw women into a system of co-exploitation of worker by worker, thereby driving women further and further apart. The work was exploitive not just because of a given capitalist employer, but because the system drove women to exploit one another. Women working for the industrial rights of women eventually concluded that the only way to reverse the submission and resignation of so many sweated women workers was to eliminate homework completely. As long as women worked in the home, they would not talk of their rights and trade unionism was impossible.

Thus the persistence and growth of sweated homework perpetuated many of the preindustrial values of working-class women. The traditional argument that women were traumatized by the factory is in one sense superfluous, because women always worked before industrialization, and in another sense false, because a majority of women workers in the new industrial society did not work in the factory. The tendency of historians to study change rather than continuity has distorted our picture of working-class women. And historians have erred in seeing the textile worker as the typical industrial woman. Because so many women worked in the home and not the factory, their work experience and value system remained largely traditional and pre-industrial.[3] Unlike some occupations (including domestic service), therefore, the clothing trades were not a modernizing agent in bringing women into modern industrial society. Working in the home maintained the link between women and the family.

In the sweated trades in the last decades of the nineteenth century and up to 1914, more and more women were working harder and longer and for less pay. If there was increasing unhappiness among

working-class women toward the end of the nineteenth century as some
have suggested,[4] this may be one reason why. The seamstress and
tailoress had been touched only slightly by the new industrial world.
The rejection of capitalism, the demand for the vote, the moral revolution, and the image of the "lady" in society, all remained distant as
the clothing trades worker toiled alone or with her sister and mother
in an industrial system that had changed but little for her. If and when
she followed working women like Amie Hicks into the public arena,
it was more often to fight for industrial rights rather than political
rights.

The experiences of women have been commonly charted by
reference to a male archetype, and the woman in history has long
been measured in terms of how well she fits this traditional male-
centered model. Since the experiences of women often do not fit, historians have spent their time explaining why women did *not* succeed
in building movements and institutions of power as did men. What
women actually *did,* that they often moved according to different time-
tables, by different methods, and out of different values than men,
has not been regarded as important. Hence, history has assigned to
women a certain weakness and sense of failure, relegating them to
the shadows of history or pressuring them to construct shaky arguments that try to prove they really did learn the rules of the game.
Nowhere has the orthodox male model been more energetically upheld in interpreting the experiences and responses of women than in
the history of work. Here success has always been seen in terms of
labor organization and political or financial power.

The problem of women's wages illustrates this myopia. Since women
were unsuccessful in using trade unionism to improve their wages,
they are wrongly dismissed as powerless. First, as we have seen,
although they did not join the union in mass, they did strike, they
did march, they did agitate for greater government intervention, and
they did stand up in labor gatherings and ask for help. Second, under
middle-class leadership women turned to another approach, the establishment of a national minimum wage. As direct industrial action and
trade unionism proved futile, women cast aside the lessons of political
economy taught by the middle class and worked for state intervention. Hence, in part at least, it appears that the politicization of some
working women grew out of their inability to direct industrial change,
and in one instance, the Trade Boards Act of 1909, the impetus for

welfare legislation came not from the Liberal party, but from the women's industrial rights movement. Aside from a few efforts to improve factory and workshop regulation, from the time of the House of Lords' sweating committee until 1909, the government expressed little interest in working women. The Trade Boards were one of the most important innovations in twentieth-century industrial relations, an important part of the welfare state, and, eventually, an aid to wartime industrial control.

One of the most notable features of the clothing trades labor force was its disorganization and high degree of stratification. Indeed, industrial disorganization kept the workers apart. Based on intense labor competition, on decentralized methods of production, and offering quasicapitalist status to many workers, outwork generated prejudices among workers and isolated them from the mainstream of the British labor movement. Outworkers were enemies of one another. Wages among outworkers differed as much as 45 and 50 percent for the same work and tended, in the long run, to shift downward. More often than not, the outworker was responsible for obtaining the work from the employer and for providing work space, machinery, and materials. The duration of employment was short, and the number of workers rose and fell with the vicissitudes of a highly seasonal trade. One of the most notable features of outwork is that the outworker seldom knew anyone else working for the same employer.

As a result, workers were antipathetic toward one another. On the surface, sexism and racism continued to divide the working class. English male workers often attributed the degeneration of their trades to competition from women and Jews, while Jewish workers traced their problems to the entry of English women into the trades. Conversely, women workers periodically voiced the opinion that male prejudices kept them from achieving their rightful place within the work community. Hence, the working class tended to become more fragmented. But the apparent instances of racism and sexism were misleading. Prohibition of outwork and banning women from unions were the only weapons men had in their war with cutthroat capitalists. On the other hand, we have found a growth in cooperation between male and female and Jew and Gentile in the London clothing trades in the last quarter of the nineteenth century.

Furthermore, outworking resulted in the embourgeoisiement of some workers. Subcontracting, the easy entry into the trade, the low capital needed, and the marginal skills required all encouraged the worker to rise from the sweating dens by the way of capitalism, not by trade unions. The factors of labor competition were intensified and aggravated by the sweating system, and, as a result, it was work and the workplace that retarded the class consciousness which ordinarily would have accompanied the workers had their labor become centralized in the factory.

Eric J. Hobsbawm has noted that skilled labor tended to see machinery as a "means of intensifying exploitation" of the worker, whereas unskilled labor often regarded it as a "triumphant promotion."[5] This statement appears to be partially true of the clothing workers of London, for the skilled worker tended to be more vehement about machinery than the unskilled worker. However, although there was some antimachine sentiment among clothing workers, particularly male artisans and semiskilled female machinists, more often than not workers were grieved less by the machine than by the process of subcontracting and subdivision of labor and the relocation of work. Year after year, workers as individuals and as organized groups protested the giving out of work to be done in the home or the sweating den at lower wages. Few industrial changes generated as much job dissatisfaction as did subcontracting and subdivision of labor.

As the outwork system grew the demands of workers tended more and more to center on the establishment of space for each worker by the employer. Workers demanded that employers and, where applicable, municipal governments, provide workshops. But, like the trade union movement, this work-on-premises movement also failed. Although the unions were strong enough to make their demands felt, they could not overcome the ineffective and one-sided arbitration system, the ambivalence of local governments, or employers' preferences for outwork production.

From the time when the clothing trades first began to experience mechanized decentralization in the 1860s, it was obvious that there were two solutions to the problem of cheap labor: either exclude such workers from the ranks of unions with the hope that this would prevent the contamination of the entire trade or bring them into the union with the intent of bringing their wages and work conditions up to the level of other workers. In London the unions and the rank and file favored the second approach, whereas the national union favored the more elitist policy. This disagreement over principle was damaging.

Time and again, especially in the tailoring trade, the strength of the union movement was eroded because of this conflict between the local and the national unions. And employers took advantage of these inter-union conflicts. For them outwork was not only cheaper, but also it was a hedge against unionism. In this sense outworking was part of the general post-1889 antiunion counterattack by employers.

There was considerable continuity in the objectives of the London clothing trades unions from the late 1860s through the 1900s. Throughout this half century the union movement was largely a defensive reaction to declining wages and deteriorating working conditions. Generally, its goals were the organization of unskilled women and Jewish workers, increased state protection and regulation, and the elimination of outworking. The continuity of these goals means that the various theories of historical discontinuity, which are founded on so-called bursts or explosions within the British labor movement (e.g., the new unionism of 1888–89), have limited application. The advance of trade unionism among clothing workers cannot be explained in terms of sudden fluctuations in either ideology or the trade cycle as much as it can be explained in terms of gradual industrial change. The organizational efforts among tailors in the late 1860s and women workers in the 1870s and the renewed activities of clothing workers in the late 1880s and 1890s follow the same general pattern: a reaction against the decentralization of labor and industry. Although new unionism gave the clothing trades union movement renewed impetus and vitality, it did not give it any new principles. The organization of unskilled workers and a belief in state intervention had long been part of the London clothing trades movement.[6] And it was the failure of unionism by 1889 that pushed women unionists in the direction of increased state intervention.

Finally, the sweating system was both a cause and an effect of poverty. Although much poverty was due to the physical growth of the city and the exodus of older industries such as dock work, heavy engineering, shipbuilding, and textiles from the inner industrial perimeter of London, the sweating system made its contribution as well. The system not only pushed many once satisfactorily employed tailors and shoemakers into poverty, but, because it was able to guarantee marginal existence to destitute families of the unemployed docker, shipbuilder, and the like if they stayed nearby, it caused a large number of people to remain trapped in impoverished neighborhoods. The sweating system thus explains why a movement of skilled jobs out of London did not result in an accompanying movement of labor to new industrial areas. Sweating was a source of social compression in that it kept people in poverty-level jobs and served the same function as the street industries — costermongering, street-sweeping, and street-selling — that Henry Mayhew so vividly described.

On the other hand, the sweating system was also a result of poverty. The relationship between sweating and the crisis in the late Victorian and Edwardian family economy is apparent. Many women became sweated laborers only because they and their families could not survive without their work. These were women (widows, wives, and young girls) who would be increasingly cared for by retirement systems, old-age pensions, workmen's compensation, or state and local social assistance. But before the welfare state, and particularly in the period of declining real wages and increasing unemployment that began toward the end of the century, many women converted their homes into sweating dens because it was the only way out of poverty. The underlying philosophy of the New Poor Law of 1834 was that the poor take care of themselves. The sweated industries, to an extent, illustrate how far this could be carried, for, in effect, sweated labor was one of the few avenues to survival for many members of the lower working class.

Above all, the experience of the workers in the London clothing trades points to a well-known but often neglected fact about economic and social change: the movement of labor and industry toward the factory system and the concomitant fusion of the working class was not inexorable. Industry, in the case of the clothing trades, was transformed not by centralization, but by decentralization. Outworking, despite its many preindustrial features, was another side of industrialization and in the long run contributed to the technical backwardness of the clothing trades industry. At its best, the relationship of the outwork system with factory system was symbiotic; at its worst, it was parasitic. The history of outwork shows that the generally accepted premise of the discontinuity between the factory and the prefactory stages of industrial growth has been somewhat exaggerated. Not infrequently, as in the case of the London clothing industry, change came in the form of unspectacular, uneven, and irregular growth.

NOTES

1. Duncan Bythell (*The Sweated Trades: Outwork in Nineteenth-Century Britain* [London, 1978]) and James H. Treble (*Urban Poverty in Britain, 1830–1914* [New York, 1979]) both argue that outwork was declining by 1890.

2. Karl Marx, *Capital,* 3d ed. (Chicago, 1912), 1: 505–15.

3. Theresa M. McBride, "The Modernization of Women's Work," *Journal of Modern History,* 49 (June 1977). Oddly, M. E. Currell (*Political Women* [London, 1974]) does not consider work to be a factor in political socialization.

4. Peter Stearns, "Working Class Women in Britain, 1890–1914," in Martha Vicinus, *Suffer and Be Still: Women in the Victorian Age* (Bloomington, Ind., 1973), 103.

5. *Labouring Men: Studies in the History of Labour* (New York, 1965), 326.

6. The impact of trade unionism on the economy has never been fully evaluated. David Landes has gone far in explaining that the period of decreasing prices (deflation) of the last quarter of the nineteenth century was due to cost-reducing innovations which allowed for the use of unskilled, ergo, cheaper labor. But as S. B. Saul has suggested (*The Myth of the Great Depression* [London, 1969], 21), Landes has not explained why these innovations led to price reductions in the nineteenth century and not in the twentieth. One answer, it appears, is that in the clothing trades of London at least nineteenth-century labor was not able to guard itself against the cost- and wage-reducing innovations. Thus the weakness of labor contributed to the deflationary tendency of the economy.

Statistics on Outworkers

THERE ARE TWO SETS of statistics on outworkers: the local medical officers' lists and the occupational census count of home-workers. The Factory and Workshop Act of 1901 required that the person giving out work must supply the local medical officer of health of the borough council with a list of all persons to whom work was given. These lists were required to be compiled twice a year (on 1 August and 1 February), and the local authorities were required to forward to other boroughs the names and addresses of outworkers receiving work within their borough but residing in another borough. This registration of outworkers was not, however, completely new, for the Factory and Workshop Act of 1891 required employers to keep lists, although since there was no stipulation that the lists be sent to the local borough council, in most cases no records were kept. Even after 1901 the system of registering outworkers was erratic, and it was not until 1904 that the medical officer of the London County Council began to enforce the law rigorously.

According to the data collected by the borough medical officers (see Table A-1) for the London County Council, the number of outworkers in London increased from 17,290 in 1904 (about 7 percent of the labor force in the clothing trades) to 32,765 in 1909 (about 12 percent of the labor force). This increase represents a growth of 89.5 percent. The size of the outwork labor force, according to the lists, reached a peak in 1908 with a total of 36,116 outworkers. It also appears that the ratio of outwork to workshop labor force also increased significantly from 0.5 to 1 to nearly 1 to 1 by 1908. To be sure, much of this growth was due to better collection and reporting, not an increase in outworkers. But the lists have some inherent problems, as well; one is that they indicate only the addresses of outworkers and not

Table A-1. Outwork Lists: The Number of Outworkers as Reported to the Medical Officer of Health for the London County Council, 1904-9

Year	Number of Outworkers	Number of Workshops	Ratio of Outworker to Workshop
1904	17,290	34,488	0.50
1905	19,399	35,187	0.55
1906	28,030	36,632	0.76
1907	32,876	37,891	0.87
1908	36,116	37,673	0.96
1909	32,765	37,782	0.87

Note. The annual figure for the number of outworkers has been calculated by dividing the number in the lists by two, since the lists were returned twice a year. The resulting estimates, however, are probably low, since not every outworker would appear on both lists.

Source. London County Council, *The Annual Reports of the Chief Medical Officer of Health* (London, 1904-9).

the number of outworkers at each address, and another is that they record the labor force only for two days of the year. As most observers noted, the outwork lists only partially reflect the number of outworkers in London. Many outworkers were not reported, either because the employer — perhaps fearful of the local inspector — failed to keep an accurate list or any list at all, or because the outworker was employed by another outworker who, naturally, did not have to keep a list. Williams and Jones estimated that only half the outworkers were included on the employers' list.[1] It is perhaps the case that the only significant value of these local outwork statistics is in pointing to shifts between workshop to outwork in specific boroughs where we know more about local conditions and inspection.

Also misleading is the census category "working at home." It was only in 1901 that the census began to distinguish between those working at home from those working on employers' premises. The census shows that overall the percentage of people working at home decreased between 1901 and 1911 from 25.1 to 19.7 percent. While the number of homeworkers in the boot and shoe trade remained roughly the same at 27.9 and 27.0 percent and the number of homeworking male tailors increased, homework among women tailors decreased. Fewer homeworkers were reported for dressmaking, millinery, shirtmaking, and seamstress work. Thus, for the industry in London about one in four workers was a homeworker in 1901 and about one in five in 1911. However, in using the census figures, we can do nothing but rely on the willingness of the head of a household to report whether or not work was being done in the home, by himself, his wife, or other members of the family. Howarth and Wilson, in their survey of West Ham (the industrial northeast of London), found that many instances of work "nominally done by one person" were the product of a number of women in the family working together: "an aunt helps with the ironing, sisters and nieces take part, and children are employed to sew on buttons and help in little ways, as well as fetching and carrying."[2] One estimate is that as many as one-third of all women workers were not counted in the occupational sections of the census.[3]

An estimate of the size of the outwork labor force can be only speculative. The census figures, as low as they may be, underscore the inadequacy of the figures provided by the local medical officers and give support to the frequent charge that the local inspectors simply were not reporting all the outwork premises.[4] The census of production officials in 1907 suggested that approximately half of those working in the clothing trades were outworkers. Assuming that this estimate, along with other estimates that between one-half and one-third of the outworkers went unreported, is nearer the truth, it is possible that for London in the first decade of the century between 100,000 and 125,000 workers were outworkers.[5]

Table A-2. Homeworkers in London, 1901 and 1911

	1901 Census				1911 Census			
Category	Female	Male	Total	% of Total Working in Trade	Female	Male	Total	% of Total Working in Trade
Dressmakers	21,342	156	21,498	34.2	17,517	182	17,699	26.4
Tailors	8,162	7,415	15,578	24.1	6,950	7,596	14,596	22.3
Shirtmakers and seamstresses	9,758	155	9,913	30.4	7,126	132	7,258	27.1
Milliners	1,482	41	1,524	13.3	1,299	41	1,340	9.4
Boot and shoe workers	1,747	7,781	9,528	27.9	1,293	6,254	7,547	27.0
Total in clothing trades	44,351	18,339	62,692	25.1	36,065	17,129	53,194	19.7

Source. P.P., "Census Returns," 1901 — London, Occupations, 1902, vol. cxx, pp. 88–89; 1911 — London, Occupations, 1913, vol. lxxix, pp. 36–37.

NOTES

---

1. P.P., "Royal Commission on the Poor Laws," 1909, vol. xliii, Appendix vol. ix, William and Jones Report, p. 390.

2. Edward G. Howarth and Mona Wilson, *West Ham: A Study in Social and Industrial Problems* (London, 1907), 267.

3. John Burnett, ed., *Annals of Labor* (Bloomington, Ind., 1974), 48–49. See also Elizabeth Roberts, "Working-Class Standards of Living in Barrow and Lancaster, 1890–1914," *Economic History Review,* 30 (May 1977), 311.

4. Ramsay MacDonald frequently carried the complaints of the WIC (that large numbers of workers went unreported by the local inspectors) to the House of Commons. For example, see Hansard (*Commons*), 4th ser., CXCII, 22 July, 1 Aug. 1908, cols. 814–16, 1231–33.

5. The census figures are found in P.P., "Census Returns for 1901," 1902, vol. cxx, pp. 88–89; and the census of production figures are in P. P., "Census of Production," Final Report, 1912–13, vol. 109, section vi, "Clothing Trades," pp. 391–92.

Location Quotient, London Clothing Trades, 1861, 1891, 1901

TO MEASURE OCCUPATIONAL shifts I have used a location quotient for five districts of London for the years 1861, 1891, and 1901. The quotient is arrived at by dividing the percentage of the particular occupation (either clothing or boot- and shoemaking) group in the district by the percentage of London's working population in the district. The quotient tells us how concentrated that particular occupation was in that district. A location quotient of 1.0, for example, means that the distribution of the occupation is co-extensive with the distribution of the working population of London as a whole. If the quotient is greater than 1.0, then the occupation is more highly concentrated in the district than London as a whole; less than 1.0 indicates a lesser concentration. This method is set out in Garth Stedman Jones's *Outcast London: A Study in the Relationship between Classes in Victorian Society* (Oxford, 1971), appendix 2, table 5.

Table B-1. Location Quotient of London Clothing Workers
in Five Occupational Districts, 1861, 1891, and 1901

Area of London* & Year	Clothing		Boot- and Shoemaking	
	Male	Female	Male	Female
West				
1861	1.27	0.67	0.82	0.27
1891	1.02	0.79	0.70	0.20
1901	0.87	0.70	0.62	0.12
North				
1861	0.96	0.87	0.95	0.56
1891	0.89	1.04	0.97	0.92
1901	0.87	1.03	0.094	0.95
Central				
1861	1.47	1.08	1.18	1.07
1891	1.07	0.81	0.71	0.46
1901	0.92	0.87	0.68	0.36
East				
1861	0.86	1.52	1.26	2.33
1891	1.82	1.47	2.17	3.94
1901	2.02	1.45	2.36	3.84
South				
1861	0.70	0.99	0.82	1.10
1891	0.63	0.93	0.62	0.38
1901	0.68	0.98	0.61	0.44

*The districts represent the following boroughs: West includes Hammersmith, Chelsea, Kensington, Fulham, and Westminster. North includes Paddington, St. Marylebone, Hampstead, St. Pancras, Islington, and Hackney. Central includes City, Finsbury, and Holburn. East includes Bethnal Green, Stepney, Shoreditch, and Poplar. South includes Woolwich, Deptford, Southwark, Wandsworth, Stoke Newington, Lewisham, Lambeth, Greenwich, Battersea, and Bermondsey.

Source. P.P., "Census Returns," 1861, 1861, vols. li–lii; 1863, vols. liii, liii.l; 1871, 1873, vol. lxxii, pt. 2; 1881, 1883, vol. xcvi.l; 1891, 1893–94, vols. civ–cvi; 1890–91, vol. cvii; 1911, 1912–13, vols. cxi–cxiii; 1913, vol. lxxvii–lxxx; and Jones, *Outcast London,* appendix 2, table 5.

Index

A Note on the Author

JAMES A. SCHMIECHEN is associate professor of history at Central Michigan University, Mount Pleasant. He received his education from Elmhurst College and the University of Illinois at Urbana-Champaign, where he received a Ph.D. in history in 1974. His doctoral dissertation, which forms part of this book, received an American Economic History Association dissertation citation for 1975. He has published articles in *Economic History Review* and *Journal of Economic History* and is a contributor to the *Dictionary of Labour Biography*.